"The man eyed me with a sullen stare, while the dogs growled and showed their teeth."

THE

HUSBAND IN UTAH;

OR,

Sights and Scenes among the Mormons:

WITH

REMARKS ON THEIR MORAL AND SOCIAL ECONOMY.

BY AUSTIN N. WARD.

EDITED BY MARIA WARD,

AUTHOR OF "FEMALE LIFE AMONG THE MORMONS."

NEW YORK;
DERBY & JACKSON, 119 NASSAU STREET.
CINCINNATI:—H. W. DERBY & CO.
LONDON:—SAMPSON LOW, SON & CO.
1857.

W. H. TINSON, STEREOTYPER.

GEO. RUSSELL & CO., PRINTERS.

PREFACE.

ONE year since, with fear and trembling, I gave to the world my testimony against the Mormon delusion.* It was not a history of that people, or the rise and progress of their singular creed. It made no pretensions even to trace them as a body through their various settlements in the Western country previous to their emigration to the Valley of the Great Salt Lake. It was designed simply as a record of personal experience—a transcript of events written from memory ; a faithful narrative of such hopes and fears, joys and sorrows, as any woman placed in such circumstances must necessarily feel.

The success of that venture emboldens me to send another barque in the same track, though this time it is the experience and adventures of another—of a man. Of course he takes a somewhat different view,

* "Female Life Among the Mormons."

but his account corroborates my testimony. He presents a philosophical view of the Mormons, with their moral and social condition as a community; but that neither softens nor modifies the nature of the facts which came beneath his observation. It was not from ambition or the love of gold, but a sense of duty to my country and the world, that the other book was written. The impostors are still abroad in the land; every month brings the arrival of their dupes from foreign shores. Again I lift the voice of warning. Beware of their arts.—Enter not the circle of their fascinations; their charms are like those of the serpent, and lead to the death of all that is holy and beautiful in this life, and all that can support the anxious soul in its moments of dissolution, and give it a happy and abundant entrance into the presence of just men made perfect.

I have been careful to preserve the thoughts and sentiments of the writer. In no case have I changed or omitted a sentence, because it did not agree with my feelings and opinions. I wished to be true to him as I had been to myself.

The writer was the nephew of my husband. Subsequent to my escape from Mormondom, but before his family were aware of the fact, he took the overland route to California, stayed among the Mormons for a time, went on to the Gold Region, caught cold from exposure in the mines, and came home to die. He was unmarried, and in the distribution of his effects his papers were given to me. I hand them over to you, kind public, relying on your candor and generosity for a charitable appreciation of the work and the motives which prompted it.

MARIA WARD.

THE EDITOR'S DESIGN.

THE public mind has begun to appreciate, with some degree of correctness, the evil influence of the Mormon faith, and the true nature of its institutions. It has at least commenced to perceive the extent of folly and wickedness that must naturally grow up under such a system, adverse alike to democratic institutions and the truths of Christianity. Priestcraft, in its worst phase, is the soul and life of Mormonism. The United States, as well as foreign countries, teem with these men and their confederates, whose morality is even more lax, whose delusion finds readier dupes, and whose designs are more sinister and dangerous than those of Rome. Polygamy and the conversion of women are accounted among the chief instrumentalities to promote their designs. To support the one and effect the other the most strenuous exertions are made. Nor is it always the case that efforts to secure fresh victims are confined to the use of persuasion and advice, but physical assistance can be rendered when necessary to abduct and carry off, in some emigrant train or caravan, such youth of either sex as circumstances throw in their way.

If either of these volumes * should be the means of warning one individual to escape their nefarious designs, I shall have been amply repaid for all my pains and labor.

* The Author here refers to the popular work entitled "Female Life among the Mormons."

CONTENTS.

CHAPTER V.

DIFFERENT SENTIMENTS—POOR CLASS OF MORMONS—MISERY OF WIVES—ETC.

CHAPTER VI.

AN ENGLISHMAN'S OPINION—ENGLISH EMIGRANTS—THEIR CHARACTER—ETC.

CHAPTER VII.

THE MRS. UNDERWOOD'S JEALOUSIES, MISUNDERSTANDINGS, AND REMOVAL.

CHAPTER VIII.

THE DINNER—A NEW WIFE—JAUNT TO GRANTSVILLE, AND WHAT I SAW THERE, ETC.

CHAPTER IX.

RETURN—OGDEN'S CITY, ETC.

CHAPTER X.

FREDERICK B—— —THE MORMON THEATRE—MRS. CANFIELD, ETC., ETC.

CHAPTER XVIII.

THE MORMON PARTY—MORMON BELLES—INCIDENTAL NOTICE OF BRIGHAM YOUNG AND HIS FAMILY, ETC.

CHAPTER XIX.

EXTERIOR INFLUENCES—YOUNG MEN—DISSATISFACTION WITH POLYGAMY—CHANGES TO BE WROUGHT IN THE SYSTEM OF MORMONISM, AND HOW.

THE

HUSBAND IN UTAH.

CHAPTER I.

UTAH—MOUNT ZION—INCIDENTS AND FIRST IMPRESSIONS—BROTHER UNDERWOOD.

UTAH! Deseret! The country of the Great Salt Lake! The region of saline plants!—the abode of the beautiful, the wonderful, and the new. Snow on the mountains, flowers in the valleys—the tall pine trees crowning the rocky heights, and the graceful cottonwood marking the margins of a hundred streams—the air redolent with the fragrance of blossoms unknown to the East—cattle grazing peacefully among the hills, or reposing in the shade—the tall spires of the Mormon temple glittering in the rich sunlight—the Mormon city, with its picturesque edifices, and busy inhabitants—bustle, hilarity, and confusion in the streets—huge family carriages filled with a mixed variety of old and young women, and children of different ages and sizes—stately Mormon elders proceeding on pedestrian excursions of business or pleasure—dashing soldiers with nodding plumes, gay uniforms, and prancing steeds—Indians in all the glory of their national costume loitering near places of low resort. And last, not least, a company of English emigrant converts to the new faith, approaching in the distance.

MOUNT ZION.

The Great Salt Lake City, called Zion by the Mormons, is pleasantly situated. They are fond of comparing it to the ancient capital of Judea, though to find any resemblance between the two, must require a great stretch of imagination. For sublime and picturesque scenery, the Mormon city has no rival in the world. Behind it, like an amphitheatre, rise the lofty summits of the Wahsatih mountains, whence never-failing streams of fresh water descend, and are conducted in small channels on either side of the streets. The city is well laid out ; the streets, which are one hundred and twenty feet wide, intersect each other at right angles, and are ornamented by rows of cottonwood trees. The houses are all adobes with the exception of the Governor's palace. They are substantial and elegant, and though generally small, a few are very large and commodious ; each house stands back a short distance from the street, and is surrounded by a small garden ; each block has a bishop or spiritual overseer, whose duty it is to know everything passing within his jurisdiction. He must examine every week into the moral and material condition of each family, and report to the Governor. With this preliminary notice of Utah, and its famous city, I shall proceed to recount whatever was most interesting, amusing, and instructive to me during my visit to that place, in the summer of 1855.

INCIDENTS AND FIRST IMPRESSIONS.

I was one of a small company who took the overland route to California, n ore for the amusement of the thing than any other purpose. We hunted buffalo on the plains, visited trappers in the mountains, and feasted with half-naked savages, till novelty gave place to weariness, and our approach to the habitations of civilized man, was attended with feelings of decided pleasure. When the saints from the United States, or other parts of the world, arrive within sight of the city, they prostrate themselves to the earth like the Mohammedans when they discover the sacred edifices of Mecca ; in our case, however, the discovery of its gleaming habitations was only hailed by a shout of joy, and accelerated speed along the well-worn road. This road, though generally good, was quite as remarkable as other things belonging to the same territory. It went bending, hither and thither, first to to the right, then to the left, winding around the mountain spurs, and the bases of hills, till finally reaching the plain on which the city stands, we entered it just as the sun was declining in the western horizon, and the shadows of night began to gather on the mountain tops. Of course our first desire was to obtain shelter and food, not only for that night, but several weeks. Zion was crowded with visitors, travellers, and emigrants, under similar necessities. There are some persons who for a consideration will supply what we want—I say for a consideration—the Mormon brethren in this respect resembling the Jews of old, who while affecting to despise the Gentiles, were at the same time strongly enamored of Gentile gold. We applied for lodgings at the United States Hotel, kept by the Hon. Mr. Kinney, U. S. judge for the territory of Utah, but to our great disappointment his house was full. He likewise expressed regret, but gave us directions to a smaller and much inferior establishment, kept by a Mormon—Brother Underwood.

"BROTHER UNDERWOOD!"

I said to myself, walking in the direction of his house, "that name sounds familiar," and I patiently strove to recall where or under what circumstances I became acquainted with its owner. Thus meditating, I reached the domicile. It was now nearly dark; there was no candle or lamp burning, and I could obtain only a very unsatisfactory glimpse of my host. Yet his manner was kind and cordial, and he spoke in a frank cheerful voice. I told him my necessities. He said, very well, he wonld see, and disappeared.

The formality usual in Eastern hotels was entirely dispensed with here. There was no registry of names, and there seemed to be no clerks or assistants, with the exception of a small boy, who acted in the double capacity of errand runner and bar-tender. At present he sat dozing behind a small counter, apparently unconscious of the presence of a stranger ; meanwhile we heard some one (whom we supposed to be our host) running up and down stairs, opening and shutting doors, and calling through the rooms, "Nelly, Nelly!" After an absence sufficiently prolonged to have cooked and prepared a good supper, he returned with the dismal intelligence that there was no one in the house who could get us anything to eat, but that he would show us to our apartments if we desired to remain. My companions angrily expostulated with the man. He excused the matter by throwing the blame on his wives ; they generally took turns, he said, in going out, and the one whose duty it was to stay at home, had neglected or forgotten it. He supposed she was at a neighbor's, though where, it would be impossible to tell. All but myself decided to depart. I was secure of a shelter, that was half I sought, and I hoped that the remainder might be forthcoming ; so taking up my travelling-bag, I bade my companions call on me the ensuing day, and with a hearty "good night," prepared to follow my obsequious host. The room to which he consigned me was a sort of little cell. He had brought up in his hand a short piece of tallow candle, contained in an iron candlestick, which to judge from its appearance, might have been coeval with Noah's ark. This he placed on a rude semblance of a table, and unceremoniously withdrew. I scarcely had courage to inspect the apartment. I hoped that the roof was tight, and the bed clean. I hoped too, that by-and-by I might be summoned to supper, though my better judgment rebelled against such anticipations. On rummaging my pockets, however, I found the remains of a broken cracker, and a small portion of dried fruit, which had hitherto escaped my notice. This I ate, and commending myself to Divine Providence, retired to bed, though determining to lie awake, at least, until the candle burnt out. The more I saw of Brother Underwood the more firmly I became convinced that I had been previously acquainted with him. At length, with a sudden flash of thought, I remembered the time and circumstances. It was in the State of New York. My introduction to him was merely casual, though with the woman he subsequently married I was intimately acquainted. How exceedingly strange! Would she know me? Would she receive me as a friend? I questioned. Only those who have been far from home and friends can realize with what delight I anticipated meeting with an old acquaintance, in whose society some of the happiest days in my life had been spent. Then it occurred to me that I might be mistaken, and having by this time relinquished all hopes of supper, I saw the candle swale, flare, and flicker without reluctance. A moment more it blazed, flashed up suddenly, then the wick fell over to one side, became saturated in the melted tallow, and all was darkness.

I cannot say that my bed reminded me of any I had ever slept in before ; for to tell the truth, it did not. Though not much inclined to luxuriousness, I found it hard, cold, and uncomfortable. It was yet early in the season, and cool nights are characteristic of the climate of Utah, even in the midst of summer. I wished for a warm quilt or coverlid, but as none could be had, determined to be satisfied without it. After all, there is no philosophy like that which prompts a man to conform to circumstances, and make the best of everything. With these feelings I composed myself to rest, and soon fell asleep. I awoke in the morning with a gnawing sensation of hunger, and actually shivering with cold. Silence prevailed throughout the house, and no one seemed to be stirring, though it was broad day. I had full leisure and opportunity to examine my room and its concomitants. I found it a hard thing, indeed, to be satisfied therewith, and unavoidably found myself wishing that its general appearance were otherwise. Notwithstanding all my philosophy, I felt that my satisfaction would be greater were more neatness and taste displayed in its arrangements. I had been accustomed to lave my hands and face in the fresh mountain springs, and could not be content with the quart bowl of water prepared for my use. Then the napkin had evidently grown old in some other employment before being applied to its present purpose. I think that if the floor had been well scrubbed and sanded, this small piece of old, dusty, faded rag carpet might be happily dispensed with. The uncurtained window looks unpleasant, the glass being so dingy that before looking through it to obtain a view of the mountains, I am obliged to wash it with the napkin, in which laudable endeavor to exercise the vocation of chamber-maid, I pushed out one of the panes. It fell to the ground and broke with a crash, probably awaking the family, as I heard them moving about soon after. In attempting to seat myself on one of the chairs, it let me sprawling to the floor, and I ascertained that, one leg being broken, it could only be retained in an upright position while standing with its back to the wall. My table had evidently been a stranger to hydropathy for a very long time. Instead of a lock, my door was fastened with a wooden button. The fireplace was filled with ashes and cinders, while the jambs were literally festooned with pendent webs.

I look around for a bell. The apartment is not furnished with any such convenience. I think of ordering a fire. I wonder when breakfast will be ready. I ponder the best way of making myself known to the landlady. I muse on a thousand other things, till tired out of all patience with waiting to be summoned below, I hastily descended and made my way to the bar-room without formality.

I found Brother Underwood in the bar. He was quietly munching a hard brown lump, designated a rusk. He looked up, and his broad features relaxed into a smile.

" Got in a hurry for breakfast, eh ?" he inquired.

I replied in the affirmative, reminding him that I had no supper the night before.

"Ah yes," he answered, "I recollect, Nelly was out."

I paid no attention to this remark, but again referred to the morning meal.

"Certainly, certainly," he said, "it will soon be ready."

There was certainly a great rush of business going on in a neighboring apartment, and as my host seemed communicative, lively, and amiable, I sat down to wait patiently and converse with him.

"How long have you been in Utah?" I ventured to inquire.

"About five years," he replied, musingly.

"And you removed from Cortland County, in the State of New York."

"Why do you ask?"

"Because your voice, and face, and name, strongly remind me of one with whom I was formerly acquainted."

"Your name?" he inquired.

I mentioned it.

He looked earnestly in my face for a minute or two. "Yes," he observed, "I have a faint recollection of your features, and I have heard my wife speak of you."

"Her name was Maria R——"

He assented, and held out his hand.

I met his grasp with a cordial pressure.

"I shall be most happy to see her," I observed.

"You will probably meet at breakfast," he said. "I wonder whether or not she will know you?"

Probably an hour elapsed before we were summoned to breakfast, and then a faded woman came to the door with the announcement. I directed an inquiring glance towards my host.

"My second wife," he remarked.

"Oh, I beg pardon."

"No apologies are necessary," he replied, leading the way to the breakfast room. Half a dozen women, all the wives of my host, were standing around. I knew Maria at a glance, though she gave me no look or token of recognition. Her husband smiled, and inquired if she had forgotten an old friend; she gazed curiously in my face, then her countenance lighted up, and she cordially offered her hand.

Our meeting, however, under such circumstances was one of painful embarrassment. I could not help speculating on the appearance of Maria compared to what it had formerly been. I had known her as one of the most tidy and industrious of girls, and now her dress and manner were indicative of the utmost carelessness and negligence, to say nothing of the want of neatness conspicuous in every part of the house. Though my hunger gave it a zest, the breakfast was anything but good. There was not a dish on the table even tolerably well cooked. The coffee was bitter and "muddy," the meat burned, the bread half dough, and the butter—but I forbear to speak of that—it looked indescribably, and I did not taste it.

"As you are an old acquaintance," said Underwood, "I shall expect you to make my house your home during your stay in this place. You can scarcely expect to be better accommodated. Quiet is a great thing, sir, a very great thing. I have no boarders except my family, and little custom. Of course, I don't want much—just a little to bring in a trifle of change, is all that I desire. It is expensive living here, very—so many mouths to fill," and he glanced at his wives.

"How long did you design staying?" inquired Maria.

"That depends on circumstances."

"You will stay with us, I will see that you have comfortable accommodations," said Maria.

"All the other houses of entertainment are full," continued Underwood. "They always are. The brethren moved out here to be separated from the rest of the world, and build up a righteous and holy kingdom, but it seems that the world cannot do without them."

Maria turned her eyes towards him imploringly.

"I should suppose that my companions would soon be here," I observed, wishing to change the conversation; nor was I mistaken. On rising from from the table, I heard voices in the bar-room. "They have come," I ejaculated, and taking French leave of the ladies, went out to meet them.

"And what do you think of Mormondom?" inquired Harry Buck, the moment we were out of the house.

"I shall reply by retorting the same question," I answered. "What do *you* think of it?"

"What will induce me to get away as soon as possible," he said. "We are going on to-morrow."

"To-morrow!" I exclaimed with surprise.

"You needn't look so scared up," he said, laughing. "Is it strange that a man should wish to leave a place where he can get no food but roasted potatoes, and no shelter but an old emigrant wagon cover."

"Has this been your fare?"

"Certainly it has. We went around to the different houses of entertainment, but all were full. We could present no claim to the hospitality of the Saints, and had not an old Indian fortunately come to our assistance, we should have been compelled to pass the night in the streets, or to have sought you out with a certainty of not getting any supper."

"And the old fellow took pity on your forlorn condition?"

"He did. He cheerfully shared his bed and food with us. It was poor and scant to be sure, and only better than none."

"Is he a Mormon?"

"A Mormon! No; he hates and despises the whole sect—says they are thieves, liars, and devils; in short, the greatest rascals in existence."

"That may be all true," I replied, "yet I prefer to have evidence of the fact. I have succeeded in finding an old friend, and shall remain some time, probably all summer."

They tried in vain to dissuade me, but my resolution once

taken was not easily moved. Various reasons which it is not necessary to repeat, influenced my decision, and the matter was settled.

I found a manifest improvement in the appearance of things at Brother Underwood's when I returned at night. The floors had been newly swept, the webs brushed away, and the dingy windows cleansed. When I ascended to my room of the previous evening, I found that the good work had extended even there. A cheerful fire was burning on the hearth, the broken chair had been removed, and so many little additions to comfort and convenience had been furnished that the transformation was complete. I could easily guess who had done this, and what motive inspired it; Maria was ambitious to make her circumstances appear in the best possible light to one she had formerly known. There was no harm, and there might be much good in that. Just at dusk I was called to a plentiful supper, at which she presided, while the other wives of her husband remained in the kitchen.

I subsequently discovered that Brother Underwood was not considered strictly orthodox. He belonged to the Mormon church, and practised polygamy, yet he was not so liberal with his money as the elders desired, and had on several occasions boldly refused to pay his assessment of tithes. He possessed, however, and in an eminent degree, one quality which Mormon husbands especially need, and which at all times and seasons they are required to exercise. This was good nature, and that easy sort of disposition, which rests satisfied with getting along "somehow." If things went wrong, "oh well, never mind." If the meals were not prepared by the right time, or not at all, it made little difference to him. He would roast a potato, or munch a crust, and expected to live just as long as though everything went on in the smoothest manner.

His wives generally partook of the same qualities. They were the laziest set it was ever my fortune to behold, and the five did not perform on an average the ordinary work of one good housewife in the Eastern States. Yet strange as it may appear, Underwood had married them solely with the view to their labor. He wished to keep a hotel or boarding-house without the extra expense of servants. When Maria's health failed, and she could not perform the duties devolving on her, instead of hiring a girl he married another wife. She refused to work, and he resorted again to the same alternative with no better success. Thus one after another had been added to his family with no advantage to him. Fortunately they bore few children, or his circumstances would have been still more embarrassed. These women divided their time pretty equally between visiting, sleeping, and going to church ; one attending to the household affairs this day, and another the next ; while such general concerns as washing and scrubbing were utterly neglected. Though these women were actually too indolent to quarrel, they had no domestic feeling, no interest in common with their husband to preserve order, and promote the family welfare. In this apathy and indifference they strongly resemble the servants, for whom they were designed to be a substitute. These things were obvious enough to a stranger; I determined to ascertain whether or not Brother Underwood regarded them in the same light. I felt little delicacy in broaching the subject, as the Mormon, unlike the Mussulman, manifests little sensitiveness in regard to his wives. They will sit for hours relating their domestic experiences, vexations, and the motives that caused them to desire so intimate a connection with so many women. Of course there will be different views, but in many cases it is my candid opinion that the husband is more to be pitied than his wives. One day, when our acquaintance had ripened into familiarity, I inquired of Brother Underwood if he considered polygamy conducive to the happiness of those husbands who practised it.

He frankly replied, "Generally speaking, I do not. One thing is certain, it has been my ruin in a pecuniary view—not that exactly either, but it has caused a stagnation in my affairs that to a person of different temperament would have occasioned madness or suicide. Fortunately I take things easy, and never suffer myself to be worried, come what may."

No one, I believe who had seen his broad, smiling, good-natured countenance would have disputed this.

"It seems to me that you might do a good business at hotel keeping under other circumstances," I remarked.

"No one can be more certain of that than I am," he answered, broadly smiling; "yet I have given up all hopes of that; in fact I care no longer about it. One or two boarders at a time is quite enough. I wish to retain what little property I have succeeded in getting; I have no expectation of ever obtaining more."

"Candidly and truly, do not you, who have tried both, consider the one-wife system to be the best pecuniarily, as well as morally and socially?"

"Not a doubt of it," he replied; "but uneasiness seems characteristic of human nature. Few men, I believe, are entirely satisfied with one wife. They find deficiencies in her which they seek to remedy, where polygamy is allowed, by taking another, and as no woman is ever perfect, the number from this same motive may be indefinitely increased."

"And no one knows exactly what a thing is until he has tried it," I replied.

"Exactly so."

"Do you not suppose that many who have tried polygamy would gladly go back to the one-wife system, could they reasonably do so?"

"I know it; but a marriage once consummated is not to be readily abandoned. Justice to the woman requires its permanency."

"And you find no difficulty in procuring second, third, or even the seventh or eighth wife."

"None whatever, so far as I am aware. It is even said, that the more wives a man has, the more he may have, especially in those families where labor is required of the female members. I have been told that many girls make it a condition in their courtship that their future husbands shall marry at least two other wives, in order that the cares and burdens of household duties, with the annoyance of children, may be lessened by being divided."

"A practical view, certainly."

"And one which serves admirably to banish whatever objections a female might reasonably have to married life. Most women strongly object to being mothers to large families, and if such is the case it is decidedly against their wishes and wills. The first child is welcomed, the second tolerated, the prospect of a third occasions tears and reproaches, and that of the fourth is attended with exhibitions of temper, ebullitions of spleen, fits of melancholy, and not unfrequently with actual dislike or hatred of the husband. Whatever unhappiness the want of children may occasion in some families and under certain circumstances, it cannot be denied by any one even tolerably acquainted with the facts of the case, that too many of them is a source of greater disquietude and discontent to those that give them birth, and on whom during infancy and childhood the care of them necessarily devolves."

"Likely enough; yet what bearing has this on the system of polygamy?"

"Much, very much. Where polygamy is indulged, few women ever give birth to more than two or three children apiece. These are soon out of the way, and their mothers at liberty; while at the same time the burdens of the husband are increased, and his application to labor or business is even more imperatively required."

"But Maria was doubtless averse to your second marriage?"

Without noticing my last remark, he continued: "I could point you to many women in Utah who are strong advocates of polygamy, though their husbands are doubtful of its utility, and hesitate about practising it."

I became subsequently convinced that there was much truth in his statement, and was forcibly reminded of Lady Mary Wortley Montague's remarks, where she expresses her belief that the ladies in the Turkish harems lead the easiest and happiest lives in the world, and also of what a young lady of good sense and respectable position in society once said in my hearing, "that she would rather be the fiftieth wife of a rich man who could support her without the necessity of labor, or the inthrallment of family affairs, than the only wife of one who would expect her to perform all sorts of menial labors, besides giving birth to and rearing a dozen children."(*a.*)

CHAPTER II.

GLANCES AND GLIMPSES—COSTUME—SCENES IN THE STREETS, ETC.

WHILE walking the streets of Zion my thoughts constantly referred to the great changes that a few short years had sufficed to accomplish. Land rescued from savages and wild beasts; redeemed from the wild; elegant structures built; a populous city, rich in the various elements of prosperity, and the resort of thousands of emigrants from all parts of the world, is a great work to be performed in half a score of years, more especially when its isolated condition, and the absence of all water communication with the ocean is considered. One thing is certain; the Mormons, whatever may be the faults of their religious or social system, are not deficient in the energy and perseverance of the Anglo-Saxon race. Yet not a tithe of the country they nominally occupy is cleared or inhabited. Little colonies of Mormons are settled here and there, at fifty, forty or twenty miles from the main settlement, to which, for various reasons they pay a semi-annual visit much in the same manner as the ancient Jews went up to Jerusalem. The appearance of these people, when seen in the streets, is much inferior to that of the natives of Zion, and you soon learn to distinguish them. They are coarse and rude in manner, impudent, staring and curious, miserably dressed in a costume half-way between that of the Indian and white man. You are surprised at the unmistakable marks of Indian descent that many of the younger ones exhibit. The straight, well-proportioned figure, long coarse hair, high cheek bones, and wary expression of eye and countenance betray to the most casual observer the mixture of races.

One thing that strikes you as remarkable, is the assemblage of different nations to be seen in the streets. Gibralter itself can scarcely be more favored in this respect. Every nation in Europe, and every State in the Union has representatives here. The tall Norwegian, fresh from his native pine forests ; the Dane, probably a descendant of some sea-king of old ; the blue-eyed German, meet, and probably salute you in a language whose strange unintelligible gibberish has no more meaning to your ears than the gabble of so many geese. These generally retain their national costume for a time, but sooner or later adopt that of the Mormons, which varies little from the usual style of English dress. Brigham Young, the patriarch, attempted to lead the fashions, and set out with a slouched yellow hat, much too large even for his large head, green frock coat, and pants large in size and loose in fit, white socks, and slippers. He was followed by some of the elders, though the young men and dandies were so intolerably wicked as to prefer imitating the people of the world.

Zion, like other cities, has its fashionable streets. In these some are dressed with foppish extravagance, and a great many in clothes of expensive material. You are tempted to wonder how so much finery ever found its way to such an out-of-the-way place.

Of course, the ladies in personal adornment must keep up with their husbands and lovers. The wives and daughters of the rich dress expensively, with good taste and effect. Many of them are attractive in appearance, and some would produce a decided sensation in any European drawing-room. These were objects of especial attention to the United States officers and soldiers, which gave great umbrage to the Mormons.

Many of the poorer class of women work in the fields. These adopted a costume something like the Bloomer, consisting of wide pants, gathered with a band around the ankle, short skirts, and a broad-brimmed straw hat of home manufacture, yet all the better for that. They were adorned with knots of ribbon, and being rather jauntily worn on one side, had altogether a pleasant effect.

The arrival of an emigrant train always occasioned a great amount of bustle and excitement, and such arrivals were of frequent occurrence. Some were bound to Oregon, others to California, but by far the greater number were foreign Mormons, who came to join their brethren in the promised land. These are hospitably entertained, and provided with homes among the wealthy saints, until they can procure some of their own. Even after that, they are supplied with cattle, domestic utensils, food, clothing, and other necessaries at a trifling cost, until they are enabled to get a "start." This seems to me a praiseworthy and humane policy. "Thou shalt not oppress the stranger, for ye were strangers in the land of Egypt," said the great Jewish Lawgiver; a maxim too often forgotten by our own people. These emigrants are a source of great wealth to the Mormon Church, besides being an important addition to their numbers. Many of them bring large sums in gold and silver; others have strong hands and willing hearts to work, and thereby increase the material wealth of the country; and all are blindly attached to their novel faith and creed.

Such emigrants are precisely the kind of people required to bring out the resources of a State. Few "gentlemen" among them, and no "ladies;" but all true-hearted men and women, inured to toil and hardship, with brawny shoulders, firm step, and coarse hands. Deficient in the exterior graces of polite education, they generally exhibit a strong native sense of right, and what is due from man to man. They soon found employment, and in most cases, were busy and satisfied. (*b.*) The exceptions were those of old people, who had left their native country for the sake of ending their days in the society of their children, and who seemed to sadly miss the old familiar accociations of former years. I was always fond of the society of aged people, and some of these interested me very much, though I could neither speak nor understand a connected sentence in their language. I was deeply struck with the appearance of two old Norwegians—husband and wife, who lived with their son and his family, in a small adobe house, on one of the principal streets. They had all the appearance of great age—long white locks, and bent forms, with that indescribable something in manner and countenance, which even among the rudest people commands veneration. They seemed inseparable—that old man and his equally ancient wife. When the air was damp or chill, you could see them sitting by the window. In warm sunshiny weather they often came out on the little porch, but it was easy enough to be perceived that the old people were not happy. There was an air of loneliness about them. They were home-sick—how could it be otherwise? They were too old to form new friendships, or seek new pleasures. They are tired of isolation from all the habits to which they have been accustomed through a long and undoubtedly happy life, besides being disgusted with the condition of the things they find around them. The wife pines for her old neighbors, her little village church, the voice of her aged pastor, and the mounds in the tidy grave-yard, where her ancestors sleep. I missed them one day from the window, and still the next they were invisible. Then rumors came that the old Norwegian woman had fallen down in a fit. Another quickly followed, that she was dead, and I felt a certain presentiment that her companion could not long survive. I attended the funeral, which was conducted after the manner usual in Norway.

The coffin was borne on the shoulders of six stout foreigners, and followed to the place of burial by a large company of foreign men and women. First, and conspicuous among them, was the aged husband of the deceased, bending beneath the weight of unutterable sorrow, and looking older by several years, than when I had last beheld him. He seemed utterly decrepid and helpless, and was obliged to lean heavily for support on the arm of his son. His frame was that of a giant, and he must have been in his best days of wonderful strength, though now he shook and shivered as if under the influence of strong convulsions.

The procession passed out into a little open plain, bounded by large rocks, and extremely desolate in appearance. It halted by an open grave, over which a solitary cottonwood waved its huge branches. After the usual preliminaries, the coffin was lowered down, when the old man tottered to the head of the grave, and sat down, with one long, earnest, straining look into its gloomy recesses. Then the son, taking his station at the foot, opened a small book, and read from it in his native tongue, what I supposed to be the funeral service of the Norwegian church, during which the whole assemblage reverently uncovered their heads. Many of these were evidently illiterate, and somewhat boorish in manner, but all seemed deeply influenced by unaffected feeling. Several of the women sobbed and wept bitterly, and the reader himself paused at intervals, apparently overcome by the depth of his emotions.

This exercise was succeeded by a few moments of silence,

when another person stepped from the crowd, and began a short address, perhaps eulogistic of the virtues of the deceased, or more probably a strain of exhortation to the living. His manner was earnest, and the tone of his voice solemn and impressive. He finished, when a few handsful of earth were thrown into the grave, when those who had acted as bearers came immediately forward, and taking some shovels proceeded to fill the grave. While this was transpiring, the son took his former place, and some one in the assembly raised a hymn, with a long, slow, mournful air. The strain was immediately taken up by many voices, while the echoes rolled and died away in musical cadence among the hills. I was deeply affected, though unable to understand a syllable.

Meantime, a man had gone into the ravine near by, whence he returned with two small branches with green leaves, that he had broken off a chenopodiaceous shrub, native to the place. He approached with the apparent intention of erecting them at the head of the grave, when the old husband, who had sat immovable, his face buried in his hands, made a hasty gesture of dissent, and pointed to a dwarf pine growing on a small mound at a little distance. The man understood his mistake, and throwing down the shrubs, proceeded to gather the pine boughs, with their green tufts of long spiral leaves and pointed cones. These were placed upright at either extremity of the grave. A few sentences of prayer were then repeated in a low voice ; the old man, assisted by his son, rose to his feet, and all dispersed. For a day or two I thought much of the old Norwegian, and the probable effect which the decease of his wife would have on him. Then I took a short trip to a neighboring settlement, where I remained nearly a week. I purchased a horse, and returned by a bridle-path, leading near the old woman's place of burial. Suddenly my horse pricked up his ears, as if listening intently, and in another moment the loud echoes of a martial strain reverberated through the woods. Riding on, I soon discovered that another funeral was proceeding. The singers were standing around a new-made grave, chanting with most impressive utterance and gestures, the national air of Norway, and simultaneously bursting into a chorus, of which the burden, prolonged in a loud, full-toned, enthusiastic aspiration was, "Gamle Norge." I reined in my horse till the pine branches were erected, when the company peaceably dispersed, and all that remained to earth of the old man, was left sleeping quietly by his wife. Upon inquiry, I found that he had been a patriot and a warrior, and that his name was honorably mentioned in his native land.(*c.*)

Many emigrant trains on their way to California or Oregon stop at the Mormon city to obtain rest and refreshment. This is obviously a great advantage to the country, and contributes largely to its wealth, by furnishing a market for all kinds of produce. These trains are not the least remarkable feature of the western world. They come from all quarters—Ohio, Indiana, Wisconsin, and Missouri, and such a combination of strange characters rarely and perhaps never meet under other circumstances. Each family is generally furnished with a large stout wagon drawn by mules or oxen, in almost fabulous numbers, and capable of accommodating quite a number of people. Hoops, bent to form a half-circle, with a coarse white cloth stretched over them, make a passable cover. These are attended by men on horseback, with hunters and half-breeds on foot. Many a time emigrant parties double in number while journeying across the plains. The Americans, or those who had resided for several years in the States, were usually well-dressed, though mostly rough and coarse, and generally fond of spirituous liquors. The men were not sociable, except when the prices and qualities of land, or the abundance of gold in their prospective home, was the subject of discussion. This, however, I attributed to a sort of jealous fear of the Mormons, whom they had learned to regard as enemies, and whose movements they incessantly watched. They took care to show the handles of concealed weapons, and managed fire-arms with dexterity, though carefully avoiding all altercations and disputes. One thing was particularly observable in many of them—a straining after effect, and an attempt to make themselves appear more wealthy and intelligent than they really were. Their language was generally ungrammatical, idiomatic, and extravagant ; excessively profane, and interlarded with obsolete phrases, and nicknames applied almost indiscriminately. Yet one of these men, who had acquired some little property, and felt very large in consequence, though he could neither read writing nor write his name, had the impudence (what else can we call it ?) to cause himself to be nominated as candidate for the legislature of his native State, was supported by an independent ticket, and obtained the office, after which he aspired to be governor. Failing in this, he conceived the idea of going West, where his talents would be better appreciated. Hence he had gone roving about, always dissatisfied because the people refused to trust him with some high office. He was evidently a singular man, uniting in himself the confidence and self-possession of the well-bred gentleman, with the coarseness and low tastes of the uncivilized boor. He would exhibit in one day the most opposite qualities. Frankness and reserve, recklessness and self-control, penuriousness and prodigality. I was told of one act which he originated and carried through the legislature, and which empowered each of the members to purchase at the public expense a leather trunk, dressing case, and gold pencil of the value of ten dollars. Could anything show the man in a clearer light ? It was amusing to witness the sharp eyes with which these men regarded the movements of their women when the Mormons were about.

There is a camping-ground on one side of the city, where such travellers as choose can pitch their tents and reside with comfort during their stay at Mormondom, which is always prolonged to a month, and sometimes much longer.

I used often to visit these companies, and when they had satisfied themselves that I was not a spy, or Mormon emissary, I was uniformly well received.

In one of the trains en route for California was a beautiful girl, of most bewitching manners, slightly addicted to coquetry and remarkably fond of society. Her mother was dead, and she had inherited from her a small property, which she lavishly expended in dress and ornaments. Her father, a man of naturally kind and humane disposition, with true parental feeling attempted to restrain the faults of his child. During their journey she had little opportunity to exercise her levity of disposition, but once encamped in the immediate vicinity of a populous town, and that town a military post, she determined by present indulgence to make amends for past restraint. Her beauty soon became the general topic of conversation, at least among a certain class, and her little coquettish arts delighted and excited the young soldiers in no small degree. Several of the younger Mormons seem-also struck with her fascinations. Like most other women, however, she preferred a military uniform, and when a young lieutenant became her constant attendant her happiness seemed complete. Meanwhile Mr. Scott, the father, forbade her lovers approaching his tent, and reprimanded her severely for encouraging them. A scene ensued. The father was violent, the daughter impetuous. He threatened her with punishment ; she defied his power. That night she fled.

I had grown quite intimate with Mr. Scott, during his

stay at the city. Friendship among travellers is of rapid growth. Utterly ignorant of what had occurred, I went the next day to his tent, and found him in a state bordering on distraction. He knew her recklessness and impetuosity, and doubted not that she had rushed headlong into the most deplorable evils.

"My daughter has gone, sir, gone," he said, bringing down his fist with great emphasis on the table; "and I drove her away, yes sir, drove her away, my beautiful Louisa, could you believe it, sir?"

"I certainly should not, except for your own words," I replied; "but what occasioned it?"

"Those cursed Mormons, sir, those cursed Mormons were all the time running after her. I forbade their coming, and talked rather savagely to her—too much so, sir; a father should never indulge his passions towards his children—never sir—that caused my daughter to run away.'"

"Perhaps she will come back."

"Never, sir; she's too much grit for that. She'll never come back unless she's brought back, sir, brought back by main force. The Mormons——"

"Excuse me sir," I said, interrupting him. "But I doubt that the Mormons had any hand in this reprehensible conduct of your daughter. It is much more probable that some one of these young officers has deluded her."

"Do you think so?" he inquired meditatively.

"I certainly do."

"I should like to know your reasons."

"I believe that Miss Scott was rather partial to the military."

"And I know she was," interposed the stepmother, who had been a listener to our conversation, and who manifested little disturbance at her daughter's flight.

I was sincere in this belief, and circumstances, as I conceived, warranted the full expression of them, not only that the ends of justice might be met, but to prevent a collision between the Mormons and the exasperated travellers, which must result fatally to the latter.

"What shall I do, sir, what can I do?" he inquired. "The camp will be moving in a day or two—and to leave my daughter, sir, I cannot think of such thing."

Not knowing what better to say, I simply remarked,

"I presume not."

"If she prefers a rascally soldier to yourself, I should say, let her go," observed the step-mother.

Her husband silenced her with a look.

Others of the emigrant party came in, and expressed great exasperation. Some persisted that the Mormons had kidnapped or abducted the girl, and proposed all sorts of violent measures to effect her rescue. Others contended, with much more show of reason, that she had voluntarily sought the protection of a lover.

"I've studied woman nature in my life," said one old man, "and I saw that in her eye which told me what she was up to. Lord! how they danced and sparkled at the sight of a pair of epaulettes! It's the epaulettes that did the business."

"Shouldn't wonder."

"She'll repent it," said a woman, who stood at the door of the tent, looking in. "Well, it's just what I expected. These beauties; I never could bear 'em, not one in ten is what she should be."

More than one of the men looked at the speaker, who was excessively homely, with a broad smile.

In a few days the encampment broke up, and the travellers moved on, leaving the young lady behind them. Mr. Scott requested me to look for his daughter, and if I obtained intelligence of her to write and let him know. This I promised to do.

I am told that it is no uncommon thing for beautiful young girls to be abducted from emigrant trains, or persuaded to abandon their parents for the sake of a Mormon husband.

I was particularly interested in one class of men, who occasionally visit the Mormon city, and who, generally speaking, are honest, brave, and liberal; I allude to the free trappers. During my sojourn in this country I was often thrown in contact with them, and can safely endorse all that has ever been said in their favor, though I have strong doubts of the correctness of many fabulous reports of the crime and violence attributed to them. True, they want polish and grace; many of them are uneducated; all are more or less deficient in the usual forms of civilized life, but for generous feelings and the combination of noble qualities, which make a high-minded man, they are rarely to be equalled and never excelled.

Generosity with them is almost a fault. Their purses, their pleasures, and their hearts are ever open to the weak, the stranger, or the needy. They have little of the sordid love of gold ; still less appreciation of caste or condition. Confide in them, and no friend can be more true.

CHAPTER III.

RURAL SCENERY—RURAL LIFE—JUDGE WHITE—HIS OPINION OF POLYGAMY—THE BRIGHT SIDE OF THAT INSTITUTION.

SOME of the Mormons are wealthy, and not a few have fine farms at some distance from the city, besides town-houses of considerable pretensions to architectural elegance. Of course they would suffer in comparison with the buildings of New York, or other eastern cities, though in this place they really look well. Usually these men have several wives with families. The first wife, with two or three others, resides on the farm probably, while the others are supported in the city, or it may be the reverse. The husband revolves between these two establishments ; blessing one place with his presence for perhaps a month, and then staying an equal length of time at the other. I understand that these husbands are greatly petted ; each wife vieing with the other to best entertain her lord. As the dispositions of women are various, in certain instances this may be the case ; in others it is not.

It was a fine, warm, bright morning when I started on a

stroll with my fishing-rod up City Creek. This stream is rapid and beautiful. It runs from a wild gorge on the north side of the city, along the banks of the principal canal, conducting the water for distribution into one part of the town. The stream was full of trout, which, however, declined to bite, and I resolved to visit the farm of Judge White, which I knew could not be far off. Certain business connections had led me to form an acquaintance with this man, who was considered a pattern saint, and who, at sundry times, had pressed me to share his hospitality. Striking into a narrow path I walked rapidly along the edge of the plateau at the base of the mountain, for about two miles, when I came suddenly on a little mud shanty of indescribable appearance. It seemed to swarm with children. A parcel were playing at the door when I approached. Seeing me, there was a hurried ejaculation, and they ran in quickly to communicate the news. Three men immediately came out, and double that quantity of women showed their faces at the door, while the lesser ones behind were pushing and crowding to obtain a glimpse. My approach had produced a sensation more than I considered safe or agreeable. Two of the men were half breeds; the other the most villainous looking white fellow it was ever my misfortune to behold. Snaky glittering eyes, shaggy brows, and sensual mouth, with an expression of countenance at once malicious, cunning, and devilish. The women were suitable matches for such men, nearly naked and undescribably filthy. I approached them frankly. The white man held out his hand. Not wishing to encounter the grasp of such a man, I took no notice of the action, but inquired if he could direct me to the residence of Judge White.

"Judge White?" he reiterated. "Really, stranger, but come in here, and we will see," motioning towards the cabin. This movement revealed the handle of a concealed dirk. That, however, was nothing of consequence ; weapons, in this country, being considered a necessary appendage to every man.

"No, sir," I replied. "Have no occasion. Will you direct me?"

"Walk in, and we'll have a game," he said, drawing a pack of cards from his bosom, where they rested side by side with the dirk.

I declined in the least offensive manner I could assume, satisfied that the man had evil designs towards me.

"But I say you must, stranger," he continued, with an attempt to be facetious, with ended in a hideous leer. "It isn't often that anybody comes this way, when they do, we must be civil and obliging. Now there han't been better liquor to be had around here since old Noah came out of the ark, than I've got in yonder. I want you to go in and taste it, come," and he grasped me by the shoulder, attempting to drag me forward. He was a powerful man, broad-chested, and long-limbed, and his grip was that of a vice ; but I shook him off, and ran ; yes, ran, with all my might across the plain. I heard a great shouting and laughing at my expense, but no one followed me.

Wandering about in one direction and another I became

thoroughly wearied, when ascending a small eminence the house I sought appeared before me. I had heard it described so often that I knew it instantly. It was a large adobe house, two stories high, with a piazza running all around. A pretty stream of water coursed rapidly a short distance in the rear, and being lined with a growth of trees, it had an Eastern appearance truly refreshing. On the other side of the way was a large and convenient barn, with other out-buildings, suitable for the rearing and sheltering of stock. The house was surrounded by a good fence, with very neat gates. The yard was intersected by gravelled walks, with beds of flowers on either side. I noticed some very beautiful flowering shrubs peculiar to the country, and others also of which the seeds had been brought from the East. Two or three stout healthy-looking boys were playing on the grass, and the sound of a spinning wheel mingled with singing came through the open door.

"Judge White lives here, does he not ;" I asked of one of the boys.

"Yes sir," said the little fellow, with a smile of intelligence.

"Is he at home !" I asked again.

"Down at the stable yonder," said the boy, pointing to a large new building. "The Devons are there, too ; he thinks a great deal of them."

While I was speaking to the child, a good-looking woman came to the door, courteously saluted me, with an invitation to "walk in."

"Run, boys, and tell your father that a gentleman wishes to see him," she said, addressing the children who scampered off with great glee.

I followed her into a large and handsomely furnished room; carpets covered the floor; there was a neat, well-filled book-case, a mirror, several pictures, fancy chairs, a sofa, and elegant harp. Bouquets and vases of flowers were tastefully arranged in various parts of the room, and there was that comfortable pleasant air, in which most Mormon homes are sadly deficient. Handing me a chair, and seating herself nearly opposite, she prepared to act the cheerful entertainer during the absence of her husband, and commenced by asking me if I was a stranger in the Mormon country, to which I made a suitable reply.

"And how do you like our people?" she asked.

My answer was rather equivocal. "Better than I expected."

"I admire your intelligence," she said with a bland smile.

"We have been greatly misrepresented. People who come among us as a general thing, are much too prejudiced to form a cool dispassionate judgment of our institutions. They see and report only one side; this is scarcely fair?"

I answered that it was not.

The extreme cases of female suffering and unhappiness reported in the books and papers which circulate through the Eastern States, are by no means general. I am told, however, that formerly it was much more the case than now. Opposition to polygamy is the effect of habit and education.

Females become reconciled to it by custom. Perceiving that she was willing to discuss the matter, I said that among civilized nations, polygamy had generally taken the name of a crime, that I believed it was rarely attended with domestic happiness, and that few women would be allowed to tolerate a rival in the affections of their lord.

She answered that jealousies and heart-burnings in such cases were preposterous, and that if there was a class of women on earth who were really and truly objects of pity, it was the wives of small farmers and poor mechanics, who, generally speaking, were nothing more than household drudges—doing work of half-a-dozen, though unable to work at all.

"You refer to the States ?"

"I do, where thousands of women are expected to bear and rear from six to one dozen children apiece, besides keeping their houses in order, and doing with their own hands all the cooking, washing, scrubbing, making, and mending for their families. Now, suppose all the sufferings of those women during ill health, all their toils, cares and annoyances—for these must exist where there are children, with discontent and unhappiness from various other causes—were all drawn in one picture, keeping the worst side constantly in view, it would show marriage in a dreadful light."

"Probably."

"No one can deny that polygamy is a patriarchal institution, directly countenanced by the Scriptures, and nowhere inhibited by them. The chosen people, the Jews, were direct descendants, not simply from the wife, but the wives of Jacob. Bathsheba, the fourth or fifth wife of David, was the lineal progenitor of Christ.

Here the conversation was interrupted by the entrance of Judge White. He welcomed me to his house with great cordiality, excusing himself for not coming sooner, by saying, that he had just purchased some very fine Devons, and wished to superintend feeding and stabling them.

Many of these Mormon farmers pay great attention to the breeding of stock, and no country in the world can boast a superior quality of butter and cheese. The bunch grass, indigenous to the climate, gives it a peculiar yet most delicious flavor.

Accompanying Judge White, over his extensive farm, I was surprised and delighted with its judicious arrangements. Whatever may be the errors of Mormon theology, or the evils of its social customs, it certainly does not disqualify a man for the business of life. I have rarely seen a place on which everything was more admirably contrived for comfort, convenience, labor-saving, and economy of space. The stable was a model of its kind, and the animals were sleek, docile, and kind ; soft and pliant of skin, abundant milkers, and excessively fond of the bunch grass.

There are extensive bottom lands on this farm, subject to be flooded by freshets, when the snow melts on the mountains. Here, the cows are pastured usually with the assistance of "herders," who are paid for their services by monthly wages. These fellows were sitting on rocks quietly tuning a rude pipe, or lying at full length on the grass beneath the shade of cottonwood trees, while the cows were feeding a little way off. The whole scene was suggestive of the pastoral ages.

The lands devoted to wheat and corn, were rather elevated, and of very fertile soil. The wheat was heading, and gave promise of an abundant harvest, and the long sward-like leaves of the corn, were of the rankest, deepest green, and rustled pleasantly as we approached. There were extensive fields of potatoes, a large garden filled with vegetables, and a young peach orchard. Several laborers were employed on the farm, and I learned that wages were much the same as in the Eastern States. At tea-time we returned to the house, and were ushered into the dining-room, where we found a table abundantly furnished with the good things of life. The lady with whom I conversed on my first arrival, presided at the table, and I was introduced to three several Mrs. Whites whom I had not seen. We all sat down together. There were no exhibitions of ill temper or moroseness, and I could not help wondering whether or not was this good nature affected, and what scenes were reserved for the special entertainment of the judge.

When the supper was finished, I was left alone with the judge for a time. The conversation had flagged for a few minutes, when my host abruptly asked what I thought of Mormonism. The question was sudden and unexpected, and I hesitated to answer it. He laughed outright, saying, "You do not know what to think!"

"Indeed, I do not," I answered.

"And why not?"

"Because no one can form a just idea of a people until he has seen them, nor even then without the exercise of great sagacity and judgment, especially if their institutions should be different from those to which he had been accustomed."

"A wise thought, happily expressed," said Judge White, "though the usual custom of tourists is to run through a country, selecting and sketching the most prominent objects, looking out extreme cases and supposing them to be general, and then, after a large blank is filled up entirely from the imagination, the world receives the benefit of swallowing the crude and ill-concocted mass. Our people are not perfect by any means. The Mormon church requires reform. I am not perfectly satisfied with the system as it exists among us, but in this age of the world, where free opinion is universally tolerated, no two people think alike. What one considers a deformity is regarded by another as a great beauty, and the very thing that one desires to preserve, another will wish to purge. We must take things as we find them, though beneath a standard of imaginary excellence. The same course is necessary in your own churches."

"I am aware of that."

"I used to be frequently amused, when listening to discussions on the relative and comparative merit of the different churches. How common was the remark, "I don't think my Church perfectly right, but only the nearest right. But whatever may be the faults of Mormonism, polygamy is not of the number."

I was glad when he touched on this point, feeling some delicacy in introducing it.

"Is not?" I replied inquiringly. "One Mormon gentleman with whom I conversed, and who had several wives, objected to the whole system, and expressed regret that he had ever been tempted to adopt it. I referred to Brother Underwood.

"Is he a man of property?" inquired White.

"Some considerable."

"Then he has probably been unfortunate in the choice of his wives."

"Very likely."

"Still that proves nothing against the system. Have you never heard men with only one wife express regret that they were ever married?"

"Frequently."

"Yet you never set it down as the fault of the system, but that of the individual."

"Even so, though I have thought, and still think, that there is more unhappiness in marriage than in celibacy. To early marriages and the necessity of supporting large families without previous provision being made for them, nine-tenths of the poverties and miseries in our large cities may be attributed."

"I believe it," he replied. "Among us it is the custom to obtain the consent of the first wife to the second marriage, not because the law requires it, but as a matter of domestic policy."

"And do the first wives consent to this willingly?"

"Generally they do," I am told.

"Of course your wife did."

"Have you been conversing with her?" he inquired archly.

"A short time this morning."

"She had no complaints to enter?"

"Nothing of the kind."

"She gets along admirably. The same as a mother with her daughters. I never entertained a thought of taking the second wife, till she, herself, made me the proposition. We had a very large dairy; it made abundance of work, and help was scarce, with high wages. What was still worse, the hired girls, if reproved, or required to do anything not perfectly agreeable, would get offended and go away, leaving us in the lurch. On one such occasion, when Betty ran off with a half-breed Indian without giving us a moment's warning, my wife thus addressed me:

"'My dear, I am utterly disgusted with this system of hiring girls.'

"'So am I; but what are we to do? You cannot possibly bear the whole burden of labor.'

"'No, I can't; but you can take another wife.'

"'Take another wife,' I said, surprised that she should propose the matter so bluntly.

"'Certainly; why not?' she answered. 'There is Sarah

Fogg, a most excellent dairy-maid, and a girl of good disposition. If you could marry her it would be much better than to hire a servant. She would take more interest in the work, and I think we could get along quite as well together. What do you say?'

"'That I will do so, if you wish it.' And the next month Sarah Fogg became my wife. Since then, I have united with others, as it seemed expedient."

"Expedience, then, is the governing principle in Mormon marriages?"

"Sometimes, though not always," he replied. "Many women are 'sealed' to a husband for the sake of salvation."

This absurdity was too much for my gravity, and I could not suppress a smile. A shade of displeasure passed over his countenance. It was but momentary, however, and he became serene and cheerful. Is it possible, I thought, that a man of such seeming intelligence and probity can cherish ridiculous notions, or is all that I have heard of Mormon hypocrisy, indeed, true? Perhaps he guessed what was passing in my mind, though too well bred to manifest anger.

We were soon joined by the ladies, all wives of my host. I believe they were all very industrious, and so many hands certainly made labor light. They came in, each with her knitting work, and all apparently cheerful and contented.

"My dear," said the husband to his first wife, who seemed a sort of sultana, "is the milking done?"

"Certainly it is," she replied.

"And the men have had their suppers?"

"They have."

"Did you give them orders to yard and stable the cows?"

"To be sure, I did."

"I thought you might have forgotten it," he returned, half apologetically.

"When did I ever forget such things?"

"Never, that I know of—excuse me."

The conversation was resumed, and I soon began to suspect that the religion of this man, like his marriages, was founded on expedience. No man of the world could have exhibited a more utter absence of all moral principle, clothed in the most specious and sophistical language.

"I think your people are fond of hair-splitting theories," he observed; "they consider it just, and right, and virtuous for a man to have three or four, or even, six or seven wives one after the other."

"But only one at a time," I suggested.

"Yes, one at a time, though if it is right to marry several at different times, it must be right also to have them at once. Virtue or vice must be inherent in the action itself, and not merely a question of time."

I replied that I was not prepared to argue the subject with him.

"But you can hear my reasons and arguments," he replied, and launched forth in a strain that I will not hazard the good opinion of my readers by repeating. .

During the evening he requested his youngest and last wife, who was very pretty, to favor us with a song. She consented, accompanying her voice with the harp. When the music ceased, and I had complimented her execution, which was very good, her husband informed me, that she was the daughter of a wealthy New England family, who, becoming converted to Mormonism, had abandoned their home and friends, and emigrated with the saints.

He considered her courage, perseverance, and eminent love of truth, as most remarkable, and said these qualities first won his regard.

When bed-time approached, the ladies took leave of each other, with a friendly good-night, and retired.

"Do you prefer to sit up late ?" inquired my host, looking at his watch, "it is now past ten."

"About my usual bed-time," I replied, rising.

Judge White rose also, took a silver candlestick from the table, and said that he would show me to my room. I followed him up stairs, to a very comfortable chamber, neatly furnished. He sat down the light, politely hoped that I would sleep well, bade me good-night, and went out shutting the door behind him.

The bed was good and well made, the apartment fresh and airy, yet I found it impossible to sleep. Judge White and his wives, their seeming intelligence, yet absurd and depraved ideas, filled my mind. It was a new phase of human nature for which I was altogether unprepared, but it filled me with greater abhorrence of the system they denominated patriarchal, than I had previously conceived.

I had not yet learned to regard marriage as nothing more

than a civil contract—a matter of mere expedience. I had been taught that it was a holy ordinance, instituted by the Almighty, and that a union thus consummated would be perpetuated in another world. But to sanction and excuse polygamy, my Mormon friend had taken an entirely different view of the subject ; he had divested it of every charm only mere practical utility ; his connections were purely sexual, with neither romance nor sentiment to clothe and adorn them. How would my pious and venerable mother regard such sophistries ? What would my venerable and white-haired father say to them ? Then I thought of the first Mrs. White ; thought, too, of Fanny Wright, and others of the strong-minded sisterhood, and their preferences for "free love."

THE MORNING.

The family were early risers. The morning star was blazing in the east, when I heard the judge arousing his men, and presently the whole house was astir. The females were busy milking and getting breakfast. I saw two from the window tripping across the dewy grass, each carrying a clean bright pail.

Descending from my chamber to the sitting-room of the previous evening, I found the table laid out preparatory to the morning meal. It was covered with a cloth, white as the snow on the mountains. The dishes were stone china of elegant pattern, and the knives and forks had been rubbed and polished until they shone like a mirror. The food was brought in by the two first wives of the judge, and breakfast was announced. The two milkers had not yet come in, and we sat down without them. I have rarely seen a table better provided with good substantial edibles. There were fried fowl, and fried bacon and eggs, with cold ham and game. There were preserved strawberries and honey. There were cold wheaten bread, and hot corn bread, hot biscuits, and hot short-cakes. There were home-made butter and cheese, with most excellent coffee. A pitcher of milk stood on the corner of the table, and glass tumblers were placed by each plate to receive it when wished for. Judge White made a short extemporary prayer, nowise different from those usually delivered on such occasions—thanking the Lord for the bounties of nature set before them, and the revelation of divine truth which had enlightened their minds. At the conclusion, the females pronounced "Amen" with one voice, and their lord requested me to "help myself," though without waiting for me to do so, he commenced piling the delicious viands on my plate. I ate heartily, and my host was evidently delighted.

"Don't you think the patriarchal institution works admirably in my family?" he inquired.(*d.*)

"It seems to," I answered.

"There is no seeming about it," he said quickly, "it is all real—matter of fact. Don't you believe it?"

"Certainly I have no reason to doubt it."

"And there is no reason why you should," returned the first Mrs. White.

I mentioned my adventure at the hut on the morning of the previous day.

"I know them," said my host, "they are mischievous fellows, and doubtless were influenced by some evil intent. I have more than once suspected them of injuring my cattle; and once I caught them in the very act of dressing one of my sheep."

"Are they Mormons?" I inquired.

"They come under the spiritual jurisdiction of our prophet, though they have no faith—no religion of any kind. We have made great efforts for their conversion, but without success."

"They seem to have adopted Mormon institutions. I saw several females with them."

"Yes; they have two or three wives apiece, and I don't know how many children."

"Does the system do well in their case?" I inquired.

"I should expect not, very," he replied. "If I had the laws to make, such fellows should not get married at all."

I looked surprised, perhaps inquiringly.

"No one should have the privilege of getting married, who had not made provision for taking care of a wife."

Thinking that the conversation might be profitably changed, I inquired what he thought of the general condition and character of the Half-breeds.

His observations and opinions might not be of much value here, though they verified my own experience of the same people. He said they combined the worst qualities of the

Indian and white man, with little of the good belonging to either; were lazy, shiftless, improvident, and lived wretchedly; rarely working at all, but depending for subsistence on the precarious supply of hunting and fishing, or the plunder of fields and folds.

I observed that they seemed quite numerous.

"They are numerous," he replied, "more so than you would suppose from your short acquaintance in this country There are hundreds, and, I verily believe, thousands of them of all sexes and ages."

Mrs. White here interposed that some of the half-breeds were respectable, wealthy, independent men, far superior to the general class of Indians, and fully equal to the whites, whose opportunities for education and knowledge of the world had been no greater.

"Oh, yes, my dear," he replied, "there are exceptions to the most general rule." He then stated as a grand climacteric to their depravity, that they were sadly deficient in religious faith; that neither their hopes nor fears of future punishments or pleasures could be excited; though he owned that they were disposed to relish and practise polygamy.

I subsequently learned that though sufficiently numerous, their isolated condition, as individuals, precluded their forming a distinct class, and that the circumstances attending their births generally threw them into association with the Indians.

They compose the illegitimate offspring of white hunters, trappers, and United States soldiers, and Indian females.

As the habits of these people are migratory, and they rarely occupy permanent residences, the mother and her child, or children, is usually left among her own people. The men are generally robust, capable of great endurance, though predisposed to intemperate habits. Their complexion is singular, taking, in matured manhood, the color of a dark red berry ; their features are those of the white man, with the black, snaky, glittering eye of the sons of the wilderness. Like other mongrels, they are said to be short-lived, and extremely liable to the attacks of infectious diseases.

Some of the half-breed females are said to be models of womanly beauty, combining in the most exquisite degree the lithe, agile figure and graceful proportions of their mother's race, with delicate features and clear olive complexions. These are frequently sought in honorable marriage by the whites, and it cannot be denied that they make good wives and affectionate mothers ; being, as an old trapper once assured me, much more modest and humble, and much less exacting and capricious, than their white sisters. The old fellow had good opportunities to know something about it, having shared his cabin with seven or eight different ones at different times, and being, according to his own account, the father of nearly a score of children.

I saw many of these women in the Mormon city. They were quite as distinguishable as the Quadroon women of the South. Some were residents with Mormon husbands, though the greater part were occasional visitors. They usually wore the picturesque costume common among Indian females of the higher class, and many times were well-mounted on valuable horses, which they rode with ease and grace. Many of them carry on a considerable traffic with the whites. They embroider buffalo robes, woollen blankets, moccasins, and similar articles, in the most beautiful manner ; are extremely skillful in knitting bead work-pockets, necklaces, and armlets ; weave mats and baskets from the inside bark of certain kinds of trees and rushes, and practise other little arts of handicraft. These articles they barter for beads, those indispensable ornaments for the toilet of an Indian belle, needles, vermilion, and similar things, though they have learned the value of money, and prize it highly. And thus it is wherever the white man treads. Love of gold, like a shadow, follows his footsteps, and all with whom he comes in contact are infected with the same selfish passion.

CHAPTER IV.

ALEXANDER BURNHAM—HIS HOUSE—TRAGIC OCCURRENCES—WEDDINGS—DEATHS.

I HAVE described, perhaps with tedious prolixity, the order and decorum manifest in the family arrangements of Judge White, for the purpose of giving an idea of the phases which polygamy under certain circumstances assumes, and the arguments by which its votaries attempt to excuse it ; yet this aspect must not be considered as a general characteristic, but only as occurring in rare and exceptional cases, where the disposition of the parties combine with pecuniary abilities, in a manner particularly favorable.

Notwithstanding all that has been said and written of the sentimentality and romantic tendencies of women, I find by observation that as a general thing they are excessively practical. They ask husbands who can support them in ease and splendor, and so long as this is obtained care little for moral character and personal habits. Do not many in all our large cities prefer living in style as the mistresses of rich men to being the lowly and industrious wives of poor tradesmen or mechanics?

Even in the Empire State I have known women not averse to polygamy. Fifteen or twenty years since there lived in Onondaga County, a man named Warner, who owned three farms, with large brick houses, and supported a wife at either place. The dwellings were in one vicinity, and the women were good neighbors to each other, frequently visiting and otherwise extending little courtesies. The younger of these women had refused the hand of a respectable, but poor man, declaring that what she asked and would have of a husband was physical support above the actual necessity of labor.

Another man in the same State had two wives, who lived in two houses close together, on the same farm. Both had families, and the children ran and played together with great harmony. This man might often be seen at public places with his wives, one on either arm. They usually dressed precisely alike, and might readily have been mistaken for two sisters. They were very friendly, and never manifested a jealous or contentious disposition.

A former acquaintance of mine is now living in the State of Ohio, with his two wives. The women seem perfectly satisfied with their condition, and assist each other in the performance of domestic duties, with great alacrity. Yet none of these women or their spouses were Mormons, and I have mentioned them to show that after all the Mrs. Whites were not the unique and singular beings that some might imagine.

Now, even in Mormondom, if the females would unanimously set their faces against polygamy it might soon be be abolished. Why they do not is referrible to particular causes. They have neither the time, nor opportunity, nor capacity for concerted action on the subject. Many of them, I verily believe, are well suited with it. Others consider it necessary because the elders tell them it is, and the remainder, being the minority, are obliged to conform.

How much the former are to be pitied I leave the theologian and moral philosopher to decide ; but the condition of the latter is most deplorable. Generally impulsive and passionate, they cannot view things with the cool expediency of Mrs. White, and not sufficiently superstitious to be governed in all their feelings and sentiments by the priesthood, their souls revolt at the associations and connections in which they are placed. Their lives become a continued scene of bickerings, jealousies, and contentions, rendering themselves and all around them supremely miserable. In such cases, as Maria Underwood informed me, the most tragic occurrences are not uncommon, yet it usually happens that the affair is hushed up, and very few either hear or even suspect the truth.

I requested her to relate without exaggeration the history of these events. She smiled sadly in return, and asked me if I ever heard of a woman in the States stabbing or poisoning her rival through jealousy and hatred ?

" Certainly, I have heard of such things," I replied.

" Then you can readily conceive what they do here under

the influence of the same passions," she answered. "Human nature is the same everywhere, and in some cases proves itself superior to spiritual wickedness in high places, though yielding perhaps to as great evils of another kind."

She then went on to inform me that the most strenuous opposers to polygamy were those who came there ignorant of its existence, or those who with little or no faith in the Mormon doctrines, had accompanied their husbands thither rather than be abandoned by them.

"And do women, who are not converts, ever come here?" I inquired with some surprise.

"Certainly they do," she answered. "There is Mrs. White."

"And what is she?"

"A believer in the doctrines of Fanny Wright."

"Is it possible?"

"Even so. She lived in Massachusetts several years, where she lectured on Woman's rights and other issues of the day."

"She seemed very intelligent."

"Of course, she is intelligent, no one doubts that."

"But, Maria," I questioned, "can't you relate to me some of those tragic occurrences of which you have spoken?"

"I could, though it might occasion trouble for me to do so."

"What kind of trouble; you cannot, certainly, be afraid of your husband?"

"Not exactly afraid of him, but it is the safest here, I

believe, as it is everywhere else, to see nothing, hear nothing, and know nothing. By professing ignorance I have frequently avoided trouble."

"But such professions will not avail you now," I replied.

She smiled, and rising, went to the door, opened it and looked out.

"Whom do you fear?" I inquired.

"No one," she answered, but proceeded to examine the windows. She then remarked, as if talking to herself: "They have all gone, I believe, but Underwood, and he is in the bar entertaining a drunken soldier, and will hardly have time to play the eavesdropper." Then seating herself, she inquired: "Did you ever know, or have you ever seen Alexander Burnham?"

"Never to my knowledge; but what of him?"

"Nothing of him, though what I am about to relate occurred in his family."

"The same thing," I suggested.

"Well, it makes no difference, but come to the window and I will point out his house;" and she led the way. "You see that dwelling yonder, seemingly isolated, and occupying a picturesque situation on the elevated plateau?"

I assented, remarking that I should suppose it to be a very pleasant place.

"It is," she answered. "The landscape is agreeably diversified with hill and valley, mountain and meadow, and presents altogether a rare combination of natural beauties; but the house—you just ought to see the house."

"What is there remarkable about that?" I inquired.

"Nothing so very remarkable, when all things are considered," she replied; "yet to one accustomed only to the square, plain, substantial buildings of the Eastern and Middle States, it would be neither more nor less than a curiosity."

"What is it like?" I inquired.

"It is a long, rambling, irregular concern," she answered. "At first it was a plain adobe structure, with three apartments on the ground floor, and as many above; but since then wings and lean-tos have been built, and domestic offices, such as kitchens and nurseries, erected; these various rooms communicating with each other by closets or small and generally dark entries.

"Then you have been there?" I said inquiringly.

"Certainly, I have been there to both weddings and funerals."

"And how many wives has Mr. Burnham?"

"Only three at present," she answered. "To accommodate these wives, the rooms are subdivided into suites of apartments, wonderfully alike in their appearance and appointments. To describe one will give a general idea of all. Each consists of a bed-room, sitting-room, and closet, simply furnished with such necessary conveniences as civilized life renders indispensable to neatness and comfort. Yet all the movables, the chairs, tables, curtains, glasses, beds, even to the scent-bottles and work-baskets, are precisely of the same color, quality and cost. In the living inmates of these rooms alone a difference exists, and that is difference indeed.

"Mr. Burnham was a well disposed man, whose character exhibited a singular mixture of strength and weakness, wisdom and folly. Though apparently wishing to make all around him happy, his well-meant endeavors frequently miscarried, through his own want of foresight and judgment. He had a pleasant voice, a kind face, and was generally liked as a neighborly, good sort of man. He was probably aware of his mental deficiencies when he concluded to embark his domestic happiness amid the quicksands of polygamy. He might have considered himself able to educe order out of that chaos in the family establishment, though it is much more likely that he thought nothing about it, but married his second wife, as most men do their first, from mere passional attraction."

"Had he been long a resident of Utah?"

"He came in with the first settlers, bringing his wife and one daughter. Mrs. Burnham was a woman of high passions, great strength of character, and unusual mental power. She was tall and commanding in stature, moved with the majesty and grace of a queen ; yet these exterior advantages were more than counterbalanced by a deficiency in moral and religious principle.

"Though the daughter of pious parents, and educated by a mother particularly exemplary, she seemed utterly devoid of conscientious restraints. Public opinion, however, exercised great influence over her, and while many doubted her goodness of heart, no one could point to any open infringement of the laws of society, or the fact of a lax morality. She was the senior of her husband by several years, and it was whispered that the marriage on his part was one of expedience, rather than affection. Whether as a consequence of this, or his knowledge of her unprincipled character, or both combined, Mrs. Burnham never acquired any great influence over her husband's mind, though her love for him was of the most ardent and passionate nature. When the Mormon missionaries came to their native village, and his easy and credulous mind was won to the belief of their tenets, she cared little, and said less. All religions, or none at all, were the same to her, and when he openly avowed his determination to emigrate to Utah, she readily declared her willingness to follow him, even to the ends of the earth, if he desired it.

"Mrs. Burnham had always been conscious that her passionate affection was not returned measure for measure, though she never found occasion to complain of neglect or ill-treatment. He was uniformly kind, and when a daughter was given to their arms, his demonstrations of tenderness were neither few nor feigned. Time, however, gradually effaced the novelty of paternity. The father relapsed into his accustomed manner of coldness and constraint, and his wife solaced herself with a mother's cares, and their reward.

"Mrs. Burnham was one of those people who never weary in the pursuit of an object. She had determined during the first year of her matrimonial life, that if she could not command her husband's love, she would at least extort his praise by good management and attention to all wifely duties. And this laudable design she carried out by the most unremitted exertions. His appetites were consulted, his tastes gratified. His home was always pleasant, neat, and cheerful, and his table spread in the nicest manner. At evening the most comfortable place by the glowing fire was kept for him, and the easy-chair, slippers and newspaper provided to his hand.

"Could Mrs. Burnham have found it in her heart to be satisfied with gratitude and esteem, anything in short but passionate affection, she might have been happy, though as it was, she continually pined and longed for the good beyond her reach. She felt that gratitude and esteem were cold and commonplace. She had given love, and she asked it in return. Thus several years passed away.

"It is well known that some time elapsed after the rise of Mormonism before its peculiar doctrines were publicly proclaimed. Had Mrs. Burnham fully understood them, it is to be presumed that she would have opposed her husband's scheme of uniting with that people. But accustomed to comply with his wishes, she bade farewell to the scenes of her youth, without a tear, and almost without a sigh.

"It is unnecessary to recount the incidents of their journey. They arrived in Utah, and Mr. Burnham prepared a home for his family, and tried with a right good will to make them comfortable and contented. But Mrs. Burnham discovered too late that she had taken a step most fatal to her peace. For the first time she had reason to reproach her husband for neglect. He would perhaps be detained from home on business of the church, leaving her without food or fuel. Then, too, she was shocked with the developments of polygamy, but true to her woman's nature, she never for a moment wavered in her resolution, to be all and everything to her husband. This she conceived would guard him against the temptation to take another wife, and through weariness and grief, and manifold discouragements she toiled and struggled.

"Mr. Burnham had been absent from home two or three days, and returned unusually hilarious and cheerful, embraced his wife and kissed his daughter with a great demonstration of affection, and then sitting down, commenced a conversation at once singular and unique.

"'My dear,' he said, addressing his wife, 'we have a nice little place here, I think. It makes no pretensions, and it is cosy and comfortable. Amy's bright face is a great improvement to it. But Amy needs a companion. Now, my dear, would you have any objection to take a child, one of the finest and freshest creatures on earth?'

"'A child! take a child!' echoed Mrs. Burnham in supreme astonishment.

"'Not exactly a child in years,' pursued Mr. Burnham, 'but a child of nature, simple, unsophisticated, enthusiastic, and an orphan, the daughter of my old friend. Though she can play, sing, dance, draw, sketch, and write poetry, it is her misfortune that she could never learn to do anything really useful. She is much too delicate for household labors; sewing she fears would spoil her fine eyes. She has no patience with children, and so is incapable of teaching, or attending on them. A being so helpless and guileless, with such a fine inaptitude for worldly affairs, must excite the sympathy of every man.'

"'I believe, however, that few women would fancy such an addition to their household,' said Mrs. Burnham.

"'It has been revealed to me,' continued Burnham, without noticing his wife's remark, 'that it is my duty to adopt her into my family. The will of Heaven must be obeyed, whatever may be the consequences.'

"A sudden and mortal sickness shot through the heart of Mrs. Burnham at this announcement. All her previous fears seemed about to be realized. Her husband loved another, and that loved one was about to be introduced into her presence, and to share her home. All her cares and toils, and the deep, deep love she had lavished on him had been of no avail. A fearful, a horrible thought flashed into her mind so suddenly and with such distinctness, that it seemed the suggestion of another. Was it the tempting of a fiend?

"That afternoon," continued Maria, "I paid Mrs. Burnham a visit. She received me with great friendliness, though her countenance bore the traces of great mental anguish. To my inquiries if she was ill, she returned the monosyllable 'No.' We had been on terms of intimacy for some time, and I pressed her to tell me what the matter was. At length the floodgates of her soul opened, and she poured forth a perfect storm of wrath, accompanied with such bitter denunciations against the little simple creature designed for the second wife of her husband, that I actually trembled, while Amy burst into tears, and wept bitterly.

" 'Only to think—to think that he intends to bring such a silly, coquettish, lazy thing as she is here, and then to insult me with talking about her fine eyes, and her helplessness, as if I am going to be her slave—her slave, indeed!' and her countenance indicated some fearful purpose. I soon took leave, determining to watch the progress of events.

"The next day Mrs. Burnham returned my visit. She seemed cheerful—even joyous. I was somewhat surprised at the change which such a short time had sufficed to bring about. She laughed outright. 'What is the use of making fools of ourselves?' she said. 'My mind has changed much since yesterday; and I have called to request that you will not report anything I said in reference to this projected marriage. It might create further difficulties.'

"I assured her that I would not, with a feeling of pleasure that the affair was likely to terminate so happily.

"The next week we were invited to the wedding-feast. There was a great company present; for Mr. Burnham was a noted man in the Church. The apostles and elders were all there—some with two or three wives, and others with only one. My attention, however, was chiefly engrossed by the bride, and the first Mrs. Burnham, who, it seemed to me, were the most dissimilar beings in existence. The former was a delicate little thing, with rather a large head; but her face was fairy-like, her voice sweet, and she really looked charming. All she said was free from effort, and spontaneous; and she had such a captivating gaiety in her laugh, that it was fascinating to hear her. She bandied jests with every one, and manifested the utmost brilliancy and enjoyment."

"And the first Mrs. Burnham?" I suggested.

"It would be difficult to give you an idea of her appearance. She was calm, yet rigid; and it was evident that her features and gestures were schooled for the occasion. Once, and once only, she was thrown off her guard, and then the nervous twitching of the muscles of her mouth betrayed a degree of internal agony painful to behold. There was a gleam, too, in her eye, as it followed the motions of the bride, that filled me with secret apprehensions I cared not to reveal.

"The husband evidently wished the occasion to be a joyous one, and—between demonstrations of tenderness for his new bride, and nonsensical remarks, designed to excite the mirth of those present—acted, as I thought, excessively silly. One of the elders breathed an extempore prayer, when cotillions were formed, the twelve Apostles leading off in the first set."

"Is it, indeed, a fact that cotillions are introduced with prayers?" I inquired.

"It is; and the effect is most ludicrous. I could scarcely help laughing outright."

"A fitter subject for weeping!" I replied.

"Well, every one to their mind," she continued. "But I could not help thinking that both exercises were remarkably similar—both seemed got up for the especial occasion. The new husband, in his zeal and fervor, quite outdid himself—balancing to this one, turning that one, and then whirling round his young wife for a final flourish, till she grew quite giddy.

"The first Mrs. Burnham presided at the table. The dinner was excellent and abundant. After eating heartily, the whole company resorted to dancing again, which was kept up with little variation till late at night. And the next day we were astounded by the intelligence that the bride was dead!"

"Dead! How did she die?" I ejaculated.

"How did she die? How often was that question asked! but who could answer? It was all a mystery. It was not even known when she died. An hour after the company dispersed, she was found by her husband in the portico of the dwelling, senseless and speechless. A physician was summoned, but the remedies came too late, and before morning she expired.

"We went to the funeral. The husband seemed inconsolable. The first wife was rigid and indifferent, though, when she approached to look at the corpse, I either saw or fancied that a momentary gleam of malicious pleasure flitted over her countenance. Amy, too, wept with unaccountable bitterness. Ill-natured people seemed disposed to suspect that all was not right; but their surmises never took tangible form or shape, and the affair was soon forgotten, like every other nine days' wonder."

"And did Burnham relinquish the idea of taking another wife?"

"Far from it. Before one month had elapsed, his versatile and fickle fancy had selected another. The courtship was carried on with all that fond intercourse usual where no wife exists. The day for the wedding was set, when the bride elect suddenly sickened and died. People thought it strange. The elders condoled with the afflicted brother, and many of them advised him to try again."

"And his wife"——

"Carried herself as usual, though perhaps a close observer might have detected a greater degree of haughtiness in her manner, and a cautious reserve in her conversation, even with her most intimate friends.

"That season was proverbially sickly. Bilious and other fevers extensively prevailed. Mrs. Burnham was among the first attacked. I was summoned to watch by her bed-side. She was wildly delirious, and raved in a manner really frightful. I shuddered, listening to the revelations of her guilt. She avowed herself a murderess, and called on Heaven to witness the truth of what she said. Her husband stood by, livid as chalk, and trembling like an aspen. She accused him of destroying her soul, by exposing her to such horrible temptations. I never saw such a death-bed before. May I be mercifully spared from seeing such again!"

"She died, then?"

"She did; and, after what had happened, it was a great mercy. Since then, Mr. Burnham has married six different women, and no doubt finds it a relief to be without her."

"And Amy"——

"Ran off to California, with a tourist old enough to be her father. But I have heard that her husband has become rich, and that, taken upon the whole, she did well."

CHAPTER V.

DIFFERENT SENTIMENTS—POOR CLASS OF MORMONS—MISERY OF WIVES—ETC.

I FIND that, even among husbands, the utmost diversity of sentiment, with regard to polygamy, prevails. It cannot be disguised that the whole system is indebted, for support, to the protection and countenance of the elders. These monopolize the fairest, most healthy women, leaving the old, ugly, and decrepid to be shared among their followers. I have known some of the most virtuous and intelligent of these people to be exceedingly disgusted with what they saw and heard, though evidently cautious not to express publicly their feelings of disapprobation. Slavery and polygamy, both institutions of barbaric ages and countries, have this in common, that while increasing the luxuries of the rich, they add to the discomforts and miseries of the poor.

A poor man—by which I mean one dependent on his daily labor for the necessaries of life—will generally find the decent support of one wife, and her little brood, quite enough for his exertions. But poverty exempts no one from the passions inherent to the race; and if a rich man indulges himself by taking six wives, his poor neighbor will imitate him as far as possible, and probably take two, though against his better judgment, and fully aware that his domestic happiness will be thereby destroyed.

In conversation with an intelligent Mormon, I inquired how it happened that they were so well supplied with women, as the proportion of the female population to that of the males was about as four to one. He replied that the ranks were thus filled by the female converts to Mormonism.

"You would imply, then, that more women than men embrace your doctrines?" I suggested.

"A great many more," he replied. "Women, in all ages, have been the most susceptible of truth, you know."

"And of imposition, too," I replied.

"The first believers and preachers of Christianity were women," he continued, without noticing my last remark.

"And the first convert to Mohammedanism was a woman," I answered.

"Your comparisons are odious and unjust," he retorted, angrily.

"The truth should not be either," I replied. "Women, from their peculiarly susceptible temperaments, are extremely liable to be charmed with novelties. While their devotional sentiments are more easily excited than those of the men, it holds, as a general thing, that her reasoning powers are much inferior; hence I question whether she is as capable of perceiving and appreciating the truth as are the stronger sex."

My Mormon friend, however, did not seem inclined to discuss the subject further, and our interview ended with manifest displeasure on his part.

Another with whom I conversed, considered this abundance of women as a providential interposition in behalf of the saints; and when I attempted to argue with him on the absurdity of such notions, he broke out in a malediction, denouncing me as an infidel, Gentile, and heathen. It is a fact that Utah, as compared with other portions of our country, is disproportionately supplied with women, and many of them excuse or advocate polygamy for that reason.

"Suppose," they say, "that only one woman was married to each man; then for one married woman you have three or four single ones. What is to be done with them? Shall we let them sink into vulgar, degraded, and abandoned habits, as they do in all your large cities? Shall their young affections run to waste? Shall the State be deprived of the children they ought to bear? And last, not least, must they spend their lives in a hopeless celibacy, because certain legislators have deemed it expedient to restrict the intercourse of one husband to that of one wife?"

When I remarked that I should fancy they would be happier single than married, under such circumstances, "They don't think so," would always be the answer. "We have no difficulty in obtaining wives."

I scarcely think they do.

The laboring class in Utah are not so comfortably provided for as might be wished, yet the question arises, Where, in the wide world, is not such the case? In civilized, Christianized, and enlightened London, to marry two wives is a crime considered worthy of transportation, though to let a next-door neighbor starve, yourself rolling in luxury meanwhile, elicits no reproach. New-York, the great, the spacious, the commercial, has its free schools and churches, side by side with dens of squalid poverty and haunts of crime. Where, I say, are the comforts of the laboring classes duly considered, or where do they take the position in society they are justly entitled to? It would be a hard thing to tell.

As a general thing, however, labor is more respected in Zion, than in any other city which I have visited; and laboring people do not form, as elsewhere, a separate and distinct class. This may be chiefly owing to the discordant elements of which society is composed, and which require mixture and fusion before the scum can rise to the top, or the dregs settle to the bottom. Yet I am inclined to think that it originates in the policy of the Mormon leaders; and, without looking further, we can find very good reasons why they should wish to have it so. Though accused of laziness themselves, the Mormon elders are "loud" against its being practised by others, and take every occasion to enforce the duty and necessity of industry. Of course, there is a class of loafers, but these are mostly outsiders, visitors, and Gentiles.

Most of the mechanics, small farmers, and day-laborers, have each two or three wives. Some of these women are very industrious, though others are not. Indeed, I thought laziness more prevalent among them than any other class. Perhaps that is owing to polygamy—perhaps to natural disposition. I do not attempt to decide. But in this heterogeneous assemblage from different parts of the earth, a great diversity of character necessarily exists. In walking out, one morning, I came unexpectedly to a miserable shanty, and called, to rest and look around. It was occupied by four women, all the wives of one man. One of them was weaving a kind of coarse cloth, and the others did not seem to have anything to do. I ascertained that the husband was a blacksmith, who had emigrated from Cayuga county, in the State of New-York, but a few years previous. One wife only had emigrated with him. He found the others subsequent to his arrival. They were aware of his condition, and that nothing better than a hovel could be afforded them, yet each one preferred sharing this with the others and a husband, to living in celibacy. I inquired if the husband followed his trade, and received a negative answer.

"Why not?"

"No particular reason, that I know of, except that he prefers to hunt and fish."

"Prefers to hunt and fish, does he? And yet I should suppose that a rather precarious manner of gaining a livelihood."

"You would, ha? We live as well as our neighbors, sir—poor people, I mean—yet, if you have a trifle to give me, I should thank you, sir—I should, indeed!"

I tossed a twenty-five cent piece into her lap, and bade her "good-day."

My curiosity was excited to look further. The cabins which I entered were usually occupied by two or three, and sometimes six or seven, very dirty women, and a group of ragged, squalid, miserable-looking children. There was but one room and loft to each cabin, or, where there were two rooms, they were occupied by two families. They were very destitute of furniture, and without any ground floor. There was no glass in the windows; and the whole scene was comfortless in the extreme. I encountered one old fellow sitting near the entrance of a covered wagon-body, which had been removed from the wheels. His countenance had a simple, idiotic expression; and I approached, accosting him with the inquiry of, "What are you doing there, uncle?"

"Nothing at all," he answered. "This is my house"—pointing to the wagon, with ineffable self-satisfaction.

"Your house!" I reiterated, in great surprise.

"To be sure; and a very good one it is," he answered. "I slept in it all last winter."

"Didn't you suffer with the cold?"

"Not much. I had a buffalo."

"Have you any family?" I questioned.

"None at all," he answered, but avowed his determination to marry at least three women when his prospects brightened a little. Thinking this idea to be a good one, I encouraged him in it, and passed on. Yet these were solitary cases.

Entering a small cabin by the road-side, I found two women, one man, and three or four children. The house and its furniture looked very well ; so did the women and children ; but a large bandage was bound over the face and one eye of the man, that gave him a grotesque appearance.

"What is the matter with your face, friend ?" I inquired.

"Burnt it," he answered, gruffly.

The women looked at each other with ill-concealed merriment, while the husband rose and went out.

"I've a great mind to tell the stranger how it happened," said one.

"Do," answered the other.

"I should like to know, certainly," I replied.

"Well," resumed the first speaker, "our husband is a little queer sometimes."

"He always is," suggested the other.

"For three or four years, however, when anything occurred to rumple him, he would refuse to go to bed, and actually sit up the whole night, dozing away his time in the rocking-chair."

"Did he suppose that plagued any one but himself ?"

"He knew very well that it plagued me ; but often I was as innocent as you were of giving him cause for offence. If the pigs got into the yard, he was mad about it, and wouldn't go to bed. If I found a word of fault with any of his arrangements, the next thing was, he wouldn't go to bed. Sometimes, by coaxing and flattery, I would succeed in getting him off; but I grew tired of this, and concluded to let him set up till he got enough of it. Yesterday, he got sullen, as usual. Neither of us said a word, or took any notice of him. When bed-time came, we retired, leaving him to his meditations. In the night we were awakened by a loud shriek. We fancied what had happened, but determined not to rise or go to his assistance, unless he requested it. We heard him going about the house, but he said nothing to us, and this morning his face was bound up, as you see. I suppose he got to sleep, and fell against the stove."

"It will probably be a lesson to him," I said, though I could scarcely speak for laughing.

"I should think so," she replied.

These women did not seem miserable. I have seen few that did. They have probably become accustomed to the prevailing state of things; and custom, it is said, is second nature. I believe that the manifestation of deep feeling, by the wife, when her husband takes his second partner, is exceedingly rare. Are they restrained by fear, or is it actual indifference, or do both these feelings come in for a share?

Maria Underwood, to whom I mentioned the subject, declared that the greater part, though outwardly calm, were inwardly dying with grief, vexation, and jealousy, and attributed to polygamy all the shiftlessness and laziness observable in certain quarters. I should doubtless have received the same impression, had I not been aware that similar habits existed among a certain class where polygamy was never tolerated. Yet there can be no doubt, I think, that it operates unfavorably on the mind of the wife, by removing the great stimulus to the proper discharge of her family duties.

St. Paul, a wise man, and accurate observer of human nature, thus remarks : " The married woman careth for the things of the world, how she may please her husband." And there can be little doubt that the chief stimulus to exertion in the female mind is the idea of pleasing the husband. " What will he say ?—How will he like it ?—Will it suit him ?"—are the thoughts constantly recurring to her mind, though, when discouraged by his indifference, she becomes weary, careless, and aimless. Maria Underwood informed me of two or three cases where the first wife had actually poisoned or drowned herself on the advent of the second, though the second cared little or nothing when the third was taken.

" Mr. Griscom formerly resided in New-Jersey, and was a member of the Presbyterian Church, yet few thought him to be a man of much principle, and many openly questioned his honesty. But he was wealthy, and wealth is respectable. Consequently his conversion to Mormonism made a decided sensation—a sort of nine days' wonder—in his native village. Mrs. Griscom had riches in her own right, but the scheming husband had contrived to get them all in his possession, thus leaving her penniless for voluntary and separate support. When he proposed to unite with the Mormons, and emigrate, her friends decidedly objected to her accompanying him. To this he manifested entire indifference, telling her to go or stay, whichever she preferred; but when she mentioned her property, he told her plainly that he should not voluntarily relinquish one cent, and that the law, under the circumstances, would give her nothing. Not wishing to become a burden to her friends, she determined to remain with him.

"After innumerable difficulties and dangers, they reached Deseret, with a company of the first settlers. The country was wild, and inhabited by Indians; but one thing was in their favor—they had the choice of pleasant localities.

"Mr. Griscom made immediate preparations for extensive grazing. He justly concluded that milk, butter, and cheese would be in extensive demand; and, to make sure of "help," in the domestic department, he hired a great, red-faced, freckled, and blowzy German girl, who immediately became a candidate for matrimonial honors. Most men are vain, and Mr. Griscom was manifestly flattered by her endearments and attentions, while his poor wife looked on in insufferable agony.

"A year elapsed, and the consequence of their intimacy became manifest. Mr. Griscom was a proud man, and she was not exactly such a woman as he would have selected, even for his second wife. But there was no alternative; she refused to leave the house. and in this determination the elders encouraged her. Finally—and, it may be, for the sake of his child—his reluctance was overcome. They were married in the evening; before morning she became a mother. On this occasion, the absence of the first Mrs. Griscom was observable. Inquiries were made, but she could not be found. Two days elapsed, still she came not. A week went by, when some hunters discovered the body of a woman floating in the thermal spring. It was soon ascertained to be that of Mrs. Griscom. The poor lady, whose prospects of life were once fair and bright, had been reduced to the last great extremity of committing suicide."

"And how did he get along with his German wife?" I asked.

"Extremely bad," she replied. "His domestic establishment embraces at this time six or seven more, but they are little better than slaves. He appoints their daily tasks, and when they fail in the performance, punishes them.

"For my own part," continued Maria, introducing the subject which I had longed to hear her touch upon—"for my own part, I didn't lay it to heart like some women would. Of course, I worried a little at first, but soon concluded it was no use to make a fool of myself. If Underwood had grown tired of me, and thought another would suit him better, why, let him try it. I was never much given to sentimentality. I always considered marriage to be of all things most exceedingly practical. I could very well be contented with beef, bread, and butter, with or without the husband. As the formation of matrimonial connections with another would not cancel his obligations to me, I raised no objections, but kept all the time thinking, with a slight variation, of the old song:

"'I think light of him as he can think of me,
Not a fig for an old man who marries two or three.'

"After the second wife came here, I determined to take matters easy, and I have done so."

"And the others have imitated your example, I guess."

"Yes; we don't all perform the labor that one industrious woman would."

Another woman of intelligence and strict propriety informed me that the general tendency of polygamy was to make husbands either dupes or despots. If they were of an easy and moderate disposition, their domestic concerns would be neglected, and the utmost disorder, waste, and discomfort prevail—while, on the other hand, if they could and would bring themselves to treat their wives like so many servants, they might get along tolerably well, though the happiness usually experienced where one wife received all the affection and care of her lord, was out of the question. Many wives, she thought, brought themselves into a state of apathetic indifference, but then they had little affection and no respect for their husbands, and generally managed to make them miserable.

Her husband, she continued, had married another wife soon after their arrival in Zion, and they managed to get along comfortably, and with little quarreling—quarreling she always detested—but, as for taking care of his house or clothes since, she hadn't done it, and didn't design to do it. She believed most men found it more difficult to get a button sewed on a shirt, where their houses were filled with wives, than to have the whole shirt made where there was only one.

"And are husbands often despotic? That is, do they often punish their wives, to enforce labor and obedience?"

Well, she rather thought not. She did not suppose it was very common, though the Germans and other foreigners had little mercy on their women. One German that she knew, accustomed his wives to working in the fields, himself standing by, with a whip in his hand, and looking for all the world like a Southern slavedriver. When reproved for such an exhibition of unmanliness, he excused the matter by saying that it was the custom in Germany, and he didn't see why the women were better here than there.

"But is there no law to bring husbands to account for such brutality?"

She guessed not; had never heard of such a thing; was pretty certain there was not. The operating laws of the Territory were all founded on the code of Mormon; and husbands, according to that precious document, could do no wrong.

"Then the safety of the wife, or wives, depends altogether on the naturally humane disposition of the husband. If he chooses to punish her, or make her a slave, he can do it with absolute impunity, and that, too, within a country famed for its enlightened and liberal institutions."

I had frequently observed that most Mormon women were cautious in the expression of sentiments adverse to the prevailing customs, and, before giving information on such points, required a promise of secrecy. To account for this, I subsequently learned that some of the more orthodox husbands chastised their wives for heresy—meaning by this, the manifestation of displeasure or opposition to Mormon institutions in the presence of Gentiles.

This brutality on the part of husbands, however, cannot be justly attributed to polygamy. Husbands, uneducated, low, vicious, and sensual, have manifested the same tempers in the monogamous state. The ill-treatment of wives is a common topic of newspaper and neighborhood gossip, and of such frequent occurrence that no one wonders to hear or read of it. Even in our Christianized and enlightened State, wives are butchered, are poisoned, are subjected to all kinds of brutality, that would sicken one's heart to hear of, if perpetrated in a distant country.

I have never yet heard of one instance where a Mormon husband has actually and in cold blood murdered his wife. Would to Heaven I could say the same of those who are not Mormons !(?.)

But there is a phase of polygamy which I have not noticed yet, and which seems really cruel, though the monogamous system is not exempt from the same or similar evils.

I encountered, one morning, in my walk, a poor woman, middle-aged, and faded, through hardship and exposure. She complained that her husband had deserted her and her children ; that her house was cold, open, and exceedingly uncomfortable ; that she had neither food, fuel, nor necessary clothing, though her lord resided with a younger and fairer wife, in a sumptuous mansion, partaking all the pleasures and luxuries of life.

Upon inquiry, I found that provision for the wife was optional with the husband, and that if he chose to neglect or abandon her, she had no legal remedy.

CHAPTER VI.

AN ENGLISHMAN'S OPINION—ENGLISH EMIGRANTS—THEIR CHARACTER—ETC.

"YOURS is certainly a most remarkable country," remarked an Englishman, who had been attached to the Hudson's Bay Company of traders—"a most remarkable country. Don't you think so?"

I replied that few Americans would be inclined to dispute it.

"In looking at your system of government, and the institutions which flourish beneath it, I am strongly reminded of the pseudo-philosopher whom Marryatt has rendered famous, and who contended that everything going on was simply a rehearsal of past events."

"Why so?" I queried.

"Because you would probably contend that your country has made the farthest advance in liberal and enlightened institutions—which I cannot deny—but where has it brought you? Right back to the patriarchal ages—the practice of polygamy, the encouragement of slavery. Who, after this, will contend for the progress of the race, when the extreme of civilization merges itself in barbaric practices !"

"But we shall probably get clear of both."

"Far from it. Slavery has become already too deeply incorporated with your social and political system, and polygamy soon will be. Even now I doubt the ability of your government to get rid of it. What will be the result when Utah desires admission into the Union as a State? She can scarcely be refused, because your Congress have no right to interfere with the domestic regulations of the States; and if she is received, and the practice of polygamy tolerated in her case, who shall decide that in course of time it may not become general ?"

"I cannot believe such a thing possible. You think too meanly of us. Our Doctors of Divinity, philosophers, and strong-minded women would all be adverse to such a state of things."

"And yet how powerless are these when acting against the inexorable law of destiny, or the equally invincible bias of human nature !"

"You are not a believer in human progress ?"

"I am not," he replied. "I look upon that doctrine as dangerous and deceitful. The history of the world disproves it. Men, systems and opinions change, but never advance. Some virtues are most fashionable in one age, and some in another. Of course, those that are most fashionable will be most practised. It is just so with vices. The ancients were addicted to some of which we are happily

innocent, while we are guilty of many that they never tolerated—and thus, in the words of the song,

"'Round and round we run.'"

"I don't clearly understand you," I said, and, in truth, I did not.

"Humanity moves in cycles, or, more properly, circles," he continued. "We who stand on one side, necessarily occupy a different position from the ancients, who were on the other side, though on a level with them. They had a class of ideas, of inventions, and opinions, precisely adapted to their tastes and wants; and we have another class, different, indeed, but no better, and no more wisely accommodated to our desires. We assume to pity their ignorance, and they would have as certainly detested our folly. Here, in your age and nation, we see mankind coming directly back to the practices of the patriarchs. What a solution to the great question of ages, whether or not the race was susceptible of indefinite perfectibility!"

Not caring to discuss a question so purely theoretical, I left the Englishman to speculate on the incongruities of our people and government, and sauntered into the streets. The Mormon missionaries seem to have driven a smart business in England, making converts and procuring emigrants. All classes of the English people are represented in Utah, with the exception of the highest aristocracy and clergymen of the Established Church. Some of them are intelligent and refined, but others are mean, selfish, arrogant, and ill-bred—regular, downright John Bulls. Their general treatment of women was rude, discourteous, and boorish. If a woman met one of them on a bridge, or at the street-crossings, she must turn and go back, giving him the way, at the risk of being thrust into the mud and water. In vehicles or churches, they always usurp and keep the best places. At the table, they rudely appropriate the most dainty pieces of vegetables or game. They seem to have no appreciation of any one's comfort but their own, and are quite as deficient of artificial politeness as of natural kindness of heart. I did not wonder that such fellows were polygamists in principle, though I really did wonder how they were ever enabled to practise it, as it does, or ought to, take two to make a bargain.

ENGLISH EMIGRANT MORMONS.(*f.*)

About twenty miles from Zion, near an outlet of the Great Salt Lake, a company of English emigrant Mormons had squatted down, and I determined one day to make them a visit. Informing Maria Underwood of my intention, she attempted to dissuade me, saying that she feared I would meet rough treatment.

"Why so?" I inquired.

"Because they will think you a spy, or something of that character," she replied.

"Are they then so afraid of strangers?" I questioned.

"Oh, I don't know what is the matter with them; but

they are singular, and have such strange notions, and are so insolent and impertinent, that I shouldn't like to trust myself among them."

"If that is all, it is rather an inducement to go," I replied, and accordingly determined to start the next morning. I was up early, ate my breakfast with a good appetite, and, being abundantly supplied with cakes by Maria, took my gun and set off across the plain. Though it was rather the wrong season for game, I congratulated myself with the idea that my appearance among them would be somewhat excusable on the plea of hunting. The morning was beautiful, the breezes fresh from the mountains, and the whole scenery delightful. I pressed rapidly forward, but before five miles had been passed over, began to regret that I had undertaken such a journey on foot. Fortunately the residence of brother Wells was near. This man was a very good Mormon, had four wives, and, what was of infinitely more interest to me, owned several valuable horses. Of course, I did not wish to buy, but to hire one for a day or two. As I approached his dwelling, two or three dogs ran out of their kennel, barking and yelping; and presently a large aldermanic-looking individual came to the door, and, seeing me advance, instantly came out of the house, and withdrew around the corner. I followed him. He was standing near a small out-house, evidently awaiting my approach. As I passed around the dwelling, I heard evidences that hot work was going on within. Children were screaming, women scolding, and abusing each other in the most vulgar language. The man looked worried, and half frightened. I didn't wonder why; for the horrible discord grew louder and louder, and I could hear to distinguish the profane and obscene words.

"Have I the pleasure of addressing Mr. Wells?" I inquired; but the noise from the house completely drowned my voice.

"Sir?" he said, coming nearer, and looking towards the window, which was literally filled with heads.

"Have I the pleasure of addressing Mr. Wells?" I repeated, making my best bow.

"Yes; that is my name. Yes"—advancing still nearer.

There was a momentary pause in the domestic tempest—curiosity connected with my appearance and business, overcoming anger for the time being. I took advantage of the silence to make known my errand with as little peroration as possible.

"I should like to hire a horse for a day or two. Could you accommodate me with one?"

"To be sure he couldn't!" screamed a voice from the window. "Do you suppose that he keeps horses for the like of you?"

Brother Wells' face flushed, and he made a gesture of impatience. I turned in the direction of the voice. A large, masculine-looking woman had thrown up the sash, and, leaning through the aperture, regarded me with an expression of low cunning positively repulsive. I neither bowed nor spoke to her, but turned again to the husband.

"Could you accommodate me with a horse?" I asked.

"Begone! you vile dog's whelp, you! Begone! I say. You want to steal the horse. You'll run away with him. You'll never bring him back. You'll"——

"Sally! Sally!" interposed Wells, approaching the window. "Go in! Go in, and be a good girl! I'll give you some money."

This woman was the complete picture of a termagant. Her features large, coarse, and flushed with anger; her uncombed hair—red in color, and standing upright—and her whole appearance, unpleasantly suggestive of shrewishness and ill-humor. She might probably have been somewhat mollified by the promise of money, had not a rival at that moment appeared and put in her claim: "You promised to give the next money that you got to me. You know you did! And I'll have it, too! So I will!"

The last speaker presented an exact contrast to the other. She was little, spare, and withered, with a countenance on which vixen was plainly stamped. She spoke remarkably fluent, and all her gestures manifested a corresponding agility. The first one turned towards her with an expression of intense hatred, but she responded to the glance with a more malignant scowl.

"Now, do go in, while I talk with the gentleman," said the husband, coaxingly. "I will divide the money between you."

"You won't do any such thing! She shan't have the first red cent!" screamed the vixen.

"I will!—that I will!" yelled the other; and she made a plunge at her antagonist.

I expected to see the husband rush in, to put an end to the *mêlée*, but he never stirred.

"Those women are fighting, sir. They will kill each other!" I said, with real concern.

"I wish in my soul they would!" he replied. "It would to me be a happy riddance of bad luggage. It would, indeed! They are the torment of my life—always mad and quarreling, sir."

"You forget my errand," I interposed. "Can I have the horse?"

"Guess you can," he said. "You will bring him back, of course, and not override or otherwise injure him?"

"I will take good care of the horse," I replied; "and return him safe and sound."

I was obliged to raise my voice to a pretty loud key, as the tumult from the house effectually precluded hearing common conversation.

"This way," said Mr. Wells. "This way, sir."

I followed, glad to escape the uproar. He led me half way down the side of a small hill, to a well-built adobe stable, in which several noble animals were standing. The master entered, and spoke to them in a pleasant voice. They recognized him with a low neigh. Surely this man cannot be utterly depraved, I thought—an affection for dumb animals having always seemed to me as inherent to a noble spirit.

"I keep my horses stabled," he said, addressing me while preparing to adjust the saddle. "The flies plague them so in the field, they are very fond of the shelter. Nancy, here," he continued, "has much the easiest gait. Steady, steady, girl!"

The mare seemed overflowing with an exuberance of animal spirits.

"So you are going to that English settlement," he remarked. "Well, they are rough customers, but take good care of the mare."

"Certainly, I will do that."

He led her out. I paid him, in advance, the hire for a couple of days; and, vaulting into the saddle, bade him "good-day," and departed.

It was now near noon, and the hot rays of the summer sun were pouring down on the plain, which offered no convenient shade. I took the main road to Salt Lake, that leads over several inequalities of ground, through a literal thicket of saline plants, which continually increased in size, abundance, and beauty. At length we came to several miry depressions, strongly impregnated with salæratus, and two or three large ponds, filled with countless wild fowl, which rose screaming into the air. I took aim, and fired. Three fell, of which I obtained two.

Antelope Island, in the Salt Lake, was distinctly visible, rearing its mountain form before me, and, though I had been approaching it for hours, seeming no nearer. Then, however, its outlines became more boldly relieved against the sky, and the rocks, ravines, and inequalities of its surface assumed a shape and distinctness. Here, also, the road forked—one branch leading directly to the lake, and the other bearing off to the southward. I took the southern track, leaving the lake, of which I had just obtained a glimpse at my right hand. I paused for some time, to take in a view of the scenery, it was so wonderfully sublime, grand, and impressive. The prospect to the north was uninterrupted for a great distance, but, stretching away southward, the huge Alps of the Western World towered in majestic grandeur, the cradle of tempests and the birthplace of a thousand streams. Nestled in their deepest recesses is the Utah Lake, a broad sheet of clear, fresh water, that ever holds a mirror to the purple heaven. Here Nature seems to exult in sublimity. In outline, everything is massive, grand, and imposing.

Following the slight traces of a road, we came suddenly upon a singular vehicular establishment. It was a sort of cart, consisting of a beam, axletree, and two wheels, to which a couple of unbarked saplings were fastened for shafts, and hitched in these, by attachments of raw-hide and rope, stood a single ox, meekly and contentedly chewing his cud. A man, poorly dressed, and with a crownless hat, was lying on the ground, in the shadow of the wagon, while two hounds were squatting on their haunches, in close companionship. The man eyed me with a sullen stare, while the dogs growled and showed their teeth.

"Good-day, friend," said I, advancing.

He barely noticed my salute.

"Is this the direct road to Brick-town?" I inquired—the settlement I sought having obtained that sobriquet, from the fact that its inhabitants were, or had been, brick-burners in their native country.

"I don't see why ye can be wanting to go there," he replied, without looking up.

"I don't know that it matters why," I answered; "though if you would give me the direction, I should esteem it a great favor."

"Well, yes. Keep right on, then, till you come to the sand, when you are e'enamost there."

"I thought this was sand," said I; and, indeed, it was.

"No, this ain't the sand," he answered. "But you'll know it when you reach it; and then keep right on through that, till you see the houses. You can't miss it."

Not seeing any probability of obtaining more perspicuous directions, I thanked him, and rode on.

I did, indeed, know the sand when I came to it, which was very soon. It was deep and heavy, with a vegetation of large flowering cactuses; but, fortunately, it did not extend far; and I soon came in sight of a long, low fringe of green, which I knew to be a belt of cottonwood trees, such as always in this country line the margin of the streams.

I soon came to the village. It was a cluster of wretched mud-hovels, with pig-sties close to the doors, and miserable little gardens, growing nothing but weeds. There seemed an abundance of women, children, and dogs, though but little of anything else. Few of the houses had either windows or doors, and their only furniture seemed to be old barrels, boxes, and such like lumber.

Of course, I attracted great attention. Heads were thrust from the windows, and the little, low doors were crowded with women of uncouth shape and feature. I have scarce ever seen females, of any age or country, more decidedly ugly. They laughed, leered, and talked to each other in a loud voice, as I passed by.

Approaching one of the hovels, which had an air of decency, compared with the rest, I alighted, hitched my horse to an old cart, and went in. The air of the apartment was almost suffocating, so hot and offensive, and great untidiness prevailed, though it is doubtful how far neatness is compatible with such a place. There was no fireplace, but a great, thick, old-fashioned cook-stove occupied nearly one-fourth of the room. I subsequently ascertained that it was the only oven in the village, and quite a public concern, as all the baking required for the whole was done in it, and that, consequently, it was reeking with heat the greater part of the time. I presume the inhabitants of the cabin had become accustomed to the sweltering atmosphere. A man, looking very dirty and dissipated, was lying at full length on the ground, smoking a short, black, stumpy pipe. A woman, with a bruised face, held to her bosom a little, gasping baby ; while another woman, who looked younger, but whose cast of feature was excessively disagreeable, supported a larger infant on her lap. There was a great girl washing some dirty dishes in some very dirty water, and a great boy tying up a dog, while any quantity of smaller boys and girls were lounging about in various attitudes, not remarkable for grace. All occupations, except the smoking, stopped ; and, though none welcomed, all looked at me.

"Well, my friends," I said, assuming an air of carelessness which I certainly did not feel, "I am something of a stranger in these parts. Can you direct me to a house where I can obtain refreshment for myself and my horse ?"

"Don't you want something else ?" growled the man on the floor. "Wouldn't you like to have some whisky now, or a swig of rum, in exchange for a broad piece of silver ?"

"No, sir," I replied. "I've no occasion for anything of the kind, though I would thank you for a drink of cold water."

"Cold water !" cried the man. "Ha ! ha ! that's too good ! Cold water in hell ! We live in hell, sir !—that's what I call it. Run, some of ye, and get some water, such as it is." But nobody stirred.

"Can you direct me to the bishop's ?" I asked, at length.

"And what do you want to go there for ?" he inquired. "The bishop is no better off than the rest of us. They hadn't nothing to eat yesterday. I don't b'lieve they have to-day."

I glanced at the women. The one with the small baby looked sad and sorrowful, while the other broke out in a coarse, disgusting laugh.

"Do you suppose the bishop to be at home?" I inquired, hesitatingly.

"Better look after your horse, I guess," said the man. "The bishop wants nothing of such as you."

"But I want something of him," I answered. "Come, here is money, if you will tell me;" and I drew a half-dollar from my pocket. In a moment, I saw the impropriety of this act. A telegraphic look of intelligence was suddenly exchanged all round, excepting the woman with the small baby. The boy let go his hold of the dog. The man rose from the floor, took his pipe from his mouth, and came towards me.

"The bishop is no better off than the rest," he said. "Shouldn't wonder if some on us is better off than him. But Jim Leek, down here, I should think likely he'd keep you. At any rate, I'll go and see."

"Where does he live?" I asked.

"Don't worry yourself," said the man. "Set down here, if you can find anything to set on. I'll find out." And he started. I was somewhat surprised at the sudden interest he manifested in my welfare, but, raising my eyes, I encountered those of the woman, who was looking at me with a gaze full of meaning. A sudden, yet fearful, suspicion flashed into my mind. Yet I said no more. I felt that the only person who would willingly give me the desired information, durst not do so; and so, not knowing what else to do, I went out and stood by my horse.

I saw the man coming; and, attracted by my appearance,

several others came and stood around. They were ill-looking fellows, and I could not but notice their significant glances.

"Jim Leek says that he'll take you," cried the fellow, "though his accommodations ain't none of the best; and I guess you can get along somehow. Come on."

I had had time for deliberation, however; and, turning suddenly around to the bystanders, said, "Will some one of you tell me where the bishop lives? I have pressing business with him, and have been already detained too long."

"He lives down there, in that house standing by itself," replied a half-idiotic fellow, who did not or would not understand the winks and gestures around him—"the house clear down furthest of any."

"Thanks, my good fellow! May you always find a friend in need!" I said; and, loosening my horse, mounted, and rode in the direction he had pointed out.

To tell the truth, however, I began to fear that my curiosity, like that of the wives of Bluebeard, would be the means of getting me into trouble. The sun was just sinking behind the western horizon. I was both hungry and thirsty, and so was my faithful animal. Even if I found the bishop at home, I was not certain of a welcome reception; but of one thing there could be no doubt—it was a nest of thieves and cut-throats, who would not shrink from the commission of the foulest crime.

The bishop's house was not a whit superior to the others, that I could discover; and I had little hope that the character of the man was much better. As I rode up, a man with a fiery red face came to the door. I bowed, and addressed him with, "Good-evening." He returned the salutation more courteously than I expected, though not so much so as I desired.

"Have I the pleasure of addressing the bishop?" I asked.

"I am that person," he responded. "What may your business be?"

"I am a stranger in this place," I replied; "and if you can accommodate me and my horse with shelter and refreshments for the night, I"——

"Can't do it," he answered. "This is a poor place for strangers. Don't see what they ever come here for."

"Different motives call them here, I presume. But, my good friend, you see I don't ask you to *give* this to me. I am able and willing to pay you abundantly."

His countenance brightened in a moment.

"Well, well. I will see what can be done. Our accommodations are none of the best, but such as we have is all that we can give."

"Certainly, sir."

He then pointed out a sort of hovel, where he said my horse could stand through the night. I requested food and water for her. "Yes, he would see how they were on it for meal," and went into the house.

In a few minutes he returned, with an old water-bucket, and a tin dish, filled with coarse meal. For water, I was directed to a spring at a little distance. Though I found it without difficulty, the water was foul and muddy, and nothing but extreme thirst could have induced the mare to drink. As the grass grew plentifully around the spring, I permitted her to feed till dusk, then led her to the hovel, and gave her the meal. Though somewhat apprehensive of leaving her in such an exposed situation, I could do no better.

On returning to the bishop's house, he met me at the door, and invited me to enter, with apparent cordiality: "Walk in, sir; walk in; and don't be surprised at our poor appearance. Take a seat;" and he handed along the only chair to be seen in the apartment.

"Thank you, sir; occupy the chair yourself. I will sit here, if you please;" and I took possession of a low bench. There was a dim light, formed by a wick floating loosely in a saucer of melted grease, and the room was swarming with mosquitoes. Presently, two women came in, saluted me coldly, and sat down.

"Couldn't you prepare this gentleman a little supper?" inquired the bishop, whom I now understood to be the husband of the two.

Neither deigned an answer, and I began to consider my chances rather doubtful. Presently, another woman came in, a third and younger wife, who, being reigning sultana for the time, desired to appear amiable. Again the bishop proposed that some one should get supper for me.

"What shall I get, pa?" she inquired.

"Oh, anything that you can. I dare say the gentleman is not particular," he answered.

"Well, I will see," she said.

She did see; but found the larder empty, with the exception of a little coarse meal and a few potatoes. Then the water was gone, the fire out, and, to judge from appearances, I was likely to make a great deal of trouble. Seeing this, I begged them to desist, saying that I could do very well without supper. The bishop, however—who probably had an eye to the pay—insisted that it would never do to exhibit towards a stranger such an infringement of the laws of hospitality; that he could get the water, while she made the fire; that it would take very little time, beginning being more than half.

"Liz, go and borrow some fire, can't you?" said the third favorite, addressing one of the others.

"No; I shan't," retorted Liz.

"You go, Sally, won't you, while I peel the potatoes."

Sally shrugged her shoulders, but made no move to go.

"Well, I can go myself, and no thanks to you?" she continued. The two women sat like dumps, apparently sullen or sulky. The bishop, meanwhile, went out, with a pail on his arm, and his wife followed, to borrow fire, leaving me to my meditations. These, it will readily be conceived, were not of the most pleasant character; but they were suddenly interrupted by a loud scream overhead.

"There! that young un's awake," said Liz, and she

mounted the ladder leading to the loft. The scream was followed by others, in quick succession, and, it seemed, from four or five voices, so multitudinous and loud was the din.

"Darn the young uns, I say!" muttered Sally, likewise ascending the ladder.

The music overhead seemed momentarily to increase, between the harsh scolding of the women and the cries of the children, varied, by way of chorus, with an occasional noise of blows. In the midst, the fire-borrower—whom I shall henceforth denominate my hostess—returned, carrying a small handful of coals between some hollow pieces of bark.

"You don't have matches here," I remarked, wishing to appear sociable.

"Matches!" she reiterated, with an accent of some surprise—"Matches! I should think there was enough of them!"

"Then why don't you use them? They are very handy."

"What do you mean?" she said. "I thought you was talking about matches—getting married."

This ludicrous misunderstanding completely upset my gravity, and we laughed together, thus becoming acquaintances and very good friends. It is astonishing how a joke will unbend the most austere; how it inspires patience and creates intimacies; how, from laughing with a stranger, you get to talking to him. It is ever so with me.

"The tempest overhead has subsided," I remarked.

"What?" she queried.

"The tempest overhead has subsided," I repeated.

"Oh, yes," she said. "I have become so used to such sounds that I don't mind them at all. Neither does pa."

"No fire yet!" said the bishop, entering the house, and setting down the pail of water, with a loud grunt.

"And little prospect of any," she echoed.

Indeed, it was becoming doubtful whether the few borrowed coals, instead of kindling a flame, would not become totally extinguished.

"Here, pa; you set down and whittle up some shavings, can't you?" she said.

"Be sure, I can. I declare, these hot nights are enough to kill the devil!" he continued.

I thought so, too, and finally left the house to procure a breath of fresh air. Outside, my ears were greeted with a concert, though not of sweet sounds. Two or three dogs were barking, probably for their own amusement, while shouts and oaths of drunken profanity came from a cabin where several men had assembled to hold a debauch. The night was sultry—not a breath of air stirring—and I returned into the house.

The bishop had sunk down on a bench, and was violently fanning himself with a handkerchief. His wife was squatting before the fire-place, quite as violently blowing the fire with her apron, of which the corners were wrapped around her hands; and the motion up and down puffed out great gusts of smoke and embers, completely enveloping her and filling the room.

"Sit down," said the bishop. "We've got a beginning,

you see, and beginning's half. There's never smoke without fire."

He was disposed to be facetious.

"I exceedingly regret putting your family to so much trouble," I said.

"Never mind that—money'll make it all square."

If he could feel so, I was satisfied.

At length the smoke cleared away, and its place was supplied by a bright, clear flame. An iron pot—which did triple service, as tea-kettle, boiler, and stew-pan—was brought out from its seclusion in the corner, filled with water, and set over the flame. Then, while the Rev. Mormon peeled a handful of potatoes with his jack-knife, my hostess mixed a corn-cake, after the most approved backwoods fashion. The dough—simple meal and water, with a little salt—she flattened, with her hand, on a long, narrow, but smooth board, and placed it on one edge before the fire. In this reflection of glowing heat, the cake soon acquired the requisite tint of brownness, when it was nicely turned, and the other side exposed to the same ordeal.

Meanwhile, the potatoes were being boiled ; and an hour before midnight my supper was pronounced ready. Though got up with extraordinary effort, it was not a very extraordinary affair. Tea or coffee was not to be thought of in such a connection. Meat was a proscribed delicacy. Sweet-cakes and sweetmeats were out of the question ; but a sharpened appetite gave a zest to the most ordinary food, and I made a hearty, though frugal meal.

During the repast, I attempted to open a conversation with the bishop about the prospects of the Mormon Church, and its connections in Europe. He was not inclined to give me the information I desired, but I fancied that he seemed dissatisfied. I learned, however, that he was a man of small property in England, frugal, contented, and happy in the affections of a small and virtuous family. But the serpent crept into his Eden—the tempter came. He whispered of wealth, honor, and distinction in the new church. The dormant passions of his nature were aroused. Thoughts and feelings in his heart that had always slept, came into strange and tumultuous exercise. He no longer relished the simple pleasures of his home. He shrunk from toil, and despised the honest and honorable occupations of his ancestors. The glowing accounts of the New World, with its Land of Promise, whose beauty of climate and fertility of soil was described as unequalled, induced him to emigrate. He sold his property, placed the proceeds in the general church-fund, and, with others of his countrymen, took passage in a ship for New-York, under the superintendence of a Mormon priest. After many difficulties, they reached Zion, in a state of want, discomfort, and disorganization absolutely indescribable. Their national spirit, however, kept them together. They hated the Yankees, and the Yankees despised them. Brigham took the matter in hand, but could not reconcile the jarring factions. Finally, he advocated their removal and settlement in a separate colony—thus forming a distinct branch of his church, with a bishop, chosen from their number, to superintend their spiritual affairs. They consented to this, and my entertainer was the one selected. Yet his promotion was merely nominal, and barren alike of wealth or honor.

He informed me that the Mormons were quite numerous in England, and had their chapels and places for public worship in many parts of London.

"Do they practise polygamy there?" I inquired.

"No; the laws will not allow it," he answered.

"And do you really and truly consider it an advantage?" I asked.

He shook his head.

"Are the Mormons in England aware of the practice here?"

"They were not, till recently," he replied. "I understand that it proves a great stumbling-block in foreign countries, and that many who would otherwise join us hesitate about doing so on that account."

Having finished my supper, the bishop pointed to a sort of cot in one corner of the apartment, where he said I could sleep; and then, after making some remarks on the lateness of the hour, and several excuses for the paucity of my accommodations, he ascended to the loft, followed by his wife, who bade me "good-night" as she disappeared.

Without disrobing, I threw myself on the cot, and attempted to sleep, but in vain. The heated atmosphere grew closer and more stifling every moment. I was assailed on all sides by buzzing, stinging insects, and yet more nauseous vermin. It was near morning when I sunk into an uneasy slumber, from which the advent of half a dozen children aroused me in the morning. They were little, dirty, elfish-looking beings, only half clad, in old, faded garments. The females soon followed, and, last of all, came the bishop himself. Not wishing for a repetition of the scenes of the previous evening, I made immediate preparations to depart, and inquired of my host what I should pay him for all the trouble that I had occasioned. Of course, I expected a pretty good charge, but was hardly prepared for the unreasonable demand of five dollars. However, I paid it without grumbling, and was rather amused at his apparent pleasure when I bade them "good-morning."

I started direct for the outhouse where I had left my filly, with some apprehensions that she might have been stolen. Fortunately, in that respect, at least, I had misconceived their characters. She was there, and recognized my approach with a low neigh. I adjusted the bridle and saddle to her head and back, and, leading her forth, was met by the man with whom I had conversed the previous evening. He was evidently recovering from a debauch of the preceding night.

"Going now?" he said, with a satanic leer.

"I am. Have you any objections?" I replied, with more complaisance than, under other circumstances, I might have manifested at so unceremonious an intrusion.

"Well, you can't go; not yet," he said, taking the horse by the head. "I've a bill to settle with you."

This was said with a voice, gesture, and manner that I find utterly impossible to describe.

"What kind of a bill?" I repeated, wishing to humor the fellow, though strongly inclined to knock him down.

"Let go of my horse, will you?" I continued—"and tell me what I can do for you;" and I vaulted on her back.

"No; I shan't let go the horse," he replied; and now he was joined by three others, quite as ugly and depraved as himself. I really felt alarmed, and began to consider the best way of escaping their clutches.

"You're a 'formant!" said one.

"A spy!" chimed another.

"I knowed that last night!" cried a third, pleased with the idea of his superior penetration.

A lucky thought occurred to me. Taking a handful of loose change and coppers from my pocket, I scattered them on the ground. The man let go his hold of the horse on the instant. His companions scrambled for a share, while I quietly rode off without further opposition.

I subsequently ascertained that they practised a regular system of sponging on travellers, and that one was fortunate to escape as easily as I did.

I stopped several times on my homeward route, to allow the horse to feed; and, having accidentally lost my game of the previous day, shot three more ducks. It was near night when I reached the residence of brother Wells. He was pleased to see me, probably because I brought his horse safely back. I was foolish enough to think that possibly he might invite me to take supper with him, though I much doubted the capability of his household to prepare anything eatable. Whether on this account, or because he was conscientiously opposed to wasting hospitality on a Gentile, he breathed no murmur of invitation ; and I plodded back to Zion, actually more hungry than I had ever been before.

CHAPTER VII.

THE MRS. UNDERWOOD'S JEALOUSIES, MISUNDERSTANDINGS, AND REMOVAL.

IN most Mormon families where polygamy is practised, I believe the superiority of the first wife to be involuntarily acknowledged. Certain it is, that the others are jealous of her, and act as spies on her conduct. If they can find, or invent with the least plausibility, any cause of reproach against her, they are only too happy to communicate the same to their lord. Thus, family difficulties are occasioned, and actions really innocent in themselves become, through jealousy and misrepresentation, the cause of great domestic trouble.

I had been admitted, as a boarder, to brother Underwood's house, yet a former acquaintance with his wife had certainly given me a right to be treated with greater consideration than a mere stranger. I had sought and obtained many opportunities of conversing with Maria, thoughtless that my attentions could be construed to mean more than mere friendly regard, or that the easy and amiable Underwood could be induced to cherish a jealous feeling. I had noticed for some time an increased coolness on his part towards me, and had half suspected that a system of espionage on my conversation and conduct was being practised.

Latterly, when conversing with Maria, a flitting shadow, the sudden fall of something, or the echo of a retreating footstep, would indicate the presence of a third person, till I really began to think that the wives of brother Underwood possessed a remarkable sort of ubiquity. They were ever hovering near you. If you sat in the dining-room, the doors would be left open, and your eyes delighted by the continual passing and repassing of petticoats. If you ascended the stairs, keen black eyes watched your progress. Where you least expected their appearance, they would be, sometimes, with a meaning smile on their countenances—at others, with a leer—but always with an expression that seemed to me extremely disagreeable. I am not naturally suspicious, and for a long time considered these little circumstances as accidental, of course, and though excessively annoying, not sufficiently so to warrant my removal from the house. Recently, however, I began to suspect that more was meant than met the eye, and determined to be as guarded and circumspect in my deportment as possible.

On the day of my return from Brickville, I went at once to my boarding-house. It was near dusk ; and two drunken Indians, and one or two soldiers, were in the bar-room, with Underwood behind the counter. He took no notice of my entrance, not even returning my evening salutation. I passed on to the kitchen, with my game. Two or three of the ladies were standing around, in listless attitudes.

"Who is housekeeper for to-day?" I inquired.

"Mrs. Maria," answered one of them, laying a peculiar emphasis on the "Mrs."

"And where is she?"

They all giggled, but returned no answer.

Not seeing anything so very ludicrous in my question, I inquired what they were all laughing at.

This redoubled their mirth, when, flinging the ducks at the feet of one, I hastily retreated towards my room.

It was now duskish, and I encountered Maria on the landing-place. She carried a small candle, and had evidently been weeping. Instantly recognizing me, she said, "So you have returned; but you must go away again."

"Where to?" I demanded.

"Anywhere. You must seek another home."

"Seek another home! Why, pray?"

"Because—because—oh, we have had such another time during your absence! My husband was so angry! In short, he is jealous of you."

"Jealous of me!" The idea was so ridiculous that I burst into a loud laugh. I could not help it.

"Do not laugh," said Maria. "It will be heard. Some one is watching us now, I expect. I dare say that this moment there are listeners to our conversation. You must go hence immediately, and return no more."

This moment I heard footsteps and voices.

"Together again!" said one whom I knew to be Underwood.

I looked around. He was standing at the bottom of the staircase, two or three women peering over his shoulders, on tip-toe, and the bar-room group leering and staring behind them. Maria retreated hastily. I stood still, facing the group; for I thought some explanation due myself and her. Addressing Underwood, I requested to know the meaning of such strange conduct.

"You know very well what it means," he replied. "Wasn't you talking just now to Maria, and she to you? Tell me that!"

"We certainly were conversing."

"What about?" asked one of the soldiers.

"Jealous husbands, and wives who act the part of spies," I replied, and passed on to my room.

The agitation of my feelings almost precluded the idea of hunger. Then Nature asserted her rights over sentiment. I descended the stairs, went direct to the larder, and helped myself. Whether any one saw me or not, I neither knew nor cared.

My first business next morning was to procure new lodgings, and I determined, rather presumptuously, not to go where there was more than one wife. My inquiries must have seemed ridiculous enough. In the Eastern cities, the number of children often determines the bargain in such cases, but with me it was rather the number of wives.

"Do you know of any place where I could obtain board for a month or so?" I said to an old Mormon with whom I had become slightly acquainted.

"Well, I don't know," he replied. "There's brother Solomon—a very good man—takes in boarders sometimes. Don't know whether or not he wants any now."

"How many wives?" I inquired.

"Only ten."

"Won't do for me."

"Why not?—the more the merrier! One is a good singer. Another plays the harp beautifully. I should think you would be agreeably entertained."

I shook my head.

He smiled.

"Is there a man in this city with only one wife?"

"There may be, though I know of none."

"Not one?"

"No. Stay—yes; there is Elder Hyde. I recollect hearing that he had but one."

"And do you suppose that he could be induced to take me in?"

"Doubtful. His wife, they say, won't suffer any addition to the family. She fears it might lead to the consequences she most dreads."

"I shall make the trial."

"You can do so, but I think it will be useless."

I made the trial—it was useless.

MRS. HYDE.

I found Mrs. Hyde, and her family, in a small, yet convenient, adobe house, situated at the eastern side of the city, in a very public place. I say "her family;" for she certainly seemed the ruling, reigning spirit, monopolizing the conversation, and manifesting her independence in a thousand little ways. I was quite charmed with her naïve simplicity, though I saw that it augured adverse to my scheme.

Addressing the elder, I inquired, "If he could find it convenient to take a boarder."

"Ask her," he replied. "I have nothing to say about it."

"We have had several applications for board lately," she interposed, with remarkable vivacity. "Excuse me, sir, but are you a stranger!"

She said this flitting around the house like a humming-bird, very busy in preparing dinner.

"Not exactly a stranger, madam. I have been in this place about two months."

"Where have you been living!" she continued, with true feminine curiosity.

"At Underwood's."

"Indeed! And why don't you stay there?"

She was determined to have the whole story, while I felt such questions to be decidedly impertinent.

"Excuse my freedom, madam, but I scarcely think that subject pertinent to our present business," I answered.

Her face flushed for a moment, then her black eyes twinkled, and she finally burst into a laugh.

"That's right!" said the elder, with mirth depicted on his countenance. "The curiosity of women is"——

"Now, hush!" said the little, vivacious wife, clapping her delicate hand over his mouth.

The husband laughed and struggled.

"There was no harm in her asking," I said.

"And there was no harm in your refusing to tell," she answered. "I understand your feelings; the rebuff was merited. Yet, in a place like this, where there is such a constant influx of strangers, it is necessary to know something of one's character, especially if he proposes to become an inmate of one's family."

This was said with such a charming air, and so deprecating a manner, that I felt half ashamed of myself, and wondered that I had attributed to mere feminine curiosity what had evidently arisen from a better and nobler feeling.

Mrs. Hyde, assisted by her husband, set out the dinner-table. Then she laid the cloth, and selected the dishes necessary to the repast, but found, in the meantime, abundant opportunity to talk.

"I made up my mind some time ago, that nothing should induce me to receive any additions to my family;" and she glanced at her husband. "I do my own housework, and I find it quite sufficient to keep me busy."

"I have told her, sometimes, that we had much better take in two or three boarders, and keep a hired girl. I think we could make it profitable," said the husband.

"No hired girl comes on the premises while I stay!" she answered quickly, her black eyes fairly snapping. "I detest the whole tribe!"

"That is a strong expression," said the husband.

"It's a true one, however," she replied. "Come, dinner is ready."

I was invited to partake, and not having received a definite answer to my proposal, was not prepared to depart, and in consequence accepted it. The food was excellently dished, and served with taste. There was no disorder nor disarrangement. Everything looked well, and ate well; for all was suitable and in place. The elder was complaisant, the lady social, and I thought she took great pains to interest and amuse him, though immovable in her determination on certain points.

When the dinner was finished, and we had risen from the table, she again addressed me: "Now, sir, not to keep you longer in suspense, I must firmly, yet respectfully, decline to receive you."

The husband looked towards her as if he wished that she had decided otherwise.

"I have one question to ask, however, which I really hope you will not consider impertinent. I wish to know what induced you to make application here for a home. It is a perfect mystery to me why so many seem disposed to abide with us."

I could not help smiling at her earnestness, but doubted the expediency of making the communication she desired.

"You hesitate," she began. "Shall I guess?"

"Certainly."

"And you will tell me then?"

"Be sure, I will."

"Is it because my husband has but one wife?"

"It is. At least, that was the inducement with me."

"I thought so." And she looked archly towards her husband. He sat apparently in meditative mood.

"Have you seen much of polygamy?" she questioned.

"I could not be in this country without seeing enough of it," I replied.

"In my opinion," she said, "it is the most abominable practice ever introduced into the world. If I had a daughter, I would much rather see her shrouded for a coffin, than married to a Mormon."

"But a Mormon might be a just and upright man."

"Might be," she repeated. "Yes, might be, as my husband is; but you have no security in law, Christianity, or public opinion. If my husband goes out, I cannot help thinking that possibly he may return with another wife. If a single lady comes to visit me, how can I be sure that she has no designs on him? And the worst of all is, I am under the necessity of concealing my feelings."

"That must be a vexation to one so free-spoken as yourself," retorted the husband.

"I have no fears that this gentleman will ever take the trouble to report my conversation," she said.

"I hope, sir, that you will not," said the elder, addressing me. "It is all unfounded prejudice on her part. Many families live happily, I believe, where there are two or even more wives."

"I replied that, after my hospitable reception and entertainment in their family, it would be the height of ingratitude in me to report anything that might tend to their disadvantage; and soon after took leave, really pleased with my visit.

THE NEW BOARDING-HOUSE.

After making repeated inquiries, I was driven to the alternative of accepting any situation that offered, without reference to the number of the presiding goddesses. Mr. Inkley had but two wives—so he informed me—and they were unexceptionable women.

"And how many children?" I inquired.

"Only four"—laying great stress on the adverb. "Very good children, too. Don't think you have ever seen better; still and obedient, to a charm."

To Mr. Inkley's I went, accordingly.

Maria Underwood was not in sight when I returned for my baggage, though two or three of the others stood around, apparently watching my motions with much satisfaction. I took no notice of them—not even saying "farewell"—and hurried away.

Mr. Inkley was a singular man, and some of his points decidedly laughable. He evidently considered it beneath his dignity to pay much attention to his guests—sometimes rudely turning his back when inquiries were made of him, and scarcely ever heeding complaints or requests. His wives were far his superiors in manners, but as they were expected to do all the work, and perform the duties of attendance on the boarders besides, it is not surprising that many things were disregarded that should have been attended to, and that it seemed the study of each to shirk the labors and responsibilities herself, by laying them thick and heavy on the shoulders of her companion. Thus, if the towels were not changed, or the chamber service duly performed, Martha accused Hannah of the remissness, or Hannah declared that all the blame was chargeable to Martha.

But I was chiefly amused, though many times half vexed, at Inkley's manner of praising himself and the arrangements of his household. It was the only subject over which he ever grew eloquent.

"What an excellent supper you have got, Martha! I declare, you beat all women for getting up good things, with little effort, though I cannot say without cost. Wish I could; it would be better for all concerned," he began, drawing his chair unceremoniously to the table, and inviting me to follow.

"We have little variety here," he continued. "Though I never fancied variety in food—a few dishes, and good ones, I say. Martha understands that !"

At this juncture, Hannah flung out of the room in high dudgeon, while Martha smiled complacently, and I looked in vain to discover some particular excellence in the dishes before me. They consisted of cold salt-meat, dry slices of bread, stale butter, and some kind of wild fruit, stewed in water, without spice or sugar. The weakest nerves could not have been deranged by the tea, which was served with blue milk only, while cakes and preserves seemed unknown or forbidden delicacies.

"Now, do help yourself," said Inkley, setting the example. "Make yourself at home, as Aaron used to say. Don't you remember, Martha, when we went to Aaron's, that time, with your sister's family, and you, being afraid that Susy wouldn't like so many of us coming at once, took along an old dress, to work in, and assist her about getting dinner ; and how pleased Aaron seemed, and how he tickled you by continually saying, 'Now, Matty, make yourself at home ?'"

"Oh, yes ; I remember it all," said Martha ; "but it was hardly necessary to repeat it here."

"Help yourself to the butter. Excellent butter we have in Deseret—far superior to that in the States," he continued, affecting to eat eagerly, though in reality devouring little.

"Now, don't stop so !" he said, when I refused the

second cup of tea, and drew back. "Why, I ain't half done yet! Bread and butter, and stewed berries, are good enough for a king.

"We have a very nice chamber in readiness for you, sir," he said, soon after tea. "My dear," addressing Martha, "that bed has been properly aired, has it not? I know you always have things very nice and comfortable, but thought no harm could come of mentioning it."

Martha replied that if he wished to know about that, he must go to Hannah.

"Well, I presume it's all right. We will go, if you please."

I followed him up stairs, to a small room, in one corner of the house, next under the roof. To judge from appearances, not a soul had entered it that day. The door was closed, the windows had been shut, and the air was as hot and stifling as that of an oven.

"A very nice chamber, this," said Inkley; "convenient and comfortable."

"Uncomfortable, you might have said," I suggested. "The heat is intolerable; the room has not been sufficiently ventilated," and I threw up a window.

"Strange!" said Inkley. "This room has always been a favorite with every one. I had some thoughts of occupying it myself, but the boarders always liked it so well, that I hesitated to deprive them of it. Hope you are not more difficult to suit than the others have been. Good-evening," and he withdrew.

That was a pretty good hint. I slept, as usual, with the windows open, and awoke in the morning, refreshed and invigorated. Various domestic sounds saluted my ears. The husband talking, one woman scolding, another laughing, with the racing, shouting, and crying of children, quite counterbalanced my natural tendency to a morning reverie in bed. I rose hastily, but no conveniences for a gentleman's toilet were at hand—neither water-pitcher, stand, napkin, or mirror. There was no bell; but had there been, who would have answered it? Fortunately, I had acquired a habit of taking things as they came, and had been too long accustomed to a camp-life, to be discomposed by trivial circumstances. Taking care that my apartment should have a good airing, at least, for that day, I removed the sheets, shook up the bed, and extended the windows to their utmost capacity.

While making these arrangements, I heard Inkley's voice calling, from the foot of the stairs, "Breakfast is ready, sir."

I descended, to find that breakfast was not ready, but only in a state of preparation. The kitchen was divided from the sitting-room by a thin partition; and it was impossible, while remaining in the one, to be ignorant of what was going on in the other. The women were quarrelling, and applying to each other the coarsest and most brutal epithets; and the husband, by attempts to reconcile them, only made matters worse. Growing vexed and wearied at this, he seized the broom, and threatened to strike the first one that opened her mouth to speak again. "And get breakfast ready in double quick time. Don't you know that the gentleman is waiting?"

"Let him wait, then!" muttered one of them.

By the time that breakfast was ready, however, Hannah had become good-natured, though Martha refused to appear at the table. The master, as usual, extolled the fare, and pronounced the lady beside him the most accomplished housekeeper in the world.

During this time, the children were scrambling for the choice of pieces, and drawing the saucer of berries from one to the other, alternately, across the table.

"Good children, they are," said the father, "though full of spirits, and a little boisterous sometimes. But we were all children once, I suppose, and probably no better than those we see around us now. People don't realize this as they should, or they would exhibit more patience with the little ones."

Having finished my breakfast, I went out to breathe the fresh air; and, walking to the banks of a small stream, encountered a party gathering honey-dew from the leaves of the cottonwood trees growing along its banks. They were in high spirits, and the valley rang with their shouts, songs, and hilarious laughter. There were old and young—men, maidens, and boys—some with spoons and saucers, and others without—but all, it seemed to me, more intent on enjoyment than on obtaining the honeyed secretion, which stood in great saccharine globules on the leaves. The saints profess to consider this substance as identical with the manna which fell, miraculously, to supply the pressing wants of the Israelites during their sojourn in the wilderness. Gentile eyes, however, cannot discover anything extraordinary in it. It resembles gum-arabic in color, but is of softer and less adhesive consistence, with more decided saccharine taste. To one unused to eating it, it is scarcely palatable.

Several married men were in the company. One, with whom I was slightly acquainted, and knew as the husband of six wives, was flirting and ogling most unmercifully with a delicate maiden of twelve years, who seemed decidedly pleased with his attentions, practising all the arts and allurements of the most accomplished coquette. A more disgusting sight I never witnessed. Stranger still, the girl's mother was along, highly elated with the scene, and seeming to do all in her power to increase their intimacy.

I did not mingle with the group, but seated myself on the trunk of a fallen tree, within sight and hearing, where I was presently joined by one of the party. He was a young man of comely appearance, and remarkably fine eyes, beaming with intelligence. I had previously seen him, and he now accosted me with an ease and grace of manner only to be acquired by mingling in good society.

"You are an Eastern man, I think, sir?"

"I am."

"Were you ever in New York?"

"That is my native State."

"Then I must shake hands with you; for it is mine, too,

and I am proud to say it," he continued, extending his hand.

We shook hands.

"Excuse my liberty—your name?"

I gave it.

"And mine is Frederick B——r. And now we may consider ourselves as acquainted, for the future, may we not?"

"Certainly."

And we entered into conversation. I soon ascertained that he was not particularly partial to the Mormon system of religious faith, and viewed the patriarchal institution they professed to prize so highly, with supreme contempt. His allusion to that subject excited my curiosity.

"Have you a family?" I inquired.

"No, sir; and never shall have while I remain here."

"Why not? I have seen several fine specimens of womanhood among your people."

"When I marry, my wife must be both virtuous and intelligent. I could not find a woman here that would meet my views in that respect."

"What do you mean?"

"What I say."

"That there are no virtuous women in Utah?"

"Just so."

"I think there must be."

"You have not penetrated beneath the veil."

"Probably not."

"I may do wrong in saying that there are none. There

must be some, I suppose. Sodom could furnish one righteous man; Noah remained a preacher of righteousness, when all flesh had corrupted their way; and there may be some who are really endowed with more correct moral principle than I give them credit for. Till my mother died, I knew there was one. Since then, I have had no faith in those by whom I have been surrounded."

"Then you have parents here?"

"My father is here. As I have told you, my mother is dead. Love and gratitude to the authors of my being, first brought me here, and the same feelings now detain me."

Meanwhile, the gatherers of the honey-dew had obtained all the sweets to be found there, and departed to look elsewhere. We were not sorry to be alone. He told me of their beautiful home in New York, and how happy they were in the society of friends and neighbors, till the tempter came.

"My father," he continued, "was simple in his ways and habits, unsophisticated and ignorant of the world as a child. My mother was gentleness itself, and of the most confiding, inoffensive, and placid disposition. Neither had enjoyed the advantages of a classical education. They were of the old school, when to read, write, and cipher to the Rule of Three, was the acme of ordinary attainment. But I have always observed that those most deficient in education themselves, seem most disposed to bestow its coveted treasures on their children. I was an only child, and they determined that I should be educated, whatever might be the consequence. This determination was, probably, the cause of all our subsequent misfortune ; for, had I been near my parents, instead of being at college, in the hour of their temptation and trial, they would not have fallen into the snare.

"A letter reached me from my mother. It breathed her usual tenderness, but I detected in it a change from the usual placid serenity. I felt, in a moment, that something had occurred to agitate or wound her feelings, though of its nature I had not the most distant idea. That day, in looking over the newspaper published in my native village, I saw an announcement that the Mormons were to preach in the schoolhouse, at an appointed time, with a preliminary view of the rise and peculiarities of the new faith. Yet I never dreamed that my honored parents could be seduced from allegiance to the church they had loved and honored from childhood. I had too much confidence in their stability of principle and abiding good-sense, and only thought of them as wondering at the defection and apostasy of others. What, then, was my surprise when another letter from home announced their conversion to Mormonism, and informed me that they had determined to dispose of their beautiful home, and emigrate, with their new-found friends, to the Promised Land! The writing was, indeed, my mother's, but I knew—I felt certain—that the spirit it breathed was not hers. Oh, no ; I would not believe that such a change had come over her whom I had always considered the most perfect of women."

"And you went home?"

"I went home, after asking leave of absence, which was reluctantly given. The stage stopped near my father's door. I alighted, ran to the house, and entered the parlor, without announcement. It was dusk, and the apartment was lighted by a lamp. I was surprised to see so much company around, and all were too busy to notice my abrupt, yet noiseless, entrance. My mother was seated near the table, on which lay a pile of papers; and a lawyer—bending over her chair, and pointing with his finger to recent inkmarks on one of them—was repeating, 'You acknowledge this to'——

"I comprehended the scene in an instant: 'Stop, mother! For Heaven's sake, stop!' She lifted her eyes, sprung towards me, and fell, fainting, into my arms."

Frederick paused for a moment, and then resumed—

"My father had been deluded into the rash act of signing over his entire property to the use and behoof of the Mormon Church; and so great was the infatuation of my mother, that she actually seemed to rejoice that the affair was consummated. She said it was their duty to lay all their possessions at the apostles' feet, as in the days of the primitive Church; and that whoever kept anything back, would risk meeting the doom of Ananias and Sapphira. To my reasonings she turned a deaf ear; she was insensible to my entreaties; and so great was the influence held by the priesthood over her, that I verily believe she regarded me, her son, as her direst enemy. I left them—in sorrow more than in anger. What else could I do?

"After that, though I wrote frequently to them, I never received a word in answer. At length, vacation came, and I went back, my heart burning with affectionate desires. Strangers occupied the mansion where we had passed so many happy hours; and my aged parents, I was told, had removed with the Mormons. I wept like a child, and my greatest sorrow was for the loss of their affection.

"Two years elapsed. I had heard nothing from my parents, and began to mourn them as dead, when a letter reached me, superscribed from the valley of the Great Salt Lake. I broke the seal with a trembling hand. It was from my mother; and such a revelation as it made! What harrowing anxiety was depicted in every line! What bitter remorse and agonizing self-reproach! Finally, she conjured me, as her first-born and only child, to come to her, saying that she only waited to behold me once more, and then close her eyes to the earth and its misery!

"Of my father she said nothing, and I could but wonder at her silence. I knew the perfect confidence that had so long existed between them, and how fully each had endorsed the other's sentiments; and I felt apprehensive lest a great gulf had opened between them, in some unaccountable way. However, my mother's appeal was not suffered to go unheeded. I made immediate preparations for joining them, and, after many difficulties and dangers, reached their abode. They were tenanted in a miserable hut, with few of the comforts and none of the luxuries of life. My father, in his old age, had actually been obliged to work by the day for wages, and my mother to beg washing of the soldiers, to obtain their daily food—they, who all their lives had been above necessity or want!

"But this was not, by any means, the greatest misfortune of my poor mother. A few months had done the work of years on her frame. Instead of the round, full, red cheeks, like ripe winter-apples, her face was shrunken and withered; her hands trembled, as if with palsy; and her eye had a gleam and glitter that made me fear for her intellect. We had sat a short half-hour together, when a coarse, red-faced woman, with a flannel night-cap on her head, came in, and seemed perfectly at home. When she went out, I inquired, 'Does that woman live with you?'

"'Yes.'

"'In what capacity?'

"Her lips quivered, her whole frame trembled, and her eyes filled with tears. It was some moments before she could reply, and then imagine my horror and astonishment on hearing that she was my father's second wife. With tears streaming down her face, and her voice broken by sobs, she went on to narrate how this ugly, greasy specimen of womanhood had been formerly attached to the harem of a priest, where she kept the whole house in an uproar. He determined to get rid of her, and so persuaded my kind-hearted parent that it was his duty to take her. The old man hesitated, and asked time for deliberation. The next morning, she came to his house, and took up her abode, where she soon usurped all authority. My mother could

not even have the privilege of making a cup of coffee without the jade's permission, and had more than once been subjected to the indignity of blows, in her moments of ill-temper. 'Your troubles in that respect are at an end, dear mother,' I said. 'I will soon make the house too hot to hold her!' She smiled sadly.

"From that moment, all power in that dwelling was exercised by me; and though naturally averse to quarreling with a woman, between this termagant and myself there were some exciting scenes. My father remonstrated. He feared the power of the priests, but I did not. She was expelled the house, and went back to her former lord.

"But my mother never recovered her serenity of mind, or physical health; and the most that I could do was to smooth her passage to the tomb. I had the satisfaction of knowing that her eyes were opened to the iniquities of the Mormon system; and it was painful to hear her, on the verge of the grave, lament that she had left her 'first love,' like those mentioned in the Revelations—that she had not been content to leave 'the first principles of the doctrines of Christ, and travel on towards perfection,' but had turned aside in the bye-paths which, she now believed, led to temporal misery and eternal death. She pined for the society of her old friends, especially for that of the pastor who had broken for her, in former days, the bread of life. Her last words were full of Christian hope and trust—'Behold the Lamb of God that taketh away the sin of the world.'

"No Mormon priest officiated at her funeral. I would

not have her remains so desecrated. Neither would I permit her to be buried in their cemetery. I selected the spot myself, and caused a suitable monument to be erected, as a record of her worth."

"And your father"——

"Is nearly superannuated, and almost imbecile; and that hateful woman is the torment of my life. She persists in visiting him; and the elder, her pretended husband, encourages her in making the most scandalous advances. He seems determined to billet her on us for support."

He concluded by inviting me to visit his father. I consented, and we walked back to the city in company.

"I have reason to believe," said Frederick, "that the history of my parents is not a solitary one. Events as tragic, interesting, and thrilling, have probably transpired in all the families around us, though unseen, and even unsuspected, by the uninitiated."

As we approached the cabin, a dirty, slattern-like woman, with a small bundle under her arm, darted from the door, and ran off down the street.

"There she goes," said Frederick. "She knows better than to let me catch her in the house! I'd like to know, though, what she has been carrying off."

"Carrying off—does she steal?" I inquired.

"To be sure, she does! She had been twice in the penitentiary before coming here, I have been credibly informed. When I reproached her with this crime, she had the impudence to attempt its justification, saying that the earth and its fullness was created for man in general, and that one, just as much as another, had a right to its blessings.'

"'And so that gown you have on is as much mine as yours, eh?' I inquired.

"'Yes, if you want it. Do you want it?' she replied, with an air of the greatest insolence, taking up, and holding out for display, her ragged, draggled skirt."

We entered the cabin.

"I have brought you a visitor, father," said Frederick.

The old man raised his head, and returned my salutation with affability. He had mild, brown eyes, with such an easy, guileless expression of countenance, that I doubted not his complete subjection to the designs of the impostors. Strange as it may appear, his faith in Mormonism was not in the least shaken; and when I commenced conversing with him, he answered by exhorting me to come out from the world and unite with the saints.

I inquired if his happiness had been promoted by his union with them, to which he replied that, whether or not, such questions were irrelevant to the subject; that they were not expecting happiness here, and must be contented to cheerfully bear minor trials, in consideration of the glorious consummation in prospect.

The simple creature then proceeded to relate the marvels and miracles that had been wrought in favor of the Mormons. According to him, their journey was attended with events almost as wonderful and supernatural as that of the Israelites when they went up out of Egypt. Springs sprang up in the desert when they were thirsty ; herds of buffalo approached when they were starving ; prowling Indians fled before their faces ; and, to cap the climax, he averred that he had no doubt, had there been a Jericho on the route, its walls would have fallen down at the blowing of rams' horns, as they did in the days of old. Why shouldn't miracles be common now, as they were then ? Why shouldn't they, sure ! Others than himself have asked that question.

When I bade the old man farewell, Frederick accompanied me a short distance towards my boarding-house.

"You see my father, what he is—a mere child. I cannot leave him to the tender mercies of these creatures. Duty, honor, filial affection, forbid it. He is weak and imbecile. Still he is my father ; and not till his earthly pilgrimage closes, shall I leave the Mormon city."

I commended his resolution ; and, promising to call again, arrived at home in time for dinner.

CHAPTER VIII.

THE DINNER—A NEW WIFE—JAUNT TO GRANTSVILLE, AND WHAT I SAW THERE, ETC.

THE dinner was got up with unusual taste, and a new divinity presided at the table. She was a little, neat woman, with brown complexion, and black eyes. Her motions were quick and graceful; and, flitting from thing to thing, she strongly reminded me of Mrs. Hyde. Inkley was highly pleased, and exceedingly loquacious. He laughed and talked, told droll stories and humorous anecdotes, pinched the lady's cheek, and jogged my elbow in a manner quite unaccountable. Hannah and Martha were invisible, but their lord did not seem to perceive, much less to regret their absence. The children, too, had disappeared, and were, probably, at that moment dining with their mammas, in another apartment.

I subsequently learned the history of this woman. It was somewhat singular. Her maiden name was Sarah Carter, and she had rich and highly respectable connexions in the State of Rhode Island. Sarah, when a child, was chiefly noted for versatility of talent and changeableness of purpose. In her studies, before one science was half mastered, she flew off to another. She abandoned French for music, music for crayon-drawing, and drawing for sculpture. She gave up school-teaching and became a public lecturer on woman's rights. Wearying of this, she became a clairvoyant, then a spirit-rapper, and finally fetched up on the shoals of Mormonism. That she was witty and graceful, no one could deny, and many would have admired her style of beauty. A Mormon elder certainly did. He saw her on the ferry-boat that plies between Jersey City and the island of Manhattan, was struck with her appearance, and inquired her name. Learning this, he presented himself, without the ceremony of an introduction, was graciously received, and soon became one of her most devoted admirers, though six or seven wives pined for his embraces at home. The lover was ardent in his protestations, liberal in gifts, and the consequences of their intimacy soon became visible. At this juncture, he persuaded her to follow him to Salt Lake. Change was her element, and she consented ; but immediately on their arrival, he abandoned her. Among strangers, and without resources, she became a pensioner on the bounty of Parley Pratt. Here Inkley saw her, was made acquainted with her circumstances, proposed for her hand, was accepted, and the marriage celebrated—all in one day. The next morning—the day on which I saw her—he brought her home, which was the first intimation that his other wives had received of the affair. They were surprised, but not angry, and at once abandoned all the house-keeping arrangements to her hands. She accepted the charge with a very good grace, and doubtless with the expectation of resigning it in her turn to another. She addressed me across the table, with great good-humor, saying that she was curious to know why I came to Salt Lake City.

Without waiting for my answer, Inkley replied: "The same that others come for, probably—to see and be seen. Wasn't that so, sir?"

"Doubtless that had something to do with my motives," I replied.

The lady then launched into a voluble strain—talked of Mesmerism, spirit-rapping, and woman's rights—said that Lucy Stone was the greatest woman of the age, that Mrs. Bloomer deserved a monument, and Antoinette Brown a wreath of laurel.

"And yet all these women are in pursuit of an idea rather than a principle," I said. "They cannot succeed, because they oppose nature."

"How oppose nature?" she inquired.

"Because man and woman never advance side by side. He leads the way—she follows. He acts the tyrant—she becomes the slave. He affects the noble and godlike—she rises proportionately. Never has woman opened a path in literature, art, or science."

Inkley laughed heartily, and the bride looked vexed.

"If anything were wanting," I continued, "to prove how completely woman is subjected by nature to the caprices of man, we have a practical exemplification of it directly before our eyes. How readily she assumes the character he destines for her! How"——

"I do not understand you," she said, interrupting me.

"I do," said Inkley. "I have often thought of the same. Many think polygamy degrading to women; that is undeniable. I can't say that I do, however. But whether it is or not, matters little. One thing is certain—they are impotent to resist it. Man wills it, and, whether she wishes it or not, woman submits."

Dinner being over, Mr. Inkley informed me that business connected with the Church would call him to Grantsville, and that he expected to be absent for several days. I immediately asked permission to accompany him, and inquired for the locality of that settlement.

"About forty miles west," he replied, and went on to impart considerable information connected with the place and its inhabitants, which tended to increase rather than diminish my curiosity and spirit of adventure.

The afternoon was spent in preparations for the projected journey. We had a cold supper, and retired early, purposing to start at daybreak. In the night, I was awakened by a loud clap of thunder, and sensations similar to those experienced in a shower-bath. It was raining violently; and the roof being leaky, and the window-casements loose, the water dripped and drove in from every quarter, wetting the bed, and standing in large pools on the floor. The night was black as pitch, except the occasional gleams of lightning, followed instantaneously by the crack of thunder, loud and terrific as if heaven and earth were coming together. In a pause of the storm, I ascertained that the inmates of the house were all up and in motion. Once there was a loud crash, and fall, as of a heavy body tumbling down stairs; then the suppressed screams of women and children, and a man's voice, in a softer key, caught my ear. I arose, but my garments were saturated with wet. Those protected by the cover of my trunk, however, were in a better condition. After long searching in the dark, I found and put them on. Simultaneous with this, the house was illumined by a blinding flash, of which I took advantage, to rush out of my room and down the stairs. The family were all in the kitchen; and a small lamp, burning on the hearth, sufficed to give a view of each blank and terror-stricken countenance. The children were weeping, the women sobbing, and all, except Sarah, huddled together, like a group of frightened sheep. She was walking up and down the apartment, wringing her hands, and making gestures of the wildest despair, while exclaiming, "Oh, poor sinners! What will become of poor sinners! The day of judgment has come!—the great day of judgment! Oh, oh!"

Seeing me, she cried out, "Are you ready to stand before the bar of the great God?"

"Compose yourself, madam," I replied. "There is no occasion for all this terror. And were it as you say, though vice has always cause for fear, virtue should stand unblenched amid the ruins of the world."

"Poor sinners! Oh, poor sinners!" she continued, shrieking—thus forcibly depicting the horrors of superstition, and illustrating the fact that, whatever may be the boasted knowledge of the age, weak minds will be terrified at the phenomena of nature.

Presently, the flashes came no more, and the thunder rolled in the distance. Then the clouds parted—one great body rolling off to the eastward, while the other settled into the south. The moon, just sinking in the western horizon, came out in its mild, pale beauty, and a few stars, seen here and there, glanced out, like the eyes of angels. Inkley remarked on the suddenness and violence of the storm, and Sarah, now that it was past, laughed at her unreasonable fears. Then all retired again to their respective chambers, except myself. I was not partial to a wet-sheet pack, just then, but stretched my limbs on a buffalo-robe, and soon fell asleep.

It was that most delicious of hours, between dawn and sunrise, when I awoke. Hastily rising, I went out. The air was fresh, delicious, and invigorating; but everywhere were to be seen traces of the last night's tempest. Trees and shrubs had been torn to pieces or overblown, fences levelled, and fields of grain bent to the ground. In all the hollows, pools of water were gathered, while the streams rushed wild and turgid down the declivities. Hearing a voice behind me, I turned, to meet the countenance of Inkley. He, too, had risen, and come out to ascertain the state of the weather. Considering this favorable, the women were called up, and immediate preparations for breakfast made.

This being over, and our small amount of baggage ready, we mounted a wagon with two wheels, exactly resembling a cart, except that it was covered with a coarse white cloth, drawn tightly over bows, bent in a half circle, and fastened, by the ends, to the wagon sides. Elder Lyman had talked of going along—more for company, I believe, than anything else. We called first at his house, and were answered, from the door, by a woman with a blowzy face, flaring from a red nightcap, that the elder could not travel in the company of Gentiles.

"Is that all?" inquired Inkley.

She said that it was.

"Where is he?"

"In the house."

"Can I see him?"

She hesitated a moment, when, finally, it came out that the worthy was taking his morning snooze.

"Let him go, and be d—d!" said my companion, in a low voice, starting the mules into a gallop.

For two or three miles, we moved on rapidly, over a tolerably good road; then the ground became soft, spongy, and, in many places, decidedly muddy. Sometimes a deep gully would intercept our progress, and sometimes we would have to circumnavigate a fallen tree. The jolting was severe and incessant, yet, as if to make up for this, the whole scenery was perfectly delightful. The day was fine—not a cloud to be seen—and the mountains flashed their summits in the rich sunlight. We passed around the elbow of the mountain range, on the lower steppe of which the city is built, and went directly north—first by the warm springs, which furnish to visitors the luxury of a bath, and then by the hot springs, of which the ascending vapor is such a remarkable addition to the scenery.

After a time, the road diverged to the left, and some very pretty farm-houses, surrounded by fields of grain, appeared in view. Mr. Inkley stopped at one of these, leaving me in the wagon, to hold the mules, with the positive assurance that he would be back in five minutes, though his stay was prolonged to an hour. He returned to the wagon, evidently pleased with the success of his visit.

"Very nice place, sir," he began. "Nice people, too, sir—very nice; though sister Laton appeared rather downcast. She finds it hard to conform to the rules of our faith—very hard, sir. But, as I told her, 'no cross, no crown.'"

Mr. Inkley interlarded his conversation with expletives, at certain times; at others he did not.

"What is it that she finds so hard?" I questioned, excusing myself, mentally, for such a breach of etiquette, by remembering that Inkley loved to tell news quite as well as any one could delight to hear it.

"The fact is, sir, that brother Laton has been seriously exercised about taking another wife. He knows very well that it is his duty, but hitherto, from respect to the prejudices of his first wife, has neglected it. The case went before the church, and the council of elders decided that, to

ensure his salvation and that of his family, he must conform in all things to the requirements of our faith."

"And Mrs. Laton"——

"Fainted away when informed of that decision."

"Who is the candidate for promotion?"

"The hired girl, I believe," he answered, with all the coolness imaginable. "Brother Laton was much affected by the distress of his wife, and it required all the arguments I could bring, backed by the influence of the church, to strengthen his resolution."

"What did the girl say?"

"Oh, nothing. Mrs. Laton was an Eastern woman, and very proud. I suppose it cuts close to have a servant elevated to an equality with herself. But the proud shall be brought low, and the humble exalted—such is the language of Scripture."

"When is Laton to marry his second wife?"

"Next week. Her bridal robes have been ready for some time."

"It must be dangerous, in Utah, to have a hired girl!"

"Rather!" he replied, laughing, and the subject was dropped.

For the remainder of the day, we journeyed over a good road, along the lake—the ascending vapor of the hot-spring hanging like a thin veil of gauze at the base of the mountains, and the city dimly visible in the rear. This, however, entirely faded from view as we descended into the valley of the Weber, and paused to rest, in one of the loveliest spots imaginable. Here the mules were unharnessed, and left to feed on the rich grass, while we sat beneath the cooling shade of some very handsome trees, or strolled, in search of wild flowers and odd-looking pebbles, along the margin of the stream. The banks were exceedingly steep and precipitous, and the water coursed along with the rapidity of a race-horse.

We crossed the Weber on a bridge, and then we had a rough and troublesome causeway of brush and poles for half a mile, through a wet piece of ground. I had heard this place mentioned, previously, as very dangerous, in miring animals ; but the falling of the river, and some repairs, enabled us to pass it in perfect safety.

Thus far we had been on the regular California route, and I was loth to leave the well-beaten road for the scarcely perceptible Indian trail which Inkley said led to Grantsville, the place of our destination. Making a virtue of necessity, however, we turned off, over a rough piece of ground, and descended the valley of the stream, amidst a labyrinth of mountains, irregular highlands, and frightful gorges, which it would be quite impossible to describe. I no longer wondered that so many travellers, hunters, and emigrant trains had become lost, in their long wandering among the mysterious passes. I even began to fear that the same calamity would befall us, and hinted as much to Inkley, who laughed, and said that there was no danger.

Of all countries, it seems to me that Utah is most lonely and desolate—most destitute of animal life. Mountains generally are the resort of game. With the single exception of wild fowl, there is very little here. You may travel a whole day without hearing the voice of a solitary bird. The buffalo never leave the prairies ; the Rocky-Mountain goats are scarce, and chiefly inhabit farther north ; grizzly bears are seldom seen, and rarely caught ; but a species of small rabbit abounds, in great plenty, and the grasshoppers in summer are almost a match for the locusts of Egypt.

Our animals had become so weary that we concluded to halt for the night, when two-thirds of our journey was accomplished. Our camping-ground was a beautiful valley, carpeted with herbage, and watered by a clear, cool stream, a tributary of the Weber. Our wagon contained plenty of eatables, which were brought out at sunset, and we had a cold but delicious supper ; for a good appetite gave it zest.

Inkley, as usual, talked vivaciously, and praised everything, even to the luxury of a hard bed on the bottom of the wagon. Slumber readily comes to weariness, and I fell asleep, dreaming of vagabonds and Indians. Our repose was undisturbed. We were up by daylight, and, having untethered the mules, let them range two hours, for pasture, previous to resuming our journey. The remains of our supper served for breakfast ; and, having dispatched this, we were soon ready for a start.

There is a certain sameness connected with this scenery that wearies the most ardent lover of nature. The mind wearies of sublimity—the eye becomes tired of resting on the great and grand. Rocks, mountains, rivers, precipices, torrents, gorges, though ever varying in shape, size, and magnificence, possess the same general characteristics.

I was really glad when the road diverged into a pleasant valley, and the village we sought appeared in the distance, though seeming little better than a camping-ground of savages. It was simply a collection of huts, built in wigwam fashion, with few of the appurtenances or appearances of civilization. The nearer we approached, the more conspicuous became these features, until I could scarcely persuade myself that I was approaching a Christianized community.

"Is that Grantsville?" I inquired, with some surprise.

"It is," returned by guide.

"Then all I have to say is, that report has spoken better of it than it deserves."

"I hardly think so," he replied. "There is a flourishing church, chiefly composed of converted savages and half-breeds; and it could hardly be expected that they would assume at once all the peculiarities of civilized life."

I assented to this, not without wondering how many vices of which they were previously innocent, had been engrafted, with this religious system, on their simple, unsophisticated natures. They were certainly the most impudent and unmannerly creatures I ever beheld. Noticing our approach, they came rushing out to meet us, surrounded the wagon, clambered up the sides, pillaged the remnants of our food, and actually began to examine the contents of our baggage, begging, all the while, in a whining, abject tone, for beads and trinkets. Inkley, in a loud voice, and with a flourish of his whip, commanded them to desist, and, showing a small silver coin, declared that he would give it to the one who should first inform the elder of our arrival. That was a sufficient inducement, and off they all ran—men, women, and children—helter-skelter, whooping and shouting, and each one trying to outstrip his companions, while we brought up the rear at a moderately slow pace.

I saw, at a glance, that Indian blood greatly predominated in the population. They were athletic fellows, but vagabonds, to a man. They had no regular occupation, but fished a little, hunted a little, and smoked and lounged a great deal. After the usual fashion of savages, the women performed the labor. Several were out in the fields, hoeing or weeding small patches of maize ; and we passed by a place where two women were busily engaged in building a hut, a man standing by, apparently giving directions, and overseeing the work. He nodded familiarly, and with an air of great satisfaction, to my companion.

"Are you acquainted with that fellow ?" I asked.

Inkley replied that he was.

"And who are those women under his command ?"

"His wives. He married them last week, both at a time, so that neither could claim precedence. They seem to be building a house."

In consideration of my hearers, I forbore the expression of contempt that was rising to my throat.

Still further on, a woman was plowing, with a very stubborn mule, that gave her an infinite deal of trouble, to the great amusement of the loungers; and many others were feeding the hogs or cattle, working in their small gardens, or performing similar labors—the men loafing around, as unconcerned spectators.

Their singularity of appearance was greatly heightened by grotesqueness of apparel. Many of the women had on men's hats and coats, and some had even put on the worn-out and cast-off breeches of hunters and travellers, which were much too large for them. The children were keen, bright-looking little creatures, nearly nude, and with an expression of countenance and agility of motion strongly reminding one of the young of wild animals. I was all eyes and ears, till the wagon drew up before a building differing little from the rest, though somewhat superior.

"Does the elder live here?" I inquired.

The answer was affirmative, with a wonder that he didn't show himself, followed by the exclamation, "Here he comes."

A man, evidently a half-breed, with a face the color of some rich, ripe berry, made his appearance, and bowed with such a ludicrous air to Inkley, that I could not forbear laughing. He had been drinking, which rendered his idiomatic pronunciation more harsh and guttural.

"He good fellow, broder," he began. "Tum in; tum in. Gad to see you," and he made a step forward, to meet us, when, his toe coming in contact with something on the floor, he lost his equilibrium, and fell prostrate. The noise brought out two women. Without noticing us, they seized their lord, and bore him, notwithstanding his struggles to the contrary, into the cabin.

"What shall we do?" said I, not relishing the idea of a drunken Indian host.

"Get out, and go in, of course," said Inkley, leaping from the wagon.

I followed his example, and, after hitching the mules to a low stockade fence, we gathered up our baggage, and entered the house, with a great train of men, women, and children at our heels. Such a motley set I never saw before, and hope never to see again. They were pushing, jamming, crowding, and trampling on each other, with the manifest intention of getting at us and our baggage. The word "swap" was continually on their tongues. First one and then another would grab at some article of my clothing, and, pulling it violently, would call out, "Swap?" Some of the women were actually determined to have my vest, whether or not; and, with great want of discretion, I displayed my pocket-handkerchief, by wiping my face with it. Its bright color instantly attracted attention, and one, more bold than the others, snatched it from my hands, and made off with it, leaving me to the consolation of thinking that the gang thereby was numerically weakened.

After being made to understand that we could not and would not "swap," they became curious to know what we possessed. Our refusal to gratify their curiosity only increased it, and, as a last resort, we unrolled our bundles, carefully separating, shaking out, and holding up each article they contained, so that all might obtain a full view. A grunt of pleasure announced their satisfaction ; and, after a long time and much persuasion, they were induced to disperse. While this was going on, our Mormon dignitary overcame his drunkenness sufficiently to sit up, and signify by gestures and an unintelligible lingo, his deep anxiety to become possessed of our things. As I watched his countenance, and noted the villainous expression of his eye, I really began to be apprehensive for our safety, notwithstanding his sacerdotal character.

Three wives and seven children composed the family of this nondescript, and all were huddled in this little cabin, with a dirty stable in the rear. One of the women, evidently the oldest, and apparently mistress of the establishment, invited Inkley to drive his mules around under the shelter, where she said they could stand in perfect security. While he was attending to them, the Indian elder became drowsy, with the fumes of intoxication. His head swayed to and fro, like a reed shaken by the wind ; and he began muttering and spluttering, in a style unintelligible to me, but which occasioned great merriment to his wives. The youngest of these, going up beside him, gave him a push that completely upset his centre of gravity, and tumbled him on the floor. In another moment he was sound asleep.

It will readily be believed that this cabin was in a state of great filth, dirt, and confusion. What else could be expected, or who could have been neat in such a place ? A dog-kennel, in one corner of the hut, was swarming with inhabitants; and while I sat, looking around, the mistress approached, seized one of the puppies by the hind legs, and deliberately proceeded to knock out its brains against the wall. I turned away my head, overpowered by a sickening sensation; and when I looked again, it was skinned and dressed. The prejudices of civilization were strong within me, and, with emotions of intense disgust, I saw her thrust it into a pot, with water, kindle a fire beneath it, and understood at once that it was designed for our supper. Her motions were not lost on Inkley. He went to her, and, with the significance of words and gestures, succeeded in making her understand that we had brought provisions with us, and consequently did not require her hospitality. With a nod, she pointed to the children—as much as to say that they would need it.

We slept in our wagon again that night, and by morning our Indian host had become sufficiently sober to enter on the business of the church. These Mormon settlements, as auxiliaries and branches of the mother establishment in Zion, are subject to her government and supervision. Brigham Young, as supreme pontiff, provides each one with a presiding bishop or elder, whose duty it is to render a monthly account of all the affairs connected with his spiritual jurisdiction—the number of births, marriages, and converts; the amount of tithes; and other matters in general. With an appearance of great sincerity, the Indian—or, rather, half-breed—praised the zeal manifested by the male members of his flock, which had run rampant to marry and give in marriage, till not a single woman could be found in the neighborhood. Several times he spoke of divorces, in connection with these marriages; and I ascertained, on inquiry, that the transferrence, or exchange, of wives, was nothing uncommon—that is, a woman would be divorced, by the church, from her husband, with the express understanding that she should marry another man. He said that scarcely a day occurred in which he was not called upon to solemnize such connections, and that he believed the want of money to pay for it, prevented many more such matches from taking place.

While we were conversing, a couple came into the cabin, though whether Indians, or half-breeds, it would be difficult to say. They were clasping each other's hands, and seemed very loving. The man stepped up to the elder, and whispered something to him which I could not hear, displaying, at the same time, a small silver coin, in the palm of his hand.

"Nodder wife, eh?" said the Indian priest, with a grin.

It would be impossible to transcribe their language, but I learned that the wives of this fellow having all deserted him for other men, he had begun taking a new stock. Not being particularly interested in their affairs, I strolled out for a walk, and, by going around the back way, and keeping out of sight as much as possible, managed to avoid having a crowd at my heels. Descending into a small valley on the eastern side of the village, by an Indian trail, I was greatly surprised to see a large emigrant wagon, with six oxen quietly feeding on the luscious pasture, while an elderly man, a young woman, and three children, were sitting and lying around, in various attitudes. They were busily talking.

"How I want to get away from here!" said the old man.

"So do I," answered his companion.

"I hope none of the fellows up yonder will discover us. They are very devils, and I shouldn't feel safe a moment if they knew we were here."

"Nor I either."

"Do you think they would kill us?" inquired one of the children.

"Don't know. Can't say. Like as not," replied the man.

I coughed slightly, to attract their attention. They started, looked towards me, and said no more. I approached nearer, and addressed them. The old man had a thin, withered, and very brown face, with a speaking twinkle in his eye. He was dressed in clothes of the Quaker cut and color—a broad-brimmed, low-crowned, grey-colored hat, white cotton shirt, open in front, and without cravat, a long-skirted, snuff-colored coat, of coarse homespun, short trowsers, of blue drilling, and heavy cowhide shoes.

"Good morning, friend," I said.

"Good morning," he answered, surveying me, at the same time, from top to toe.

The examination was probably satisfactory; for his countenance brightened, and he inquired the time of day. I gave it to him, when he continued the conversation—

"Right warm weather."

"It is, indeed."

"And flies swarming like bees."

"Yes."

"Going to California ?"

"I shall probably fetch up there, though, at present, I am staying at Salt Lake."

"Come from the East ?"

"Yes."

"What State ?"

"I have been a resident of several States."

"How long have you been here ?"

"Two or three months."

"Reckon you ain't a Mormon ?"

"Why so ?"

"Because ye don't look like one. I can always tell a Mormon, when I see one. They carry the mark of the beast."

"Father !" interposed the woman.

He looked at me, inquiringly.

"You have guessed rightly," I said. "I am not a Mormon, and never shall be."

"Then what are you doing here ?"

"Looking around."

"Well, if you've seen much worth seeing, you've had better luck than I have had," he replied.

The woman laughed, shrugged her shoulders, and said, "Whether you've seen much or not, you have found out some things."

"I'm blowed, but I know that I've found out that the Mormons, with few and rare exceptions, are damned rascals! There! now I've said it. But you won't tell?"

"I certainly shall not."

"You'd better go on with us."

"I rather think not."

"Yes, you had. My daughter there is a widow."

"Ah, indeed."

The young woman blushed scarlet, and tears sprang to her eyes as she ejaculated, "Oh, father!"

"But that's of no account," he continued. "I'm a widower. My wife, and her husband, both died since we commenced our journey. I buried them both, with my own hands, on the prairie. I only hope that the wolves haven't found their graves."

These remarks might have seemed heartless, and yet there was something in his manner that indicated feeling, rather than the want of it. His daughter began to weep.

"Whence have you come?"

"All the way from Ohio."

"Alone?"

"Not all the way. We started in company with some Mormons. I didn't know them, then, as I do now, or I would have as soon undertaken the journey with Old

Scratch himself. I've not a particle of doubt that all my misfortunes were owing to them."

"Think so?"

"Stranger, I know it! You see, my wife was glib of tongue, without the least bit of deceit. She couldn't and wouldn't put up with all their vile practices. She couldn't bear to see the women so free with the men, and the men so fond of the women, and she would and did say it. I used to caution her against exciting their ill-will, but it did no good. She had no fear; and you might better attempt to bridle the wind, than a woman's tongue."

"How can you talk so, father!" said the woman.

"There was a young girl in our company, the daughter of a widow considered rich, and certainly beautiful. She was a great favorite with the elder, who, though possessing several wives already, made a formal proposal for her hand. A young hunter, from Illinois, not a Mormon, was likewise her suitor. My wife—who must have a say in everything—favored his pretensions, and attempted to dissuade the girl from marrying the detestable polygamist. The elder said little. Had he said more, I should have feared him less. Your talkers give vent to their anger, and that's the end of it; but your silent, plotting men—beware of them! I left the camp, one day, to hunt; but, somehow, I didn't feel right, and went back, long before night. I found my daughter vainly trying to soothe the dying agonies of her mother and husband, who were both writhing in strong convulsions. I knew, instinctively, that they were poisoned, and inquired what they had been eating.

"'Nothing but some fruit.'

"'And the fruit—where did it come from?'

"They found it. It was such as we had all eaten. It could not be the fruit. So they all said; but I knew better. It was plain to me as a book. They died that night. The next morning their flesh, spotted with black and green, confirmed my suspicion. Think you, after that, I would travel in their company a moment longer? Not I! We waited till they were gone, and then came on alone."

"But the girl—did she marry the elder?"

"Oh, I don't know, but I expect so."

He then informed me that he had mistaken the way, because he refused to inquire of the Mormons, or have any intercourse with them.

"And now," he continued, when I was preparing to depart, "don't tell them fellows that I am down here. I wouldn't have 'em to know it for any money. I shouldn't feel certain of my life for an hour longer."

I promised to remain silent, as he wished. Then, inviting me to visit him, if I ever came to California, and could find where he lived, we bade each other farewell, I believe with mutual regret.

CHAPTER IX.

RETURN—OGDEN'S CITY, ETC.

THE next morning, bright and early, we started on our return route, which lay through Ogden's City, another auxiliary branch of the Mormon Church. Inkley was very conversable, and found something to commend, even in the detestable manners of the brutalized inhabitants of Grantsville.

"You should have seen these people one year ago, sir—one short year ago—and then you might form some estimate of their advance in civilization. Why, bless my heart! they were savages then—had little knowledge of a Creator, none of a Saviour, and, if not exactly worshipping idols, had no regular attendance on public exercises of devotion. Yes, sir, their improvement has been little short of miraculous."

Such a palpable and manifest misrepresentation excited my risibility. He laughed, too, for company.

"My character is original," he began, after a moment's silence. "I am aware of that. Most people delight in finding fault; it is my abhorrence. In the ugliest countenance I always look for, and generally find, some redeeming feature. Beneath the most vicious character, I can detect the similitude of virtue. I find something or other to praise, wherever I go. It may be a little, still it is something, and it always makes me feel better myself, and think better of my kind."

"And what did you find at Grantsville?"

"That woman's ready hospitality struck me as a beautiful trait."

I turned my head aside at the recollection.

"You view the subject altogether in a wrong light," he said, reproachfully. "She was preparing for us the best that she had, and what she considered excellent herself. Could the most polished female have done better? Would she probably have done as well?"

"But what proofs of an advance in civilization could you discover?—for, to tell the truth, I thought their manners much more disgusting and insolent than those of the wild, untutored natives."

"You must make allowance for the many foreigners, of all classes and nations, that they are in the habit of seeing, and whose manners they insensibly imbibe. Ogden's City, however, is far superior. I think you will be pleased with it and its inhabitants."

OGDEN CITY.

About five miles from Ogden City, we stopped at an exquisitely neat adobe house, standing a short distance off the road, with a beautiful pine in front of it. The windows were without glass, but drapery, of snowy muslin, restrained the currents of air, and admitted light. The master of the house, a hale, companionable fellow, gave us a gracious welcome, and his wife looked so happy, I wondered if polygamy could be there. Everything was neat; nothing costly. Taste, not ornament, had evidently been consulted in the arrangement of the furniture. There was a table that had been polished with soap and sand, till it shone almost like a mirror; several benches, white and clean as wood could be made; a small dresser, on which some very nice patterns of queen's-ware cups and saucers were upturned, in the most approved style, while plates to match were ranged on their edges behind them. A small iron-furnace stood in one corner of the fireplace, supporting the tea-kettle, bright and shining as a new dollar. Above this, on a nail, hung a spider, as free from soot as if it had never been touched by smoke. A rifle, powder-horn, and shot-pouch hung above the mantelpiece, while some fishing tackle garnished the wall opposite.

We had been seated but a short time, when the husband glanced towards his wife. She understood the signal, and, rising, with a smile, took her tea-kettle to a pail, very white and sweet, that the husband had just brought in, brimming full of cold, fresh water. Then, while she was filling the kettle with the fluid, he kindled a warm, light blaze in the furnace, over which it was placed for the second time. Not wishing to prolong our stay until after tea, I proposed going, when both the man and wife seemed disappointed, and pressingly invited us to share their hospitality. My companion, however, excused us, on the plea of the lateness of the hour, the darkness of the night, and the miles we had to travel, before reaching our destination.

I inquired of Inkley if this family were Mormon. He said they were not, though the saints had made great efforts to secure their conversion. He thought they were incorrigible, and given over to hardness of heart.

After dark, we found much difficulty in keeping the road, there being frequent forks, and nothing to guide us. We crossed two or three brooks, and several miry places, while I began to grow impatient, when a cluster of lights appeared in the distance. We soon reached a long, low cabin, which Inkley said was brother Ripley's, and that we could be comfortably entertained. This was, indeed, good news. The door was shut, to keep out the mosquitoes ; but, hearing our steps, the good man came, opened it, and asked us to enter. It was cheerful and comforting within, and formed an agreeable contrast with the damp, dark night. A bright lamp diffused a mellow light through the apartment, and a balsamic odor breathed from the low fire of scented wood. A door to the right, opened to the background of supper-table and kitchen ; and a nice, stout, hale-looking, but oldish lady, in a neat cap, came forth to welcome us, while a boy was dispatched to attend to the mules.

When we were somewhat rested, supper was announced by a negress, in a very white bib, and a very red turban. There were several preparations of swine's flesh, fresh fish, chicken, wheat and corn bread, with very rich short cakes, and two or three kinds of sweetmeats. Both tea and coffee were served, and water, cooled with the luxury of ice.

After supper, while Mrs. Ripley was absent from the room, superintending her domestic affairs, Mr. Inkley inquired of our host whether or not he had taken a second wife.

"I have not," said Ripley, "and probably never shall. One good wife, like mine, is worth more to a man than a dozen poor ones. I have long thought that."

"But it is the duty of the saints, you know."

"I don't know any such thing. If a man chooses to curse himself with more than one wife, I have nothing to say. If he remains contented with one, it is quite as well, in my opinion."

"You will probably change your mind," said Inkley, "when the right one crosses your path."

"I think not," answered Ripley. "For twenty years I have lived in an atmosphere of domestic happiness. My expectations of connubial felicity have been fully verified. In sickness and in health, in poverty and wealth, my wife has been the sun that diffused life and light and joy through the sphere in which I moved. At my advanced period of life, with my knowledge of womankind and the world, it would scarcely be policy to attempt the experiment."

Here Mrs. Ripley came in, and the subject was dropped Her husband arose, and presented her with a chair, with all the gallantry of youth; and it was beautiful to see the little courtesies and attentions they bestowed on each other, and which are generally so sadly neglected in the marriage state. I could not help hoping that the great good-sense and real happiness of this amiable old gentleman would preserve him from ever listening to the tempter, whose counsel, in his case, at least, would be a certain prelude of misery and disappointment.

The room in which we lodged that night, was one of the best I had seen in the Mormon country. All its appointments and furniture bespoke the neat and thrifty housewife. Nothing at loose ends, or out of place. Nothing neglected for some one else to oversee. Our bed-chamber was a house in itself, separated from the main building, though connected with it by a platform or gallery in front. The window-sashes had been raised, for ventilation, and their places supplied by mosquito-curtains. Two stuffed easy-chairs stood near the fireplace, each with a tub of tepid water, to bathe our weary feet, before it, while a small lamp shed just enough light to render the apartment pleasant. Everything for comfort and convenience was so much superior to what I had been accustomed to see in this country, that I could not help noticing and remarking on it to my companion. Strange to say, however, he was rather disposed to cavil and find fault, thus revealing a phase of character by no means singular.

The next day we visited the elder, and, through all the Mormon empire, I have not seen a man more truly and really lovable and worthy. To my infinite surprise, he had no wife at all, and his house was kept in order by a youthful niece. Though a rigid Mormon in other respects, he was bitterly opposed to polygamy, and had several times refused his niece to the solicitations of men with families. His example had not been without its influence. A majority of those within his spiritual jurisdiction had but one wife—few, if any, had more than two; and I was ready to make the inquiry, if the superiority of Ogden's City over other Mormon neighborhoods was to be attributed to this fact.

Accompanied by the elder, we visited the tabernacle, which was not remarkable for architectural taste or beauty, though answering all the ends of a roomy structure. It is large on the ground, very low, and has a wretchedly tame appearance. However, father Smith, our guide, informed me that when the church became sufficiently wealthy, another and better building would be reared, and the present one removed, and applied to other purposes.

Many excellent farms are in this neighborhood. Fine meadow and pasture lands border the river on which the city stands, and which bears the same name. I noticed very fine herds of cattle, and sheep of improved breeds.

The whole region had an air of pastoral simplicity, blent with romantic associations, and I became insensibly in love with it.

The city itself (which is merely a thickly-settled neighborhood, or large village) is near the mountains—huge, frowning battlements, that seem to pierce the clouds. Along their sides you can trace the wavy paths made by the moccasined feet of the Indians, in finding their way to their inaccessible dens and caverns among the heights.

Ogden's Hole, a noted place in this region, is celebrated for one of those desperate encounters between white men and savages which are fast becoming traditionary. Who knows but that the future pen of the novelist may make it famous as Ellerslie and Wallace's Cave. It is simply a quiet, sequestered nook of the cañon, whence the river flows, in which one Ogden, with a party of white hunters, made a successful stand against a host of Indians.

It is noted, too, as the scene of a romance of softer character and more recent date : One of the Indian chiefs had a beautiful daughter, who was sought after, in marriage, by a roving hunter, named White. The belle of the wilderness could not resist the fascinations of the white man. They were married according to the Indian mode, and took up their residence in Ogden's Hole. The luxuries and appliances of civilization were wanting in their retreat, yet they were happy and comfortable. His rifle supplied them with food. He contended successfully with the grizzly bear, and dragged the panther from his lair. Such exhibitions of strength and bravery gave him great influence over the natives. His retreat, sheltered from tempests, remained green the entire year, and he gathered about him a remarkably fine herd of cattle. These he drove off to California, and returned with a splendid lot of horses. His reputed wealth tempted the cupidity of his Mormon neighbors. Then he was not a believer in their faith, and did not hesitate to reprove their practices. He went out hunting, one day, but did not return. His wife was alarmed, and, with her relatives, instituted a search. They found him dead, from the effects of a bullet that had penetrated his brain. But who aimed the murderous weapon? Alas! the rocks and deep glens had no tongue for mortal ears. His property was seized, under some pretense, and eventually distributed among the dignitaries of the Mormon church, though, to the credit of father Smith, be it said, he returned his portion to the bereaved widow and her orphan babes. I heard of many such instances, and cannot wonder that the Mormons are greatly detested.

Ogden's City boasts, likewise, a drinking-house or tavern, which I visited, from sheer curiosity. I had been informed that one Goodall, a man famous through all the West for his narrow escapes and daring exploits, was there to be seen, with his men; and I went to look at them, as to a collection of natural curiosities, or a menagerie of strange animals. They were lounging around the door, and in the house, which seemed filled with them—swarthy Mexicans and Indians, of nameless tribes, dressed in their native cos-

tumes. There was also a Lipan, with the keen, fiery eyes peculiar to his race; and two Pinos, from the interior of New-Mexico. A number of thieving, murdering Camanches exhibited their hateful physiognomies; and the whole company had such a vagabond look, that I wondered Goodall was not afraid of them.

Goodall hails from New-York State, where he left a wife and several children, though he has since assumed the marriage relation in nearly or quite all the native tribes among whom he has traded. It gives him influence, and, no doubt, the Indian belles are glad to secure so attractive a lover. His costume is decidedly picturesque. It consists of richly embroidered buckskin pants and moccasins, exhibiting a great degree of taste. A gaudy belt around his waist, garnished with weapons, giving him the appearance of a finished mountain-rover. Several very large dogs, of the Newfoundland and Spanish breeds, were attached to his train, and he rode, when in motion, one of the finest horses I ever beheld.

I was strongly reminded of Dick Turpin's favorite Black Bess, while listening to the anecdotes related of this wonderful animal. Goodall declared that he could do everything but talk, and had a way of expressing himself that no one could misunderstand. He seems to be perfectly aware that he is a privileged being—allows no one to mount him but his master, and domineers like a despot over every other horse or animal that comes in his way. Marvellous stories are told of him. How he saved his master's life, by bearing him through the floods of a swollen river, and, again, by outstripping a band of mounted savages, running eighteen hours, without pausing for a moment until he reached a place of safety.

Goodall was no friend to the Mormons ; it was business, and that alone, which induced him to pass through their territory. He had a drove of sheep, quartered at a little distance in the valley. At first, he took me for one of the Mormons, and was rather shy ; but ascertaining that such was not the case—that I was simply a tourist, travelling for instruction and amusement—he became communicative, and invited me out to see his camp. The sheep—long-legged, coarse-woolled, and black-nosed animals—were quietly feeding, in a beautiful pasture-ground near the "corral," into which they were gathered at night, and which consisted of upright logs, stockade fashion.

I inquired if there was not danger that some of the animals would be stolen.

"Danger !" he replied. "Of course, there is danger—otherwise there would be no necessity for keeping a gang to watch them."

I asked whom he feared. His reply was characteristic, and to the point—

"The Mormons, of course."

I replied that the Mormons seemed to bear rather a bad name, but I supposed that there must be honest men among them.

"Not a damn one !" he answered, quickly. "Not a damn

one! Stranger, I've always knowed 'em. I knowed Jo Smith, and a greater rascal never trod shoe-leather. I knowed Brigham Young when he was a boy. We went to school together. I knowed Elder Gould, and hundreds more; and I never yet knew one that could be trusted. To lie, and steal, and cheat, is a part of their religion. I say it is!"

"But I should think that among so many, there must be some good and sincere men."

"Not a damn one! Not a damn one!" he repeated. "It takes a good while to find them out, sometimes; but the knowledge will surely come."

"I hope it may not."

"Stranger," he continued, "until I came among these Mormons, I had faith in human nature. I have none now. I had faith in virtue, in purity, and in goodness. It is all gone. I curse them, because they have cursed me with the sight of their inborn depravity. They will curse you in the same manner."

I could hardly forbear smiling at his earnestness. The hunters and traders cherish, very generally, an ill-feeling towards the Mormons. This might partly be explained without accusing either party of dishonor or actual dishonesty. The Mormons have contrived to absorb most of the Indian trade; and the herding business is much less profitable, since so many have embarked in it. Then, too, the hunting-grounds have been materially lessened in extent, the game rapidly diminished, and the natives thereby incited to acts of violence and opposition to the wishes and interests of those they had formerly treated and regarded as friends. "What everybody says, must be true," is an old adage; and all agree in telling one story about the Mormons, and attributing to them the grossest deception and the foulest vices.

CHAPTER X.

FREDERICK B——.—THE MORMON THEATRE—MRS. CANFIELD, ETC., ETC.

WHEN we returned to Zion, the Mrs. Inkleys informed me that a young man had been there twice, and both times inquiring for me. At first, I was utterly at a loss to conjecture who it could be.

"Did he give his name?" I inquired of Hannah, the only one present.

"It was not me, but Martha, whom he asked," she replied.

"Martha, did that young man give his name?" she cried.

"No—yes—that is, it seems that he did. Fred— Frederick; that's it."

"Frederick B——?"

"That was the name. He said that he wished you would come round there, when you got home."

"Was that all?"

"That was all."

It was then quite late in the evening. I was weary, and

so postponed going until morning. When morning came, breakfast was later than usual, and it was near ten o'clock before I could obey the summons. My heart misgave me. I felt almost certain that something unusual had happened, though its nature I failed to define. I quickened my pace, only pausing to salute two or three acquaintances, and soon arrived at the place. The door was shut, and I knocked softly.

"Come in," said a voice that I knew to be Frederick's. I entered the apartment, when the first object that met my view was the old man, apparently in the last agonies. His son was bending over him, with all the tenderness of a woman, wiping the death-damps from his brow, moistening his parched tongue, and otherwise administering to his physical comfort. He pressed my hand, in silence, glanced at the sufferer, and resumed his post by the bedside. I sat down on a low bench, an interested spectator in the scene.

The old man's senses were wandering. He muttered, scarce intelligibly, of the days and events of his youth. His marriage, the birth of his child, and their happiness in the cottage-home, all came back, in pleasing retrospect. At length his tone changed, his words became fewer and more distinct, and he suddenly woke to recollection. We both knew it to be the last flickering beam of life and intellect, and he felt it so himself. Holding out his hand to his son, he said, "I am going to meet your mother, Frederick. She was with me, just now; but her garments were white, and her face was that of an angel's."

Overcome by the violence of his emotions, the strong man sobbed aloud.

"Now, don't—don't—my son," he said. "I am an old man. My time has come. It is meet that I should go. I die in the faith."

"What faith, father?"

"Of the Lord Jesus Christ," and he fell back, dead.

Frederick lifted his hands, and said, "May you meet my mother in that land where there is neither change nor apostasy!"

"O God, it is a fearful thing,
To see the human soul take wing!"

More fearful, perhaps, in the stillness, and gloom, and sorrow of a home to be bereaved, than in the earthquake, the storm, or the battle, where all the softer and tenderer emotions are wrought to an intensity of excitement that borders on sublimity.

After the lapse of a few moments, I arose, and proceeded to perform the last sad offices of affection for the dead, disposing the decent limbs, folding the meek hands over the quiet breast, and sealing the waxen eyelids in an attitude of slumber. The next day was appointed for the funeral, which Frederick decided to keep secret as possible. With the assistance of a few friends, a coffin was procured, and the robes for the dead prepared.

"No Mormon has been spoken to," said Frederick. "I hope they will remain in entire ignorance of what is going on."

"For your sake, I hope so, too, though it is rather unlikely."

A slight noise at the window attracted my attention, and, looking around, I beheld a pair of glaring eyes.

"Who is there?" I whispered to Frederick, pointing towards them. But, before he could turn, they had disappeared.

"The vultures will soon be here," he said, and he spoke truly. When a Mormon dies, the church assumes the right to look after his property, if he is possessed of any. In half an hour, a priest was at the door. He came in without ceremony of knocking, and deported himself with an insolence altogether unbearable.

"So our brother has gone," he said. "Peace to his memory! Dying happily, as a Gentile never dies; and certain of taking his place in the promised land, at the last day."

"My father died in the faith of Christ, and in no other," said Frederick, somewhat tartly.

"Ours is the faith of Christ," said the priest. "He was one of us; our brother. He loved our institutions; he followed our practices. What are you, to assume the dictation of affairs? That prerogative belongs to the church."

"Begone!" said Frederick. "I have not words to waste on such a reptile."

The countenance of the priest actually assumed a fiendish expression. "Time will manifest who is lord here," he muttered, and went out.

"He has gone for a reinforcement," I observed.

"This is dreadful!" said Frederick. "The necessity of quarrelling over the body of so near and dear a relative!"

In a few minutes the priest returned, leading the woman who, in the Mormon ritual, had been "sealed" to that old man as his second wife, and whom Frederick had expelled from the house.

"The church," said the priest, addressing her, "delegates you the mistress here. Take possession and authority."

"She shall not!" said Frederick.

"She shall!" said the priest. "He is her husband."

"He is my father."

The hag, meanwhile, stood a silent, though apparently well-pleased spectator.

Seeing how matters must terminate, I slipped from the room, without saying a word to any one, ran to the hotel of Colonel Kinney, where I knew that the officers of the military were boarding. Fortunately, the commandant was disengaged. He received me graciously, listened to my statement of the pending difficulty, and immediately dispatched a corporal, at the head of his platoon, to occupy the premises, and see that order was maintained.

As I anticipated, the house was filled with Mormons, on my return. Frederick was lying, bound, on the floor, and that hideous woman sitting beside the corpse. They were evidently disconcerted when the military appeared, and the priest grew wonderfully respectful when addressing the officer. He seemed to comprehend affairs at a glance, ordered them all to disperse and depart, assured the woman that it was no place for her—that she looked much more like going into a wash-tub than to a funeral—and carried out his commands by compelling obedience. The priest asserted his right to stay, as a minister of religion ; but the gallant soldier plainly told him that his orders were imperative, without distinction of class or profession. Uttering imprecations against the soldiers, the government, and everything in general that might dare to interfere with the liberties of the saints, he departed.

Released from the ignominious cords with which his enemies had bound him, Frederick stood again beside his dead. The soldiers—hushed, reverent, and uncovered, in the presence of death—occupied one side of the house. I sat near, conscious that the mourner required my presence, as a support in this hour of affliction.

To avoid the public gaze—above all, to prevent the attendance of those whose faith he loathed, and whose presence he hated—Frederick determined that the burial should take place at midnight.

"The hour is unseemly," I said, "for such as your father—a peaceful and good man. It would do well for a brigand—a man of war and bloodshed—but not for such as him."

"We are among brigands," he replied, and his resolution remained unchanged.

That night, therefore, when the city was silent with slumber, the procession moved from the house, and slowly down the street—the strong soldiers, in their scarlet uniforms, bearing the coffin with ease, and Frederick, with myself, following as chief mourner. Side by side with the tomb of his wife, had a new grave been made. There they paused, and, after a little preparation, lowered down the coffin, by the strong glare of torches, held high above their heads by the others in attendance. Then followed the striking of spades in the gravelly earth, and the ringing of clods on the coffin—sounds so fearful and ominous to the human heart. When the cavity was filled, the soldiers, at a word from their commander, moved silently and reverently away, leaving us alone, with the deep solemnity of darkness around us, and the stars watching above.

But others than the stars had seen us, and noted our proceedings. I accompanied Frederick to the house we had left, and going, he remarked on the silence and apparent desertion of the streets, exulting secretly, as I thought, in having so far outwitted his enemies, and the betrayers of his father's peace. The cabin, too, when we reached it, was dark and silent. He unlatched the door—we entered. Whence the impression arose, I know not, but I felt intuitively that another presence than ours was there—that some influence had been to work in our absence, and that we might expect a surprise. I am not naturally superstitious, yet the midnight burial, the hour, the darkness, and the recent presence of death, were not without their impressions. Frederick, meanwhile, was groping around, to procure a light.

"The table stood here, I thought, with a candle on it," he said; "but now I cannot find either."

A light broke into my mind, but I said nothing. He passed around the room, in the darkness, and finally, with outstretched hands, caught hold of me.

"One of two things is certain," he remarked—"that we have either mistaken the place, or those wretches have been here and stripped the house in our absence. Fortunately, if I cannot find a candle, I can strike a match."

He did so, and applied it to some fragments of dry wood, which instantly illuminated the apartment. Every vestige of the furniture had been removed—the table, chairs, and bed; in short, all the movables.

"This is more than I expected!" said Frederick, with a look of blank amazement.

The whole affair was so singular, I could not wonder at his surprise.

"Only another proof of their artfulness, and the constant espionage they practise," he continued. "Many a time the uneasy consciousness of the probable presence of some one when I was not assured of his or her being near, has made me nervous. I suppose they feared that something might escape their brigandism, if they waited till morning. Well, I hope they are satisfied."

Very heartily I echoed the devout wish, and proposed that we should adjourn to my boarding-house.

"Do you live with a Mormon?" inquired Frederick.

Being assured that I did, he declined the invitation,

Side by side with the tomb of his wife had a new grave been made. There they paused, and after a little preparation, lowered down the coffin by the strong glare of torches.—PAGE 193.

because he had formed the solemn resolution never, on any condition, to accept hospitality from a people by whom his parents had been so grievously wronged and deceived.

"Where, then, will you go?" I inquired.

"To the house of Mrs. Canfield, my mother's best friend."

"Mrs. Canfield, the actress?" I echoed, in some surprise.

"The same."

"But she is a Mormon."

"You mistake. Policy induces her to assume a friendliness towards them, which she is far from feeling. Come, let us be going."

Together we left the empty house, and passed along the street; but I could not reconcile it with my notions of propriety, to ask, at such an hour, the hospitality of a stranger-lady, and so we separated, for the time.

I cannot tell how the next day passed. I suppose like many others that leave no abiding impression. I never look out for adventures—they are wearisome. I care little about incidents—they are commonplace. But that night I went to the theatre. Yes, friends, a veritable Mormon theatre; for, whether you do or not, you should know that these worthies are quite as fond of carnal pleasures as the Gentiles, though not quite so well fixed for enjoying them.

The building dedicated to the worship of Thespis bears little comparison to those of the same character in our Eastern cities. It wants their style, their finish, their elegant adaptation to comfort and convenience; yet this deficiency is more than made up by the novelty of everything around you, and the singular appearance of the heterogeneous crowd that throng on every side.

The Mormon theatre is always well filled. There meet the hunters from the head-waters of the Colorado, the falls of the Columbia, and the great northern lakes of Canada. Here the Santa-Fé trader and New-Mexican stand side by side with the Dane, Norwegian, and German. Here soldiers in uniform jostle plain citizens, or stately Indian chiefs, in all the glory of war-paint and feathers, bend their stern brows inflexibly and immovably over the scene. Last, though not least, are the stately elders and their fair spouses. The High Priest usually appears with ten or a dozen, Kimball with as many more, Dr. Richards with nine, and Parley Pratt with an equal number.

I was there early, and it was really amusing to see these dignitaries of the church provide seats for the members of their harems. The gentleman would come in first, followed by his wives, in the order of two by two. He would look around, as if calculating distances and numbers. If there was an empty seat, well and good. He took possession of the middle, and his ladies ranged themselves on either side of him—the youngest and fairest, next his person ; the oldest and ugliest on the outside. Let me hazard the comparison of some stately knight of the barnyard, on his perch, accompanied by his numerous and faithful retinue of females The youngest ladies, as the favorites of their husbands for the time, were the best dressed, and many of them were decidedly beautiful. How they could consent to occupy the position of ninth or tenth wife to old and not particularly handsome men, excited my wonder; and I was beginning to speculate on the weakness and folly of women, in a manner that would have gained me no credit among the strong-minded sisterhood, when my meditations were disturbed by a little Frenchwoman, who came in and seated herself very unceremoniously beside me.

Mademoiselle was not timid. It made no difference to her that we had not been introduced; and my gallantry would not permit me to treat a lady with rudeness, under any circumstances. With the utmost familiarity she began a conversation, and my curiosity impelled me to listen and reply.

"How do you know that she was a Frenchwoman, if you were strangers?" says one.

I knew it by her appearance; by the becoming taste manifested in her dress; by the knots and bows of ribbon, the sprigs of flowers, and pearl ornaments, conspicuously displayed on her person, to say nothing of the thousand little graces and arts, which others may imitate artificially, but which seem natural only to them. All the world over, you can tell a Frenchwoman; and, before she had spoken, I knew, intuitively, that she was such.

"Do you see dat beautiful lady, yonder?" she asked, with the most charming confidence.

"Where?"

"Dat one setting next Brigham, de prophet."

Mademoiselle spoke with sufficient foreign accent to render her conversation interesting, but she was much too artful to disgust a fastidious English ear by an ungrammatic or idiomatic style.

"I see her."

I did, indeed. I had rested my eyes, for some moments, on her sylph-like form—her fair neck, bosom, and arms, veiled, not covered, by a thin scarf of gauze lace—her bright hair, her patrician features, their damask bloom, and the flash of conscious triumph that lighted her eye. Why had she come here to practise her fascinations!

Mademoiselle recalled my wandering thoughts.

"Dat lady be forty years old."

"Impossible!"

"Fact! I know. We came to California, in de same steamer, from la belle France—cher Paris. Den we come here."

"What for?"

"Oui; Monsieur mustn't be curus! Ver good reason; ver good, indeed."

I assured her there was no necessity for telling, and turned my attention to the play. The Frenchwoman, however, was not to be put off. She touched my elbow. I looked around.

"Dat lady—would Monsieur like to hear her history?" she asked.

"Perhaps so, at some other time."

"Oui; Monsieur wishes to see de play."

"I do."

"Ver well, not hinder," and she turned away. After sitting a few minutes in silence, she arose, flirted away, and sat down by another gentleman, with whom she was soon deeply engaged in conversation. He evidently admired her, and was not bashful about making it known, while a woman, probably his wife, sat on the other side of him, and manifested great uneasiness.

The utmost latitude in manners prevails at the theatre. The private drawing-room of Rosanna Townsend would never have tolerated such scenes as are publicly enacted there; and the worst of it is, there is no distinction. In our theatres, the disreputable characters occupy certain places—here they are mixed up with the rest.

The acting was on a stage, raised three or four feet above the floor of the room occupied by the spectators. The play was the Lady of Lyons, of which the Mormons are excessively fond. It ran season after season, with little variation, and they were dissatisfied when another was substituted in its stead.

On this occasion, the performance was good, and might be relished by one able to divert his mind from other scenes passing around him. Some of the chief actors exhibited decided ability. Among these, Mrs. Canfield, as the mother of Claude, performed her part admirably, and Mrs. Wheelock, who represented Pauline, to the life.

The latter is very beautiful. Her face beams with intelligence, and her voice is thrillingly melodious. Her husband having been absent in Australia nearly two years, a multitude of saints, prophets, and apostles are in full chase after her. According to Mormon theology, the absence of a husband releases the wife from all obligation, and she is at perfect liberty to form a union, at pleasure, with another man. One of the most eager in this pursuit, is the man who enacted the part of Claude, and whose passionate protestations had an air of the sincerest reality. Neither were the other actors indifferent to her charms. Indeed, their manifestations of gallantry seriously interfered with the performance intended for the public amusement.

MRS. CANFIELD

Is an English woman, from Bath, who, having been deserted by her husband, has been obliged to resort to the stage, to obtain bread for her children. I called on Frederick, at her house, to-day. She received me with great affability, and related, for my entertainment, many interesting incidents connected with her travels and adventures. The room was garnished with pictures and mementoes of her native city, and her eyes filled with tears, while explaining the particular points of interest, or relating the associations that gave to each its relative value. She was not a believer in Mormonism, as she assured me, but necessity impelled her stay among them. At first, she tried to obtain a livelihood by sewing, and found plenty of employment, but little pay. Then she resorted to school-teaching, with even worse success; and finally, as a last experiment, attempted the stage.

Here her fine talent for music procured her notoriety, and she might have found it profitable had it not been for the unusual number of free-tickets, which admit the elders and their families.

I could not but be aware that one so good, beautiful, and intelligent, could not remain long in Mormondom without a train of suitors, and I subsequently learned that her hand had been sought by several men, some of whom were already husbands. But their offers were firmly, though respectfully, declined. Her conscience would not permit her to form a second marriage, until she was assured of her husband's death; but, under no consideration, would she ever be united with a sensual polygamist.

CHAPTER XI.

THE TABERNACLE—FORM OF MORMON WORSHIP—SPECIMEN OF PREACHING, ETC.

NEAR the Mormon theatre, and somewhat resembling it in appearance and capaciousness, is the Tabernacle—not the first one that was built, though it occupies the same situation. The first building was large on the ground, and presented the appearance of an immense oblong box. In 1854, this was taken down and removed, to make way for the magnificent temple that stands there now. It is handsomely built of stone, and makes some pretensions to architectural beauty, though chiefly remarkable for its immense size. It is said to be capable of accommodating five thousand persons, with ease ; and is surrounded by a high wall, reared with immense cost and labor. You enter by large folding-doors in the east end, which face the platform occupied by the priests and elders in the west. The seats are arranged in the form of an amphitheatre, and all are enabled to gratify their devotion and curiosity, by a plain view of those who conduct the worship. I attended once, and but once, there being little in the service that could interest the sympathies, and still less that could affect the understanding. Wanting in the plain, severe simplicity of the Protestant worship, it has none of the pomp and gorgeousness of the Catholic ceremonial. Yet Mormonism is in its infancy. It wants the prestige of age, to render it venerable ; it requires the combined efforts of literature and art, of good taste, sound sense, and elegant ideas, to perfect its form of worship. Centuries of toil, study, and the most approved methods of art, combined with unbounded wealth, have given to the Catholic Church its perfection in appliances to captivate the senses.

What may not the Mormons in eighteen centuries become? I could not help thinking this, as, under the guidance of Elder Snow, (*g.*) I went up to the Tabernacle, one Sunday morning, and saw the immense assemblage gathered there from the four quarters of the globe. Unlike the Eastern polygamists, the Mormons do not attempt to confine their wives, or keep them secreted from the gaze of others. All entered the church promiscuously, and sat just as it happened, though, generally, the husband placed himself in the midst of his wives. It was a strange assemblage, yet, who could expect anything better? And think you the followers of Christianity, in the first century of its existence, appeared much more respectable to the votaries of the fashionable religions of the day? How would they have characterized its professors as low, debauched, stupid, ignorant, and even deficient in the common attributes of humanity! How would they have scoffed, and jeered, and mocked them, prophesying their utter extinction in a few short years! There was an extinction, it is true; but who were the victims. The old faith disappeared—the new triumphed.

The rites of the Mormon worship open with singing and a full band of music. Many of the females had good voices, and the strain was solemn and impressive. When this was concluded, Brigham Young offered a prayer, for "Zion in the tops of the mountains" in particular, and for the saints all over the world in general. The Gentiles, of course, were excluded from the benefits of this petition. His discourse was short, yet pertinent. He exhorted them to obedience and union, and reminded them that many females were yet unprovided with husbands, who ought to be married, and giving children to the church. "I think," he continued, "that I have set you a good example. My wives outnumber those of David, and children, like olive-plants, gather about my table."

He finished, and sat down, when the music struck up "Bruce's Address," followed by "Old Lang Syne." It ceased, and Elder Cumming arose. He is tall, and remarkably strong-built. While surveying his athletic form and sinewy limbs, joined to a countenance not particularly expressive of intelligence, I thought how much better he was adapted to agriculture, or some useful mechanic art, than in dealing out harangues on subjects of which his audience were quite as well qualified to judge as himself. His discourse abounded in anecdote, all relating to what seemed of chief interest to them—taking new wives. He rated those women soundly, who, having the opportunity, neglect to get married; and said that a brother was deserving of "hell-fire" if he permitted a woman to remain single without making her an offer. "Who cares if she is old, and ugly, and deformed?—her child will be young, and probably beautiful. If she has no child, why, God has ordained it, and you have done your duty. When walking along the streets, I make it a practice to inquire of every stranger woman I meet, whose wife she is. To this, many of my sisters here can testify. If she tells the name of her husband, I bless her, and say, 'Go on your way rejoicing; have children, and rear them up for Zion!' If she has no husband, I bid her begone, and get one."

There was no evidence of a devotional spirit, though much that was said elicited the boisterous mirth of the audience. While listening to these discourses, I could not help thinking that the Mormons seemed to regard marriage not as a means for promoting social happiness, but solely as a method for the most convenient propagation of the race. Yet this view is not novel, and has been frequently entertained by restless and aspiring spirits. Augustus, after devastating the earth to promote his schemes of ambition, sought to replenish it again, by recommending, and even in some cases enforcing, marriage; and complained bitterly of the dancing-girls, and other women, who refused to "give children to the republic." Yet, why did he wish this? To increase the sum of human happiness, or promote the welfare of the race? No such thing; but that his empire might be replenished with taxable subjects, and his armies filled with new soldiers.

Bonaparte had the same idea in view, when he said that the greatest woman was the one who had borne the most children—which is certainly a great scandal on the sex, as it must be better, nobler, greater, to bear, bring up, and suitably educate two children, than to simply give birth to a dozen poor, miserable, little outcasts, who ultimately come to the state-prison, poor-house, or gallows.

The great desire of the Mormons to have children, and increase in population, displays, to us, some ulterior motive. They are looking forward, down the long vista of the future, to wealth and power—to independence, rank, and distinction, among the nations of the earth. The examples of Moses and Mohammed are before them, and the lessons of ages have not been lost.

But the service was yet unfinished, and another speaker was on the floor. His words were nearly as follows :

" Now, my dear friends, what a dreadful thing it would be, if, after all your trials and afflictions, your perils in crossing the deep (for many before me have come from countries beyond the sea)—after all this, and your difficulties and dangers in the howling wilderness, what a dreadful thing it would be to lose your inheritance among the saints !

" Other sins are venal, other transgressions may be forgiven, but there is no hope for him who, having once known the good way, has turned back. And, my sisters, I hear strange reports of you, which it grieves me to mention. I hear that some of you have become dissatisfied with the institutions of our holy religion, and have dared to refuse a brother in marriage, because he had already a wife. My sisters, it is nothing to me—you must not imagine that it makes a particle of difference with me—whether you are married or not; but it does make a difference to you, and that a very great one. Why, know you not that unless a woman is sealed or married to a man, and that man a true disciple, there can be no hope of her salvation?

"Consider well, then, that if you lose your souls—your precious, immortal souls—by remaining single, you have nobody but yourselves to blame. I have told you. You know that. And the good brothers are ready and willing to assist you, if you will only let them. Let them! Why, a woman, rather than remain unmarried, should ask some elder or saintly brother to bestow on her the seal of salvation.

"And, my dear sisters, there are other subjects on which I wish to speak. I have been informed that some of you have laid stumbling-blocks in the way of your husbands when they have proposed to seal other females. You have tried, by tears, and protestations, and rebellion, to hinder them from performing such duties. Know ye not that these things are deserving of damnation? Know ye not that, in all things, your husbands are your superiors; that they stand to you in the place of God; and that obedience—unqualified, unquestioning obedience—is your first, I had almost said your only, duty, as in that all others are comprised.

"Now, my sisters, an important thing for you to remember is this: If your husbands want more wives, you must help to get them; and then you must be peaceable, and not quarrel, and lie, and filch from each other, but live in harmony, with all loving-kindness and charity. What a dreadful thing it would be if the soul of one woman, through your opposition to her union with your husband, should be lost! And, being in torments unspeakable, would she not forever cry out against you?"

There was much more in a similar strain and to the same purpose, though, as literary efforts, they were beneath criticism.

I returned home for dinner, and, while we were at table, Mr. Inkley inquired my opinion of the last discourse, declaring that it met his unqualified approbation.

"Then you will be on the lookout for another wife, I suppose," was my reply, glancing towards Sarah, who sat at the table. She tossed her head, with an expression of the deepest scorn.

"That such is my duty, I own," he said, with affected gravity; "though it sorely taxes my energies to provide for those I now have."

"Well thought of!" ejaculated Sarah.

"It would be a pity," I said, "for any woman to lose her immortal soul, because no man could afford to find her in bread and butter. She might be sealed, to secure her salvation, and then left to take care of herself."

"That is the way with many of them," said Sarah.

"Of who?"

"Why, these women that work about as nurses and assistants in families. You saw that very old lady who sat just before you, I suppose?"

"That one dressed in black, who seemed so deeply interested in the services?" I asked.

"The same," she answered. "Well, that old woman is eighty-five next September, and she has been sealed to Brigham Young just one month. She came on here with her children, though an unbeliever. But, recently, she became a convert, and the next thing was to be sealed. In consequence of her age and infirmities, the brothers hesitated to perform the duty, until the first and best one of all, touched by the consideration of her necessities, consented to become her husband, on the condition that she should remain with her children, and not be dependent on him for support or a home."

"Then I suppose that the prophet has many such wives, or sealed ones?"

"He has, indeed, more than any one knows of—probably more than he remembers himself."

"And this is considered a certain guarantee of salvation?"

"It is; and hence young girls and maidens are often sealed long before the age of puberty. I have witnessed the sealing of children not more than eight years old."

"I have never heard of this before."

"Very likely. There are many things among us that you

have never heard of ; many rites and ceremonies known only to the initiated ; many plans and purposes you could never guess."

"But this sealing of young girls is against nature and religion."

"Not more so than betrothals among the Jews, and yet this people had a warrant direct from heaven for all they did."

"The examples of the Jews have been frequently quoted to furnish props for bad and mistaken conduct or ideas, by bad or mistaken men," I replied. "It is not for me to define or limit how far such practices were expedient under their laws, and the circumstances of their society. It is enough for us that here, and in this age, the marriage relation is thereby degraded, and the happiness of thousands unrelentingly sacrificed. What sensations must the betrothal of a child to a man old enough to be her father excite ! How can she ever regard him with those feelings of affection which are indispensably necessary to render the marriage state one of happiness ?"

"She can at least be obedient."

"Seriously and candidly, Mrs. Inkley," I replied, "can you find it in your heart to approve of these things ? If you had a young and beautiful daughter, would not all the better feelings of your nature revolt against her forming such an unnatural connection ? Could you in silence behold the sacrifice of all her prospects of happiness, and know and feel that nothing in this wide world was left for her but obedience to the caprices and whims of a tyrant ?"

"Really, sir, I cannot argue this question with you," she replied. "Yet the Scriptures require obedience in the wife, you know, and make the husband stand in the same relation to her that Christ does to the church."

"And again I must say that how far such passages are to be received in an unqualified sense, I shall not pretend to decide, but that they were ever meant to compel any woman, immortal and accountable, under any circumstances whatever, to submit to polygamy, and practices so detestable as these 'sealings,' I venture to discredit."

"And so do I," said Martha Inkley, who had entered the room unnoticed, and seemed glad of an opportunity to disagree with her rival. "These 'sealings' of children are—I will not say what."

She had caught the expression of her husband's eye, but it could not silence her.

"There was brother Haywood's daughter," she continued, "a beautiful little girl, in short skirts and pantalets, who came into the room, to be sealed to a man four times her age, while crying for her doll and baby things ; and when the new-made husband attempted to embrace her, she fled, screaming that he was big and ugly, and she did not like him. Is it likely that, as years advance, she will grow fonder of him, or more reconciled to her lot ?"

"An extreme case," said Inkley, blandly.

"Not exactly an extreme case, either," replied Martha. "You know very well that Hannah May had to be held by main force while the ceremony of her sealing was going on. How she shrieked, and screamed, and protested against it, declaring that if she couldn't have Frederick Barnes, her youthful playmate, she wouldn't be married at all!"

"But she hadn't arrived at the years of discretion," said the husband.

"Years of discretion or not, it was a shame and an abomination to force her into such a connection!"

I thought as much.

"Why," continued Martha, "a man will marry two or three sisters, as brother Warner did. He married one, and then, to please his wife, he took her sister, and, finally, the mother of both, and they all had children by him. I asked sister Warner what relationship the children held to each other. She only laughed."

During our conversation, the people were gathering for the afternoon service. Their singular appearance attracted my attention. One man passed along with his six wives, three on either side of him, lovingly locking arms. Another company passed, the man ahead, and his four wives following in single file. There was no established rule or fashion, but all were at perfect liberty to walk single, double, or treble, as suited them best. Suddenly, my attention was arrested by a female walking alone, and without any apparent connection with the passing crowd. She looked towards the window where I sat, and I had a very distinct view of her features. She was beautiful, though somewhat faded.

"That lady—who is she?" I asked, addressing Mrs. Inkley.

"What her name may now be, I cannot say," she replied. "Her maiden name was Scott."

"Miss Scott! I have known her. Where does she live?"

"I cannot say. I know nothing about her, though I have heard that—that"——

"That what?"

"That she had been the mistress of a soldier who had deserted her, and that now she was picking up a living as she best could."

The remembrance of her father's anxiety, and my promise to him, flashed into my mind.

"I must see her," I said, seizing my hat.

"You have just seen her," said Sarah, laughing.

"But I wish to talk with her."

The women glanced at each other.

"I was acquainted with her father," I said. "He was very anxious about her."

"That was perfectly natural," said Sarah, with something like a sneer. I said no more, but walked out at the door. Miss Scott, however, was nowhere to be seen. I walked up one street and down another, all to no purpose. Inquiring would have been useless, and I thought that possibly she might have gone to the Tabernacle. So thither I went, but the immense concourse, even greater than that in the forenoon, effectually precluded individual recognition, and I was glad to get away long before the service closed.

CHAPTER XII.

THE COUNCIL OF HEALTH—MIRACLES—DREAMS, AND SOME OTHER THINGS.

THREE months among the Mormons, and thus far treated with consideration and respect.

"Oh, I pity you," says one, "shut up in the seclusion of the Great Basin for three long months."

But my good friend, there is no occasion for your pity; my time has passed pleasantly, I might say happily. I have found, and I trust made, friends.

Long ago I learned that if only one spot of sunshine appeared, to monopolize it; if only one flower grew in my path, to be sure and notice that; to scrutinize ugly faces for the one handsome feature, and to look for something cheering in all dismal prospects. I confess that sometimes my resolution has almost vanished, and that while looking at the Mormons my faith in human nature has been sorely tested. I have grown weary of describing unpleasant scenes. I would much rather write of virtues than vices; of good, and pure, and honest men, than wicked and dishonest ones. Byron said that he described men as they were, not as they should be, and that nothing in his descriptions or characters had ever equalled the reality.

In the propagation of a new faith it usually happens that dreams, visions, miracles, and supernatural appearances and occurrences are the stock in trade. It is comparatively much easier to influence the imagination than convince the judgment, hence credulity rather than reason is addressed.

The Mormons will tell you of great cures wrought by their priests. They will tell you of instances where the sick have recovered beneath their magic touch ; they will point out on the necks and limbs of their children the scars of great sores that have been healed ; they will tell you of the blind having recovered their eye-sight, and the deaf their hearing. Shall we dispute that such things sometimes occur after the recent experiments in electro-magnetism, especially when we consider the powerful influence of imagination over a certain class of diseases.

The question arises, are the priests impostors, or are they the dupes of their own credulity? I am inclined to think the latter. Few of them have any knowledge of the natural sciences, or the philosophy that traces effects to their cause.

"There can be nothing supernatural," I remarked, to Mr. Inkley. "Your people should be too enlightened to believe in miracles, in the general acceptation of that term."

"The most enlightened men in your Gentile Churches believe in them," he replied, gravely.

"Not as you," I answered.

"And yet, you must know that had not your church inculcated the belief that miracles were of common occurrence eighteen centuries ago, the Mormons in this age would never have dreamed of promulgating such an idea. But the possibility of supernatural events being granted, the cavil all rests on a question of time, which is nothing. (*h.*)

In conclusion, Mr. Inkley invited me to attend with him a meeting of the Council of Health, at Social Hall. To my inquiries, if I would not be considered in the light of an intruder, he replied in the negative, and said that the sisters were always pleased with the attendance of gentlemen, particularly strangers, for whom a seat was left empty.

"Is it then a meeting of the sisters?" I asked.

"Certainly."

"Then you have your strong-minded women here. I thought that class peculiar to the North."

"With this slight difference, your strong-minded females are generally old maids, in whose bosoms the milk of human kindness has become sour, whereas ours are—are"——

"Married women," I suggested, "whose lives are embittered by the neglect and indifference of their husbands; a fate to which that of the old maid is ten times preferable."

I found, on further inquiry, that the sisters assembled at this meeting to talk over their various aches and complaints, and discuss the most approved methods of cure. All physicians are entitled to a seat among them, with a voice in their deliberations; so are the priests and elders, while strangers are admitted to see and be seen. We went early and obtained good seats. At least sixty-five females were in attendance, who, so far as I could discover, presented nothing remarkable in appearance. They looked exactly like any other promiscuous gathering of women, old and young, gay and sad, pretty and ugly; coarse and vulgar in some cases, but intelligent and refined in others.

The meeting was called to order by Dr. High, who made some appropriate remarks on the blessings of health, and the violation of physical laws, to which all diseases must be attributed.

He was followed by Dr. Speight, who begged leave to dissent from his worthy brother in many important particulars. It was very plain to him that sickness was often superinduced by a direct interposition of Divine Providence. Pestilence fell on the Israelites as a judgment from Heaven, because of the sin of David; Job was smitten with a horrible disease to try his faith, and even in our own age, he contended, that similar events had happened, and might happen again.

It was easy to see that the last speaker was a particular favorite with the sisters, especially those whose countenance, appearance, and manner indicated the lower class of ignorance. The female mind is naturally prone to superstition in its uncultivated state. Sister Newman, one of this stripe, was evidently aching to get the floor. She manifested great uneasiness, wringing, twisting, and rocking to and fro. The moment he sat down she bounded up, and began a tirade against such infidel teachers as Dr. High. She knowed, indeed she did, that sickness went just where it was sent—that God was pleased to afflict some people more than he did others, and that the best ones generally were most afflicted.

"You know I am nearly always sick, but then I feel that it does me good. Last winter in that spell I had I could almost touch the hem of His garment"——

"Because I gave her so much opium," whispered Dr. High.

"Could touch the hem of His garment," she continued, "and that's just the way, when I am well, if the heavenly dew descends, I am so much like a cake of tallow, that it rolls off and leaves no impression, but when I am sick, why then, my dear friends, I am just like a muslin sheet, one drop wets me all over."

The absurdity of these comparisons excited a slight titter at her expense, when she dropped spitefully into her seat, and sister Harris arose. She was a little vulgar-looking woman, with a countenance expressive of dissipation and sensuality, and her speech was a strange compound of superstition and absurdity. She commenced by expressing her belief that the devil was let loose, and that Mormon women were the especial objects of his wrath and hatred. This she declared to be all wrong—said that they ought not to be subject to pain in any case, but that disease and even death, must be banished from among them, and go to the

Gentiles to whom they belonged—that God was about to glorify his name by cutting off the rotten nations of the earth, when all would be Mormons, and in a state of felicity somewhat resembling the denizens of Mohammed's Paradise.

She was succeeded by sister Lippincott, who seemed to think that all their difficulties and troubles were occasioned by their not loving their husbands enough, and being as obedient to them as they ought. It was a rambling tirade, and as often happens at female meetings, those least capable of speaking monopolized the floor. She concluded by recommending catnip tea as a remedy in certain complaints, at which sister Gibbs started up, declaring that catnip tea was good for nothing, but that enough lobelia would drive all the devils out. The quantity necessary to perform this wonder she did not prescribe. At length she began jumping up and down, clapping her hands, and crying out, "The spirit is upon me, the spirit is upon me, even now as it descended on the Apostles at the day of Pentecost." Then she broke forth into a strain that they called speaking in an unknown tongue. She was certainly phrenzied or intoxicated. I am inclined to think the latter. Her language and gestures were actually indescribable, but soon ended in complete exhaustion, when she fell to the floor. The sisters crowded around her, raised her up, and laid her at full length on one of the seats. One of the elders then arose and attempted to interpret what she said, but the noise and confusion had become so great that it was impossible for me to hear what he said.

Inkley, who seemed amazed, and I fancied felt disgusted at the scene, proposed to go away. Several of the more respectable and intelligent women actually departed. I wished however, to see the end. The inspired sister soon fell asleep, and order was restored. Sister Sanders then arose, and expressed her firm belief that all diseases, acute or chronic might be cured by the exercise of faith and the laying on of hands, and dealt largely in her own miraculous powers. She could ease the most violent toothache, she said, by simply rubbing her hands over the part affected, and commanding the pain to depart. She could stop hemorrhages of the most extravagant character, and last, though by no means least, a word from her would restore a dislocated joint, or mend a broken bone. Her sister's arm had been badly injured by some unlucky accident, and she roundly asserted that it had been instantaneously recovered by the exercise of her power. One woman had a daughter present who was afflicted with some cutaneous disease, and who desired to have the remedy applied. The sisters, with the priests and elders, crowded around her, laid their hands on her head and person, when one of the most eminent was moved to bless her in an unknown tongue. The oracular utterances were interpreted to mean the invocation of great blessings, both temporal and spiritual ; she was to possess all necessary good, all that the heart or sense could desire ; her seed was to outnumber the stars, and thence kings and priests were to arise. She looked, however, as if some guarantee for the comforts and necessaries of life would be much more acceptable. She was scarcely sixteen, and yet had been married for some time. One child held to her clothes, another was in her lap, and there was evidently the prospect of a third. There were unmistakable indications of poverty in her general appearance. She was poorly clad, and, I doubt not, ill-fed.

After this others came forward ; some had aches in one part, others had pains in another. One was bruised, another wounded, a third was sick, a fourth had the fever ; in short, I was strongly reminded of an excellent old lady, who was great for visiting among her neighbors, and whose enumeration of the complaints incident to her family was summed up in the following amusing style : "Jemmy has a boil on his hip, and Jerry a cut on his leg ; my husband is very poorly, and so much ails me that I really don't know what to complain of." It really seemed that there was not a sound person in the community, at least in the house. All were full to overflowing of the troubles and afflictions which had befallen their neighbors or themselves. Yet this trait of humanity is not peculiar to the Mormons. For a grievous list of ailments and sicknesses, commend me at any time to a party of old women in the lower classes of life. I was once greatly amused by a woman of ordinary intelligence, who, according to her phraseology, "never saw a well day," who always kept a dish of "systic," or some other kind of herb tea in the corner, and who was exceedingly angry if the physician did not call at least twice a week to inquire after her health, though he could never find her at home.

This interesting part of the business being finished, it was proposed to adjourn. Sister Petit, however, objected, as she had a remarkable vision to narrate. This was neither more nor less than a tremendous conflict between the Lord and the devil, which closely resembled in its minute particulars the famous fight between Apollyon and Christian, recorded by Bunyan, in the Pilgrim's Progress. For a long time the battle raged with equal spirit on both sides, but the Lord triumphed in the énd, and his sooty majesty was driven away. There was much more of similar absurdity. In review of these things, we find ourselves involuntarily asking how it could be possible for a system of religious faith, like Mormonism, to arise and flourish as that has done, unless some equally superstitious tendencies of education were at work on the public mind?

Looking at Mormonism philosophically, we shall find little in it that is original. It is an offshoot of Judaism, with a little borrowed from Christianity to make it palatable to the present age. Thus, if you deprecate to a Mormon the idea of paying tithes, he will refer you at once to Abraham, who gave tithes of all he possessed to Melchisedek. If you complain of polygamy, he will tell you of Jacob, and David, and Solomon, and thus to the end of the chapter. Think you if priestcraft had not so flourished in other countries, it ever would have abounded as it does in Utah? It is not difficult for a believer in spirits to believe in the spirit rappings.

Yet it argues little for the progress of the age that this spurious and prurient birth should belong to the afternoon of the nineteenth century. We might have hoped and looked for better things. Is it not significant of an unpalatable truth? Does it not prove conclusively that the advancement in moral and religious ideas has not kept pace with that of the physical sciences; that, notwithstanding railroads, steamboats, and telegraphs, we are yet hanging to the skirts of the past, fettered by its superstitions, and imitating its vices.

Let no one think that I am attempting to excuse or palliate the vices of the Mormons. I quarrel with no man's creed except so far as it tends to make him vicious and dangerous to the community. Many things are simply absurd, and an assembly of old women, like those attending the Council of Health, could scarcely have deserved a passing notice, only as tending to show how human hearts, even in this enlightened age, may be darkened by superstition. In any other view, it was probably one of the most harmless assemblages that ever convened in Utah.

But there are things for which we must and do blame the Mormons, more even than for polygamy and kindred vices. Great as may be their sins of commission, those of omission are certainly greater. They will meet you on all sides with Scripture quotations, and bring the examples of patriarchs and prophets to sanction their adoption of old customs and ancient usages, but it is only on the side which tends to blacken and deform humanity. The great and eminent virtues of these same men are never set up as examples for imitation. Their honesty, their truth, their moral integrity their unflinching adherence to the right, is made of little or no account ; but the one fault into which they were betrayed by the age, or the circumstances in which they lived, oh ! that is something to copy and applaud. We must blame the Mormons for reading our Bible as they do. You cannot open this book without finding on its eldest or newest leaves the purest and holiest lessons of truth and virtue, given in words that burn after the lapse of ages, yet all this they pass over with neglect and indifference.

We blame them that they have retarded the progress of the age, and blackened the development of great and good ideas in the womb of time. The world; mankind, the nineteenth century all demanded a teacher not to instruct them in the doctrines of a new faith, but to diffuse vitality into the old. They demanded a knowledge of the Infinite God, of the real man, not the fabulous, of actual divine Scriptures, not pregnant with dead forms and meaningless ceremonies, but filled with love, charity, and good-will to men. They wanted a live religion that should manifest itself in all the daily walk and conversation, as well on the broad highway of letters, business, science, politics, or morals, as in the quiet seclusion of the cloister or the domestic shade. They asked a leader in a great religious movement, a progressive enterprise. All things betoken this. Never before has the world witnessed such a grand conflict between the powers of light and darkness, between science and ignorance, between the crumbling systems of the past, and the rising phœnix of the present. We must blàme the Mormons for rising up at such a time to deceive mankind with an egregious system of folly that copies the past in its vices, and looks for its future to the worst passions of men. We must blame them, that with such opportunities for doing good, they failed to do it, that in such a vast field of culture they only planted the old, dry, unprofitable weeds, which civilization and Christianity had thrown away as vile and noxious, though superstition and barbarism had preserved the seeds.

What if their followers are the poor, the lowly, even the stupidly ignorant, or the vile. Publicans and sinners were the companions of our Lord at table ; it was to babes in knowledge that the glorious tidings of the Gospel were revealed. Does it not show a remissness in our churches that these weak ones, whose souls, however, are as precious, and whose happiness is as much worth caring for, as that of the monarch on his throne—that these weak ones, I say, should be left to herd with impostors, and swell the number of their dupes. Does it not prove that Christianity is no longer the glad tidings of great joy to all people, but rather to the rich and great.

CHAPTER XIII.

REMOVAL—MY NEW LANDLADY—MISS SCOTT, ETC.

MR. INKLEY came to my room one morning before I had arisen. There had never been any lock to the door, and entrance was readily effected. Greatly surprised, I bade him "Good morning," while he seated himself with equal composure on the side of the bed.

"Your sojourn with me has been pleasant, sir, very pleasant," he began. "I have striven to make it so. I believe I have succeeded."

"Yes," I replied, in rather a stereotyped phrase. "I have been quite as happy as could be expected."

"And more so," he answered. "You could not certainly have expected to find such friends as you have found. Haven't I administered to your comfort in every way? Haven't I gratified your curiosity, even at the expense of disgracing the church of which I am a leader? And this room—what a beautiful room it is—so apt and fit for lodging."

I replied that the apartment was quite satisfactory.

"Then you will feel regret at leaving us, if only on that account."

"Leave you, when? I had not thought of leaving you till I left the country," I said, with some surprise, "unless, indeed, you desired it."

"I have not desired it, no sir, not I; but a husband, though, presumed by the law of the States to be one with wife, is rather overshadowed when the number expands to three or four. Family peace, sir, is a great thing—a very great thing; a man must make sacrifices to secure that—sacrifices, too, that are sometimes very trying to his feelings."

"Am I then to understand, sir, that your wives desire my departure?"

"Exactly so, sir; at least Sarah does."

"In what have I been so unfortunate as to offend that lady?"

"Women are captious, sir—very captious, capricious, and whimsical, of course you know that. Domestic peace, sir, is a great thing. Sorry that it is so, but can't help it; spoiled children must be humored."

"I understand; if my presence has become obnoxious to Mrs. Inkley, I can only express sorrow for the fact, without the least idea of the cause."

"Nothing, sir, just nothing. I believe it all originated in that conversation the other day, in which you rather favored the opinion of Martha."

"But Mrs. Inkley certainly cannot blame a man for the free expression of his opinions."

"Oh, she don't know herself. She's whimsical, that's all —but domestic peace"——

Yes, domestic peace, and the idea that even my absence would secure that in a family with three wives, had something in it strangely in contrast with the nature of things. I was not disposed, however, to make ill-natured remarks, especially as he offered me a letter of introduction to Mrs. Farrow, an amiable Mormon lady, who lived at the eastern end of the city.

After breakfast I started out, soon made my way to that part of the town, found the good woman, presented my letter, and was well received. I was much pleased with the situation of her adobe cottage, and her own mild, intelligent countenance, and we soon struck a bargain. I removed thither immediately, and was accommodated with an agreeable, well-ventilated chamber, the windows of which looked out on some grounds, well laid out, and planted with beautiful flowers, native and exotic. The prospect is extensive, and stretches away on the south to a great distance; north and east the mountains appear, through which the emigrant trains find their way into the valley. Mountains likewise appear on the western side, their summits tipped with snow the greater part of the year. Antelope Island, in the Salt Lake, is distinctly visible, though at a distance of twenty-two miles. Thus, the sublime and the beautiful of nature are wonderfully and harmoniously blended.

Mrs. Farrow was an active, kind, and lady-like New Englander ; a rigid Mormon on all points except polygamy, which she seemed to thoroughly detest. She held a prominent position in society, and her house was the frequent resort of visitors. Among these Eliza Snow shone conspicuously. She is a pale, mild-eyed, silly-looking girl, though she aspires to poetic honors, and many of her productions have received the unqualified approbation of the immaculate Mormon leader ; yet, considered as literary efforts, they are beneath criticism. Her conversation is not more delectable than her poetry, and for conceited egotism was really unmatchable.

"I am not appreciated here," she said. "I cannot associate with kindred spirits ; there is no one to sympathize with my feelings. I must have a field of labor. I must go where I can spread myself." This she repeated several times, to my infinite amusement, while Mrs. Farrow's fat sides fairly shook with suppressed laughter. Miss Snow, however, did not seem in the least offended, and her excessive vanity is rendered pardonable by her great good nature. She came one day, and brought a poem in manuscript, from which she read extracts for our entertainment. There were words without ideas, and ideas struggling through a redundancy of words ; figures, metaphors, and similes without order or arrangement. When she finished, not a word was spoken, though she evidently expected the homage of flattery. The sincerest admirers of good poetry are always most deeply disgusted with bad, and I really had the imper tinence, on a subsequent occasion, to say that young damsels could be much better employed in household labors than in stringing together unmeaning rhyme. The poetess looked at her white and dimpled hand, which she boastingly asserted had never been soiled by dish-water.

Her father is a man of considerable property, and the brother of Judge Snow, mentioned in a former part of this work. He evidently desires to make a fine lady of his daughter, and for that end has had her taught certain accomplishments, which here seem rather out of place. Mrs. Farrow grows facetious over the fact of her continual visiting here, and the repeated invitations I receive to dine at her father's house. This gentleman, who bears the title of elder, called on me one day with his daughter. He was a little bustling man, with an affected consequential air. We conversed for some time on general topics, when suddenly, and without any preamble or apparent confusion, he introduced the subject of his business by making some inquiries regarding mine.

"You design to stay some time in our country?" he said, inquiringly.

"That depends on circumstances."

"How would you like to make it your permanent residence?"

I wished to be guarded, and returned an equivocal answer

"It is a very fine country; great chances for men of enterprise and talent. Large families can be supported with ease."

"But I have no family."

"I suppose not, just now, but will have probably."

"Rather doubtful."

"I should think otherwise. You must be in pursuit of a wife, what else could have brought you here?"

The idea of going to Salt Lake city for a wife was decidedly new, and excited a broad smile. The young lady tossed her head, tried to blush, and simpered, "Oh, papa!"

"Yes," he continued. "I've hit the nail on the head—that must be it. Very well, it's all right. There must be marrying and giving in marriage till the day when we become like the angels."

"I am afraid there is no such good luck in store for me."

"Afraid! why man, how silly you be. The finest belles in Utah would consider themselves honored by your preference. Just try."

I shook my head.

"I know it; ask my daughter there, she has a strong predilection for Gentiles."

Again came the shrug and the simper, "Oh, papa!"

"I declare she has," he continued with a loud laugh, "she told me so herself."

Here the young lady really blushed in earnest, and I was half tempted to kick the old fellow out of the room.

"But you don't permit your girls to marry among the Gentiles, do you?"

He twisted his mouth and features into the most ludicrous and extraordinary grimace imaginable, as much as to say what a great spoony you must be to take professions for more than they intend.

"It is contrary to the rules of our church," he said, presently, "but girls will be headstrong, and parents easy, sometimes; indeed I know of fathers, and mothers, too, as to that matter, who would rejoice to give their daughters to Gentile husbands, provided, in all cases, that their personal connivance to the affair could be kept concealed."

"I thought that according to your creed a Mormon husband was essential to the salvation of the wife."

"Yes, according to our creed, and there are many things in the creeds of certain sectaries, which in their hearts they know to be false. At any rate, speaking for myself, I would risk that for my daughter, if she could thereby obtain an advantageous settlement for life."

He spoke seriously, and with great deliberation.

"Are there no such chances for a young and beautiful woman, among the people of your church?" I inquired, doubtingly.

He scanned my countenance with an eager yet curious expression, and said:

"What I want for my daughter, and what some other parents wish for their daughters, is a home, and a true, faithful, loving heart, solely and unquestionably hers—that will bear with her weaknesses, and strengthen her virtues. Ask your own knowledge of us, if such prospects as these open before a woman in matrimony, where custom, public opinion, and even religion, sanctions the espousal by the husband of so many wives. Polygamy never looked hateful to me till my daughter had nearly become its victim."

"Your daughter!"

"Yes, sir, my daughter. One of our neighbors, a great burly Briton, with seven wives, is a candidate for Eliza's hand, and Brother Brigham recommends the match. But she hates and despises him, and we cannot find it in our hearts to force her inclinations. And yet, according to our creed, disobedience to the prophet is a mortal sin."

All this was said with a smiling countenance and affected good nature, yet it was easy to see how deeply the parent's heart was touched.

"Is your daughter's suitor a man of property and intelligence?" I inquired.

"He is not," replied the unhappy father. "Last winter his family were in a state actually bordering on starvation. He will not work at his trade, which he pretends is degrading, and his only ostensible means of livelihood is that of a comic actor at the theatre. I could not describe the huts in which his wives are kept, and though on the boards he is all fun, frolic, mirth and glee, his private life is whispered to be quite another thing. And now, to come to the point, could not you prevent the marriage between him and my daughter ever taking place."

I was surprised beyond measure, and the young lady arose and left the room.

"I prevent the marriage! how, pray?"

"By marrying her yourself. I speak plain, necessity impels it."

"Sir, I could not do that," I replied. "I respect the lady, but never thought of her as a wife; you may command my services in any way that will not compromise my personal freedom and honor."

I really sympathized with the father, who seemed pained and disappointed.

"I fear then, that my poor girl must go to the altar of sacrifice," he said, "Persecution will be brought to bear upon us, and ultimately we shall be forced to yield."

"Has she no relations to whom you could send her?"

"She has relatives to be sure, but how could she ever reach them? I could not think of exposing her to the difficulties and dangers of such a journey."

"You are an elder in this Church," I said, "why not have its iniquitous practices and laws abolished?"

"They are too deeply interwoven in our social system," he replied; "too many are interested in perpetuating them; polygamy, like slavery, may be regarded as an evil by the very ones who practise it. Then, too, the real power of the church, all exists in its acknowledged head. The elder comparatively is little more than the meanest member."

"But, sir, you must have sensible and honest men among you, who once convinced that polygamy is an evil, would unite their energies to extirpate it. Whether or not they regarded it objectionable as husbands, if appealed to as fathers, their hearts would respond.'"

He shook his head doubtingly.

"You have sensible and honest men in the South, who question the policy, justice, and humanity of the peculiar institution which flourishes there, yet who are utterly impotent to remove it."

After some more desultory conversation, the elder took his leave, his daughter having previously gone, when curiosity led me to make some inquiries of Mrs. Farrow.

She informed me that Elder Snow had six wives, who resided together in one large house—that Eliza was the daughter of his first wife, a woman of some intelligence who evidently abhorred polygamy, and whose matronly instructions had not fallen on barren ground. She laughed heartily at the elder's absurd proposal, and said she had been expecting it, though she gave little credit to his expressions of paternal feelings, and declared that other and sinister motives were at work in his mind.

"Mormon fathers," she continued, "make no scruple of offering the hands of their daughters to marriageable men, and when the girls are beautiful or wealthy, they always require a consideration. They are not yet so lost to all feelings of shame or decency as to call it by its proper name, a *bonâ fide* sale."

"What, then, do they call it?"

"Oh, an exchange of gifts,—or the son makes a present to his new father, or lends some valuable article or animal to him, with the understanding that it shall not be reclaimed."

"Do you think such things right or honorable?"

"No;" she replied with emphasis.

"Yet they are distinctive features of your Church."

"I know that very well, I know that doctrine was propagated as a Revelation from Heaven, by the immaculate Joseph, yet I can tell how, in my opinion, the prophet was deceived."

"I should like to hear."

"Why, Satan came to him in the form of an angel, and not being sufficiently fortified by faith and prayer, he was not able to detect the cheat, but received the devil's instructions regarding polygamy, and kindred customs, as the veritable truth."

"Well, that is saddling more on the Prince of Darkness than I should think him guilty of. There is no worse devil than a wicked man."

Mrs. Farrow, however, said that she was careful not to talk loud, as she should hardly feel safe if the elders knew of her heresy.

"Yet you do not suppose that they would injure you?"

"No, but they would probably expel me from the church with a curse, and then I should be overtaken by all sorts of calamities."

"None the more for that you wouldn't," I said.

"Oh, but I should," she replied, "I well know that. One man whom they cursed and expelled from the church, was struck by lightning the very next day. Another was bit by a serpent, swelled and died in the greatest agony, and Sally Harman, whom I knew much better than I do you, became insane, and wandered among the mountains where she was eaten by a wolf."

"But, Mrs. Farrow," I said, "all this is superstition. Such accidents always occur in the regular course of nature. The lightning strikes indiscriminately, the serpent bites an intruder, and insanity comes as the result of disease or the violation of a physical law, but in no case can it be superinduced as the result of such agencies as you suppose."

The worthy dame, however, persisted that one fact was better than a thousand theories, that she had experienced in her own person the potent influences of the blessing of the church, and that nothing should induce her to try the experiment of daring its curse. Of course I was silenced, though not conquered.

Notwithstanding her superstitious motives, Mrs. Farrow was a woman of decided intelligence, shrewd, ingenious, and keen as a brier in driving a bargain, when opposed to a wealthy or speculating character, though no one would more readily melt at a tale of woe, or respond with more heartiness to calls of charity. She kept a small shop or variety store, which was tended by one of her daughters, and was altogether a profitable concern. The sale of ready made clothing was not, perhaps, the least thriving branch of her trade, and the assistance it enabled her to give poor women, was one of its most satisfactory results. She bought grain, flour, pork, beef, anything eatable, which she retailed in small quantities, to such housekeepers as worked for her, or if they preferred money, it was readily given. It was not in her nature to grind the poor for the increase of riches, and many a blessing have I heard invoked on her head, by the miserable recipients of her kindness and charity.

One day, while sitting in her snug little parlor, which was a model of neatness and comfort, I caught the glimpse of a woman just entering the store. It was but a glimpse, yet something in her carriage and appearance forcibly reminded me of Miss Scott. The door between the two apartments being partly open, I could hear the plaintive tones of a melodious voice, without being able to distinguish the words. When she retired, I observed that she carried with her a small bundle, probably of sewing, and a basket that contained something covered by a paper. Mrs. Farrow soon came into the parlor, and her eyes were red, as if with recent tears. I was reading a novel, which observing, she remarked, with a sad smile, "How many scenes in real life exceed in misery and despair the most high-wrought creations of fancy."

"And yet," I answered, "misery of that description is mostly self-made."

"So much the worse for the sufferer; for then to his or her other tortures are added those of remorse. A young woman just left me, whose whole appearance was so indicative of sorrow and destitution, that without asking her name or requiring a reference, as usual, I gave her the work she desired, and added thereto a small quantity of provisions.

Poor thing! her expressions of gratitude really overcame me."

"Then you did not know her?"

"I did not."

"I wish you had."

"Why?"

"Because I half suspect that she is a girl in whom I am deeply interested."

A blank look of amazement settled on the countenance of the worthy dame.

"Oh, I hope not, indeed, I really hope not," she replied.

"Can you tell me where she lives?"

"I cannot," she answered, gravely. "But why should you wish to know?"

I had sunk immeasurably in her opinion, and deemed it necessary to exculpate myself from the rumor the unworthy suspicion aroused in her mind. So, without further parley, I related all that I knew about Miss Scott, with her father's deep anxiety, and the interest which, for his sake, I had taken in her fate.

Mrs. Farrow listened attentively, and when I had finished, expressed her conviction that Miss Scott and the person with whom she so deeply sympathized were identical. She would make further inquiries, she said, and if the supposition proved correct, we would take measures for restoring her to her father.

I was not kept long in suspense. The next day she

returned with the work, and Mrs. Farrow at once introduced the subject, by inquiring if her name was Scott.

She replied, with some little hesitation, that it was.

"And you came hither in an emigrant train for California?" continued the matron.

Her auditor assented.

"And would you be willing to return to your father should an opportunity present?"

"But would it be possible for my father to forgive and receive me?" she said, bursting into a passion of tears.

Mrs. Farrow assured her that there could be no doubt of it, and concluded by recommending her departure in the first emigrant train, declaring that she would supply the funds for all necessary expenses. Miss Scott expressed her readiness to go, and gave a general outline history of her trials in Mormondom.

She had never ceased to regret the first false step in her life; her carelessness and neglect of parental teaching and advice. Disobedience, she said, led her to form an acquaintance, and ultimately a more intimate connection with the young lieutenant. Disobedience led her to fly with him from her best and truest friend, and then, as the meed of her folly, she had met shame, desertion, and disgrace. Before she had lived a month with Fitzgerald, her seducer, he became weary of her, left her for days, and even weeks, without fuel or food, at which times she would be obliged to go out and beg a scanty supply from her neighbors. These generally were most ungracious, and never failed to express their abhorrence of her degraded condition ; for, strange as it may appear, the sixth wife of a Mormon holds in supreme contempt the unfortunate female who may become a mother without the sacred name of wife, or one whose connection with a lover has not been sanctioned by the marriage tie.

She could have borne all this, she said, as a merited punishment, but the Mormon libertines taking advantage of her unprotected condition, began to insult her with disgusting proposals, of which even Fitzgerald urged her acceptance. This aroused her temper. She reproached him with her betrayal and ruin ; he retorted. Words changed to blows. He struck her with the flat side of his sword, and left the house. She never saw him afterwards.

Dependent on her own exertions, without relatives or friends, she drank deeply the cup of bitterness and humiliation. Her first efforts were at nursing, but she soon became disgusted. There was plenty of employment, but little pay. Then she was cheated by one, swindled by another, while a third would accuse her of laziness, and refuse her remuneration on the plea that she earned nothing. What was almost equally as bad, many families were so crowded in small inconvenient rooms, that the recovery of the patient was almost impossible, when the blame, instead of resting where it ought, would be thrown on the nurse. In one family there were three wives, eight children, and one old grandmother, with the husband and grandfather, besides a table, chairs, one bed, two benches, a cupboard, and cook-stove, all in one small apartment, eighteen by sixteen. The bed contained the sick woman, whose recovery, for a long time, was doubtful, though the only wonder was, how, amid so much noise and heat, pestiferous vapor, and suffocating smells, she could have ever recovered at all.

But Miss Scott had other difficulties. The husbands in whose families she found employment, almost invariably solicited her to become a member of their seraglios, and sometimes she found it extremely difficult to escape their importunities. For this she had been persecuted in various ways, and it was extremely difficult for her to supply herself with bread.

The next day I sought the commander of an emigrant train, about to depart for California, and gained permission for her to accompany it. Frederick B—— also departed with them.

CHAPTER XIV.

CONVERSATIONS WITH AN ELDER ON POLYGAMY, AND THE FUTURE OF THE MORMONS—THEIR NATIONAL AND SOCIAL POLICY, ETC.

THOUGH a rigid Mormon, Mrs. Farrow was too much of a woman not to delight in speaking her mind, and her natural ideas of right and wrong were much too clear and perspicuous to be readily confused by the chaos of Mormon opinions and practices. Then, too, as not a particle of deceit harbored in her heart, she could not bear to see it in others.

"It's just as I thought," she said, one day at breakfast, "Eliza Snow has become the wife of Brother Brigham."

"I thought the governor favored her marriage with another man."

"Well, I suppose he did at first, but she was averse to marrying him, and declared her determination to take a Gentile husband."

"And to prevent this he concluded to marry her himself?"

"I suppose so."

"Rather unprofitable business," I said, and taking up my hat, went out for a walk. Sauntering along the streets, I came to a beautiful garden, the property of a man by the name of Sayres. His wife is a rigid Mormon, though he denounces the whole system as an abomination. He came here to gratify her absurd notions, and, for the sake of family peace, tolerates her ridiculous absurdities. Gardening is his ruling passion. He is an extravagant lover of flowers, and many a floral curiosity has he found in this region. He contemplates making a collection of all the plants native to the Basin, which will be a valuable addition to botany. A large plot of ground is thus most tastefully arranged, and clumps of beautiful and ornamental shade trees, stationed at regular intervals, with garden-chairs and benches for the accommodation of visitors. Several ladies, some bright little girls, and two or three of the elders, were promenading the walks. One of them came up, and courteously addressed me. He seemed an agreeable man, and we soon entered into conversation. He was decidedly intelligent, and appeared to anticipate all the objections that could be raised against the peculiarities of their social system. He seemed candid, sincere, and tolerant, though whether with reality or not I cannot pretend to say.

In reply to some remarks of his, I said that it seemed to me that the elders and leaders of the church were permitted to exercise a permanent influence upon the character of the people, through their legislative and social power; and that such influence could scarcely fail to be undemocratic, unjust, and unsuitable to the jurisdiction and general principles of the federal government, though not unpardonable, and probably not incapable of salutary change.

"It must be evident to the most casual observer, that the exercise of power by one part of the people over the remainder will affect unfavorably the character of the whole," I continued, "and the more readily the poorer and weaker class submit to the tyranny of the richer and mightier, the greater will be the injury to their true interests, and the deeper their moral and political degradation."

He replied, with perfect good humor, by referring to differences in opinions, feelings, and sentiments, and expressed his firm belief that polygamy had been, and would be, a great blessing to both male and female, individually and socially, though, if I understood him rightly, the advantages were prospective rather than otherwise, after all. He said that polygamy would be much more salutary and effective than law, public opinion, and religion, or all combined, to eradicate certain evils, which always had, and always would flourish under a system of monogamy, to say nothing of the fearful diseases and such crimes as infanticide, which almost invariably attend illicit connections, though rarely if ever occurring under a system of marriage so extensive and complicated as that of the Mormons.

"Your Eastern cities," he said, "point the finger of scorn at us in their true pharisaic spirit, yet how well might we retort by referring to the courtesans that throng their streets, to the innocent infants, mutilated, drowned, or left to the tender mercies of strangers, that swell their criminal reports, of deaths occasioned by nameless hideous ways ; all of which prove that in their midst is a vice stalking at noonday that their most stringent laws have no power to remove or obliterate. And of all these crimes we are clear, thank God !"(*i.*)

"You mean that in name these crimes do not exist among you ; in fact, they certainly do," I replied.

"As how? There is no such thing as concubinage, because all are married ; there can be no illegitimate children, because all are born in wedlock ; mothers are never induced by shame or the sternness of public opinion, to sacrifice their offspring ; how then can you say that the crimes which I have instanced as part of your system belong to ours ?"(*j.*)

Our conversation was long, and his defense of polygamy sophistical and eloquent. Gradually I led him on to speak of the future of his people—of their hopes and aspirations.

Yet few Mormons are idealists. With the single exception of the Jews, no sectaries are more truly practical. Their sermons and conversations relate particularly to prosperity in this world. Only a part of the females, the stupidly ignorant, and the half-insane, are visionaries. The remainder are much more ambitious of honor and wealth in this world, than desirous of the treasure that neither moth nor rust can corrupt. The Mormon leaders, as a general thing, are cautious and discreet in the expression of their views or plans for the future. It is against their purpose to excite suspicion, or arouse the jealousy of a government which they secretly hate. Only on extraordinary occasions they wax eloquent, and you can gather from cautiously-worded phrases, a sufficient insight into the boldness and originality of their schemes.

"Mormonism," said the elder, "has escaped the serpents that would have destroyed it in its cradle—the Protestant and the Catholic church. Great events which it will take centuries to ripen, are in embryo. The beginning of the end is at hand. The miserable intrigues and subterfuges that deny to us the right of self-government, cannot always be tamely endured. We have yearly accessions of wealth and strength, and shall soon be in a position to command respect before the nations of the world."

"Do the Mormons, then, desire to establish an independent nation?" I inquired, coming at once to the point.

"Such may be their destiny in the nature of things. We have all the elements of a distinct nationality. Our country is peculiarly fitted for self-reliance and defense. The Great Basin, with its own system of lakes and rivers, its fertile soil, mild climate, and mineral productions; above all its central position on the great line of travel from east to west, from north to south, could easily support millions of people, whose mountain passes would be as capable of stern defence as Thermopylæ, and whose warriors in the cause of freedom and religion might defy the world."

"But will your people have the temerity to rebel against the Federal Government?"

"Nothing can be further from their thoughts than rebel lion in the present state of things, or while the Federal Government continues the liberal and enlightened policy which mostly distinguishes it; but secret agencies are at work, the seeds of revolution have been planted. In less than a century, two distinct and separate confederacies will arise, phœnix-like, from the ruins of your present government. Then it will remain for us, on the western border, to assert our rights, our dignity, and our independence, with a prospect of success."

"If you wait till then, it will be a long, a very long time," I said.

"But what matters that?" he continued. "We can afford to wait for great events, or the acquisition of some abounding good; and compared to eternity, or the long lapse of future ages, how a century dwindles into insignificance! Yes," he continued, clasping his hands with fervor, "we can afford to wait for that which will surely come."

"But suppose it ccmes not?"

"That were impossible from the very nature of things. The clouds have already gathered on the horizon, there is the deep mutter of the earthquake which precedes the shock, the hollow moan of the volcano that indicates an explosion. Look at your Congress, wasting their time in silly intrigues and worthless cabals, while the real business of the administration, and the true interests of the people are neglected. And does not every year witness a further dereliction from duty, a more wasteful expenditure of the public money, a more shameful and shameless disposition to discord, and the subjugation of public business to private animosity. As the states expand and the population increases, the nature of your government requires the increase of the representatives in exact ratio. This accession of numbers will augment rather than diminish the difficulty. It is idle to suppose that a country so vast, with such separate interests, and clashing institutions, can be held together by the bands of a government so complicated in its machinery, and so defective in all that constitutes the true muscle of administrative power. Your laws are much better adapted to secure the happiness of a small state than consolidate the provinces of a Continent in one huge Empire."

"And do you believe all this?"

"Most certainly I do, and your people believe it, too, however loth to confess the fact. Very few have faith in the perpetuity of your institutions. Some openly prophesy the rupture; others fear, yet deprecate the idea, but it has found a place in the minds of all."

"That is certainly too much the case."

"Manifest destiny has a meaning with us," he continued "The Mormon church has been denounced as a humbug, and compared with Millerism, and other sects of ephemeral existence, but such is not the case. It is not a sect, but a faith, and the only faith at present in the world, that has a future before it."

"I do not understand you," I said.

"I mean," he resmed, "that as past religious history

belongs to the East, the future depends on the West. Christianity has had its day. It arose in Asia, passed steadily over Europe, and gained the Continent of America, reflecting in its passage some scattering rays over the northern parts of Africa. But the Catholic church can never be more powerful than it is. Protestantism has reached its culminating point. Mohammedanism is without either prestige or power, and the future is ours."

I smiled at his enthusiasm.

"You think me an enthusiast; very well," he went on. "But great effects spring from little causes. We know that the Genoese navigator never dreamed of discovering a new world when he set sail for Cipango and the distant regions of India. When the Apostle of Mecca explained his first Revelation to a jeering, hooting crowd, what stretch of imagination would have reached the vast empires to be subjugated in his name. In the earliest days of Christianity, who would have thought it possible that the instrument of torture to a malefactor would become the symbol of rank and honors—that warriors would carry it on their standards, and kings on their bosoms. Yet Christianity progressed with slower steps than Mormonism has done; at the end of three years Mohammed had made one convert, and that one his wife; Joseph Smith had as many thousand followers in that length of time. Has the world ever witnessed a parallel to our success?"

"Seldom, I believe."

"Yet our mission is only begun, our destiny, instead of

being accomplished is only commenced. We have a vast interior and almost impregnable country, stretching away to the north and the south, the east and the west; and all this country is to be filled up with people of one faith, actuated by the same designs and desires."

"But you forget that this country is already inhabited and occupied."

"By whom?" he inquired, with some surprise.

"The natives, of course."

"Oh, that is nothing," he replied with contempt. "The Indians are doomed to extirpation, or extermination. That is their future, quite as certain as the other is ours."

"And the Mormons, you think, will remain peaceful members of our Confederacy until there comes a general rupture between the North and the South."

"Probably, if our social and domestic institutions are not meddled with—if we are not required to abolish polygamy, or the union of church and state; but under other circumstances our allegiance would be doubtful."

"Yet, what could you promise yourselves by rebellion against a power so much stronger than yours?"

"Not so much stronger, either, when all is considered. Our mountains and deserts would supply the place of fortresses and armies, and our triumph would be secure because defeat would be impossible."

"There might be something in that," I said, wishing by a seeming harmony in views to lead him on.

"You must know, and your government must know, that

our dependence on it is by a very precarious tenure. We have laws with their administration, regulations with their prescribed forms, social institutions with their ceremonies, and a religious faith with its priesthood and ordinances—and all of our own. We are necessary to them, not they to us."

"How will you make that appear?"

"How will I make it appear?" he replied. "I should think it would be obvious to the most casual observer. What would be the fate of your emigrants if they had to traverse a hostile country, or if refused the necessary rest and refreshment after their long travel. Might not a descent on the Gold Region be tempting on one side to human cupidity, and extremely dangerous and detrimental on the other. Your government can well afford sacrifices to conciliate us. We ask nothing of it only to be left alone."

There can be no doubt but that this man spoke the truth. The Mormons desire no affiliation with us, our faith, or social institutions; all they ask is to be left alone. It is the wish of their leaders, it is in the hearts of the people. You will hear it verbally, and tacitly expressed in a thousand ways. "We can take care of ourselves," is their constant and oft-recurring sentiment—"We want nothing of them," "Why do they follow us?" These, and similar expressions are common with all.

In no country have I ever heard such frequent reference made to spies. If a beggar comes to the door and solicits charity, he is instantly suspected of being a spy. If a stranger passes along the streets he is supposed to be of the same character. Such constant suspicion argues to my mind anything but the consciousness of innocence, or the firm rectitude that never shrinks from observation.

"And you consider this country capable of supporting a dense population !" I said, addressing the Elder.

"I do not know of one whose capabilities are greater," he replied, "or whose resources for undeveloped wealth are more vast and complicated. Extensive territories wait for men to come and possess them. A soil never broken by the plow only asks tillage and cultivation to rival the famous fertility of the East. Hidden ores and metals sleep uncared for in the bowels of the earth. We might supply the world with salt for centuries, without exhausting the abundance of that indispensable article. Our hills are richer in pasture than the famed and famous Land of Goshen. Think of the time when all these facilities for exhaustless wealth shall be in progress of development, when telegraphs shall span our mountains, and railroads traverse the valleys, while every ship wings to us from all quarters of the globe the glory and honor of the Gentiles, and the devotees of our faith pour out their treasures in offerings on its shrines."

Whether or not the Mormons are destined to occupy the distinguished position in the world to which they aspire, is at present problematical. That stranger things have happened, is undeniable; that weaker beginnings have astounded the world with mighty results is equally certain, and no one who has sufficiently examined their prospects and character, will be surprised if long before the vexed question of slavery is laid aside, another should arise in connection with them quite as intricate and complicated.

It seems to me that few have looked on them or their creed in the philosophical light they deserve. The one is considered a humbug ; the others dupes and impostors. Yet similar humbugs have been of vigorous growth and long continuance, and what finds favor among men in the present age will probably be quite as readily received by the next. But whether these speculations have a foundation in fact or in fancy, the future must decide, and another generation will probably be able to judge with certainty.

Our long colloquy ended, and I bade my friend farewell with a feeling of regret. He was a graduate of Old Harvard, and was closely connected with some of the most distinguished families in Massachusetts. We parted near the Tithing office, and I never saw him more. Two days after, I received intimation that he had been dispatched on a secret and highly important mission to a foreign land.

Yet this man, according to Mrs. Farrow's statement, had three wives, one of them old enough to be his mother, another middle-aged, and the third a mere child. I know very well that such things appear incredible, but they are no less facts, nor was he a solitary example of misdirected intelligence. Elder Snow had made the tour of Europe, and conversed with ease and elegance of the beauties of art in

Paris and Italy, while the companion of his travels, Elder Smith, was a graduate of Yale, and possessed an extensive acquaintance with ancient and modern languages, and general and classical literature.

CHAPTER XV.

THE MARKETS OF SALT LAKE CITY—SHOP-KEEPERS—STREET-VENDERS OF MERCHANDISE—MANUFACTURES AND MECHANIC ARTS.

IN a city of twenty-five or thirty thousand stationary inhabitants, with an almost equal number of transient visitors, the markets cannot be an insignificant feature, though not connected with the most pleasant associations, or suggestive of the most refined ideas.

But the markets are capital places to study the varieties of life. The work-shops and small stores present at every step subjects for characteristic sketches, and set forth the every-day aspect of the common people. The piety of the Mormon does not at all prevent his being extremely fond of a good bargain, and, ten chances to one, if it stands in the way of his committing a regular, downright swindle, should an opportunity occur.

The markets are well supplied with the usual comestibles of civilized life ; fish, flesh, and fowl abound, with all sorts of vegetables, butter, and cheese. Little tables are usually set out in conspicuous places, with cakes, candies, and confectionaries, around which gather gay groups of soldiers, women, and children, laughing and chatting with all possible familiarity. You are surprised at the quantities of foreign wares conspicuously displayed in the windows. You had scarcely expected to find French gloves or Wellington boots. You think, perhaps, that the display of silks, costly shawls, and velvets, must be rather out of place. You begin to question in what manner they could ever have come here, forgetful that gold possesses a magic power that attracts everything which can be exchanged for it.

But there are many shops of less pretention, devoted to the sale of second-hand or inferior articles, with clothes, hose, and similar goods of home-made manufacture. You soon discover that the keepers of these establishments possess a peculiar aptitude for trade. In dexterity and cunning they seem even to surpass the Jews. You are surrounded in a moment by a dozen eager traders, all intent on selling you something, and each seeming to vie with the others in setting forth the value and utility of his wares. You cannot help feeling amused at the strange mixture of barbarous English, guttural German, and idiomatic French that reaches your ears; for these shopkeepers are nearly all foreigners, and by them almost every nation in Europe is represented. You are attracted by a little Frenchman, whose use of his tongue seems most dextrous, and enter his door with the fixed determination that you will not purchase anything, because just then there is nothing you want. The Frenchman is all assiduity and attention.

"What will you have, sir? Boots, stocks;" and he runs over a long list of articles with a glibness of tongue perfectly astonishing, meanwhile watching your eye to discover on what article it fastens. As yet you are unacquainted with his art, and look carelessly and indifferently around, till a beautifully embroidered buffalo-robe meets your gaze. Of course you have no use for that; it is in the midst of summer, and you are thousands of miles away from home. It would be preposterous to swell your baggage with useless articles, but you can ask the price. The Frenchman, however, anticipates you.

"Monsieur has well chosen," he says. "This is the most beautiful article of the kind in the market. Lord George Gordon, I think it was, won't be sure about the name, but at any rate he was an English lord, bought three of them from an Indian princess. One he designed as a present to Queen Victoria, the other he wished to keep for his lady, and the third I obtained as a reward for doing his lordship a very great service."

"Indeed!"

"Just look, what soft, long, exquisite fur. I have been in the fur trade these many years, and never yet saw its equal."

After much chaffering and bargaining, more for amusement than anything else, you are induced to name a price, though not a fourth of the sum that he has named as the lowest he can take. The words have scarcely escaped your lips, when he flings it over your shoulders, and the only course left for you is to count the gold.

The shops devoted to the sale of second-hand goods are quite as characteristic and interesting. Surely such a collection of worn-out dilapidated merchandise was never before seen. The people are as singular as the wares offered for sale. Here are two women holding a solemn council over a superannuated frock, which one would think entirely worthless. Close by is another, driving a hard bargain for a battered bonnet of Parisian make, which has served as an ornament and protection to probably a dozen heads, and has finally found its way into this repository of antiquities. Here is one of the few places in which you will find a crowd. In general the streets are so broad, and the houses cover so small a portion of the ground, that you might almost fancy yourself in a town deserted by its inhabitants. But here the crowd, and throng, and press, are sufficient to make it all up. You look around, and wish yourself away, and the wish precludes the attempt to get away. In this you are obstructed by some venders of street merchandise, who cry their wares in your ears with downright effrontery, or blockade the passage, so that you must either stop or run over them ; of course you prefer the former. It is amusing to see how the associations of polygamy have entered into all their ideas of life. They do not seem to think it possible that a man can have one wife without more, and they take it for granted that he has one. If you deny it, they will not believe you, but persist in urging you to buy combs, needles, pins, tapes, and similar articles indispensable to the female toilet, though of no possible use to a bachelor.

"Buy this for your wife, sir, and this, and this—all alike, or one just as good as the other ; can't be no quarrelling then."

"But I have no wife, never had."

"Never had a wife ; that can't be. You are joking ; you look like a sensible man, and sensible men always marry."

"Do they, indeed ?"

"Ah, yes."

"But I am too young."

"Too young ! That's a good one. Ha ! ha ! ha ! But a man who wears a moustache is always old enough to have a wife."

"That may be ; but age does not always decide these things."

"Well, one thing is certain, if you have no wife, you are no Mormon."

"No, I am not."

"Well, let that go then, but you must buy something."

You shake your head.

"Yes, you must ; these things were made to sell and to use. By not buying, you defeat the intention of the originator ; you take bread from the mouths of my wives. Buy them, for charity's sake."

"Wives"—you catch at the word, if only for the sake of relieving yourself of his importunities.

"How many wives have you?" you inquire, dubiously. To suggest that he had only one would probably be considered an insult, as some of the Mormons rate their respectability by the number of their wives.

He tells you three, four, or probably six or seven, not unfrequently representing them more numerous than they really are.

"Do you not find it difficult to get along peaceably with so many women?"

"I pay no attention to their squabbles. I find that much the best plan. If they get to quarrelling, I let them take it out over the face and eyes, and I tell you what, they have pretty warm work sometimes."

You perhaps tell him that the whole system is an abomination, when he laughs in your face, refers you to great examples, and persists in teasing you to buy. Finally, to escape the persecution, you purchase something, a trinket, perhaps, or fine-tooth comb, but be sure it is something you do not want, and for which you have no use.

Manufactures are rarely carried on in youthful communities, with the approved appliances of machinery driven by steam or water power. Flour is indispensable to human life and comfort, consequently we find that mills are among the first appendages to all civilized societies. Next come the manufacture of cotton and woollen cloths, and the simpler mechanic trades of shoemaking, tailoring, and the like. Both wool and flax of very good quality abound in Utah, and many of the more extensive farmers take infinite pains to improve their breeds of sheep. There can be no doubt that when the increase of population demands it, and sufficient inducements are offered, extensive manufactories rivalling those of the East will be put in operation. At present, the females card, spin, and weave much after the fashion of our grandmothers, and some of the most beautiful blankets and the finest linen I ever beheld, was shown to me, with commendable pride, as being the work of their skillful fingers. It must not be supposed that the Mormons are all concentrated in Salt Lake City. A vast extent of territory is being rapidly filled up with them. In the country, too, that is, on the farms, where the women have constant and regular employment—where one weaves, and another spins, the third attends to the dairy, and the fourth is housekeeper—where there is plenty of the comforts, and many of the luxuries of life, polygamy seems to be attended by fewer evils, and to be the occasion of much less discomfort than in more confined situations, though of course the immorality of the practice is the same.

The attention of the Mormons seems to have been early attracted to the manufacture of sugar from the beet-root. In 1852, a complete set of machinery for that purpose was imported thither at immense cost, and, after some delay, put in operation. The raising of beets excited a *furore* for the time in Mormondom, almost equal to the Multicaulis mania in the Eastern States. Gardens, fields, and even house-yards were planted with the saccharine vegetable. But the want of sufficiently experienced and competent workmen was severely felt. The cost of sugar production was found to greatly exceed that of importation, to say nothing of the superior quality of the latter. The experiment, though not a success, could not be considered an absolute failure. The practicability was tested, and probably some future age may reap the benefits of it.

The Mormons are exceedingly adverse to dependence on outsiders, characterized by them as Gentiles. This disposition might tend to facilitate their progress in the mechanic arts, but they are almost equally opposed to profiting by the superior skill, knowledge, and attainments of those who, from education or principle, are opposed to their domestic institutions and their church.

CHAPTER XVI.

SCHOOLS—LITERATURE—INTRODUCTION TO ELDER KIMBALL, ETC.

AS might be supposed, the Mormon schools have nothing to boast of, being little more than an appanage of the church, where the children and youth may be trained in its doctrines, and brought up in habits of unlimited obedience to its requirements. The elders appoint the teachers, select the books, and superintend the general affairs of all connected with them. The Catholic Church in its palmy days never manifested more jealousy of heretical doctrines, or was more vigorous in the expulsion of all works considered of that tendency.

"What sciences do they teach, then?" you question. "What principles of political or domestic economy are instilled into the tender minds of their youth?"

My dear friends, I cannot tell you; but of one thing you may be sure; it is nothing of a democratic tendency, it is nothing that can be presupposed to give them an independence of thought or feeling, but directly the reverse.

The school teachers are generally old, decrepit persons, who would be objects of charity if not thus provided for. One of these ladies, females are all ladies in this age, came one day to the house of Mrs. Farrow to purchase necessaries, as she termed it. These consisted of half a pint of molasses, half a pound of coffee, three candles, and an ounce of tea. I thought she must be well qualified to give the children lessons in economy. She was altogether one of the most remarkable specimens of womanhood I had seen in Utah—tall, though much bent, stout, bony, square-cornered—with cold, yet eager grey eyes, grim aspect, and great volubility. A paralytic attack had deprived her of the use of one side, her arm was useless, and she was obliged to walk with a crutch. Indeed, she was down on the list as a pauper, till Brigham Young, actuated either by motives of charity or the desire to relieve the church of a burden, gave her the appointment of school-teacher, with the understanding that in such a situation she must take care of herself.

Yet this singular woman had seen better days. Somewhere in the states she had a husband and children, but their hearts having proved too hard to be softened by the new revelation, she abandoned them in the company of the first Great Prophet's family. She had one thousand dollars in her own right, and after managing to get hold of this the rogue, by the power of a special revelation, delivered her over to the keeping of another. She remained with him a year, when he died, and she was left without friends or means. But she had great industry, and having cast her lot with the saints, would not be separated from them. So she floated along in the current of emigration to Salt Lake City, working all the time like a slave.

"How many scholars, have you ?" I inquired, when informed of her profession.

"No particular number, sometimes near forty, and at others not over ten."

"Then the children are not regular in attendance."

"I don't think it makes much difference," she replied. "They do little besides knitting, sewing, and saying their catechism."

"Manual labor, and theology," I suggested. "Do you not teach grammar ?"

"Grammar, no ; what's the use of grammar ? I never could see any sense in it, and very much doubt if any body else can. I wish my scholars to understand what pertains to their salvation, rather than the wisdom of this world, which fadeth away."

"But, madam, life and its trials are here."

She turned curtly away and made no answer.

Yet so far as I could learn, she was a tolerably fair example of the class of school-teachers; but priestcraft, all the world over, has been afraid of knowledge. The spirit of the age demands a school of some kind. It might be dangerous to refuse, hence the school is established, but is contrived to be only an accessory of superstition.

The Mormons have what they call a Library, though it

is not very well supplied with books. To make up the deficiency, however, the works, as a general thing, were well selected. Hume and Paine found a place side by side with Robertson and Volney. The most approved histories of ancient and modern times were conspicuously displayed, but there was little poetry, and less light literature, though a few standard novels were there, among which I particularly noticed the works of Dickens and Marryatt.

While conversing with the librarian, Elder Kimball was seen approaching. I knew him to be one of the first men in the place, and when he entered we were introduced. He was very sociable, expressed great pleasure at seeing me, though I doubted his sincerity, and even went so far as to insinuate a desire that I would make his country my permanent home, declaring that it was one of the finest places on the earth, that the beauty of the climate, the magnificence of the scenery, and the fertility of the soil were altogether unsurpassed. He then expatiated largely on the unity and brotherly love that prevailed—the obedience and fecundity of the wives—with the wealth and generous tempers of the husbands.

I was not disposed to controvert his position, but made some inquiries about the general appreciation of literature, and whether or not the use of the library were permitted to all indiscriminately.

The librarian looked at the elder, and for a moment his countenance changed.

"To all indiscriminately," he replied, "with certain reservations and exceptions, that mean nothing."

"But meaning nothing, why are they made?"

He laughed lightly, and turning to the librarian, inquired if I had seen "those choice manuscripts."

As I had not; they were immediately produced.

The one was a volume of poems by Eliza Snow, of which the principal ones have been published in the Deseret News. They were written in a fine, though legible running hand, and were much more interesting as a specimen of chirography than as poetry. The other was on the subject of theology, by Parley Pratt.

"These works have never been published?" I said.

"They have not," he answered. "We prize them very highly, and that is probably the reason why they have never been published."

"Indeed."

"Certainly; there can be no doubt that if given to the world there would be a diversity of sentiment about them; at present there can be but one."

"An original reason, truly."

"You must remember," continued the elder, "that the Mormon church is yet in its infancy. Under the pressure of persecution, misrepresentations, and false doctrines from without, there could be little encouragement for the exercise of original genius. We value these works rather for what they portend than for what they are. The Mormon people are yet in a Chaos; every part of the globe has contributed a quota to swell our numbers. They come with dissimilarity of tastes, feelings, sympathies, and views. When these discordant elements are blended into one, will be the time for us to produce great things in art, and make striking discoveries in physical science—and not till then."

"You design to monopolize the future?"

"In part, and to speak in common parlance, who has a better right? Our people are now accomplishing the first part of their mission—the conquest of material nature. Long ages antecedent to Homer, the Greeks produced nothing in literature worthy of the name, but they were preparing the way for that lord of song. What generations succeeded the advent of Plato and Demosthenes, of Phidias and Praxiteles! The eternal city was in the bloom of its matured strength before the birth of Cicero and Virgil, and the Italian people did not at once burst out into Dante and Michael Angelo. What felling of forests, maraudings, and piracies preceded in Germany the appearance of Goethe, Schiller, and Jean Paul, with wars of the Roses, Crusades, and martyrdoms in England, before a Shakespeare or Milton could see the light!"

"Heaven grant that the Mormon people may be spared such an ordeal," I said, half involuntarily.

"Amen," he responded. "But do you then cherish a fraternal feeling with them?"

"As belonging to the great brotherhood of mankind, I must, and do."

"I honor your sincerity," he replied. "Few come here with any other purpose in view than to turn us, and all we possess, into disgrace. They determine to be dissatisfied from the first, and with the utmost want of politeness and good breeding themselves, demand the most rigid courtesy of us. In their sight, we are no longer men, but beasts. I suppose they would deny us the privilege of living or breathing if they could. One woman who stopped here on her way to California, made great complaints that she was not treated with proper deference, because some men on the other side of a bridge preferred to walk over previous to her. Yet this same woman, lady I will not call her, never hesitated to quiz any one and everybody who came in her way, demanding of women how many wives their husbands might have, and questioning little children about their father's families."

"Disagreeable, certainly."

"Outrageous, scandalous," he persisted. "If they do not like us, all they have to do is to let us alone; it is all we ask; our protection and dependence is all of ourselves. We ask no assistance from an arm of flesh."

I have reason to believe, indeed I know, that similar feelings are generally cherished. They only wish to hold communication with the "Gentiles" when such intercourse can be made beneficial to themselves, and contribute to forward their impious designs.

After much more desultory conversation, the elder invited me to attend a cotillion party at his house, which was to come off in a few days, and to which the principal dignitaries of the church had been invited.

In reply, I informed him that I had made arrangements for departure from that place, but would postpone my journey for a few days, and should be happy to attend.

CHAPTER XVII.

DECEPTIONS—RASCALITIES—DUPES—IMPOSTORS—PARLEY PRATT—HIS SCHEMES TO RAISE MONEY—A BEREAVED HUSBAND AND FATHER, ETC.

MORMONISM, from first to last, is a system of delusion and imposition, consequently the votaries of that faith can only be regarded in the light of impostors. Yet we cannot for a moment doubt that many of the weak-minded and ignorant men, and still more of the women, are actually sincere in their belief, and would probably endure martyrdom rather than renounce their faith. The elders, many of whom are men of decided talent and intelligence, seem to have brought deception to an art, and to practise it systematically. Foreign countries present, of course, the most eligible theatre for their operations, and hundreds of missionaries are constantly employed. These expatiate on the wonderful facilities to acquire wealth, and possess happiness, in the Mormon country—on the beauty and healthfulness of the climate, the exuberant fruitfulness of the soil, the dowry of land and stock, with the great demand for mechanic labor. Sometimes they mention polygamy incidentally, though it is but too evident that many come here without the least suspicion of being brought into contact with such an institution, but whose disgust and horror, when informed of it, cannot shake their faith in the seductive imposture.

I was much pleased with the appearance of a beautiful little girl, who came on errands to Mrs. Farrow's store. She belonged to an English family of the better class, was very talkative and intelligent, and so prettily dressed that with her large, limpid blue eyes and floating curls, she looked like a fairy.

"Is that lovely creature's home contaminated by the plurality system?" I queried of my good landlady.

"No, indeed. I should as soon expect to see the summer turn to barrenness as Edward Cunningham with a second wife."

"Is he then an opposer of polygamy?"

"I should think that he was."

"And his wife?"

"It would kill her, at least she says that it would, and I cannot doubt it. Never was a woman more devoted to a man. Yet they do say," continued Mrs. Farrow, "that some of the elders have exerted all their influence to induce him to take another wife."

"I cannot see why they should have so much interest in the matter."

"They say such examples are bad for the women whose

husbands have polygamous tendencies—that it makes them jealous, discontented, dissatisfied."

"I presume they will conquer in the end. If he believes their creed, it is scarcely possible that he can escape the contaminating influences brought to bear upon him."

"He not only believes their creed, but is one of them," she answered, "or, perhaps I should say, one of us; for though I am opposed to some things the elders do and teach, I am professedly a rigid Mormon."

I could not refrain from smiling.

"Well, as I was saying, Mr. Cunningham is a man of business capacity, holds a subordinate position in the Legislative Assembly, and is much honored and sought after, though Mrs. Cunningham declares that had she known of polygamy and some other things, she would never have come here."

"Then they did not know of it."

"They never dreamed of it till somebody in St. Louis told them. But Mr. Cunningham asserted that it could not be, and persisted in his belief that the whole story was a scandal, got up by the malice of their enemies, till he received ocular demonstration of the fact. Heighho, our elders are but men."

Subsequently I had the pleasure of making Mrs. Cunningham's acquaintance, and learning further items in their history. She had a family of beautiful daughters, and her maternal apprehensions with regard to their future fate were easily excited. Lascivious eyes had already been cast upon them, and John Taylor, an old man, deformed and crippled, who had been wounded when Joe Smith was killed, and who was the husband of six half-starved wives, had actually presumed to solicit that one of the blooming creatures might be sealed to him.

"Why," said the passionate woman, her face flushing with excitement, "I would rather see my child dying at my feet, than know that such a doom awaited her. The hideous old ogre!"

She went on to tell how they had been cheated and deceived in various ways, prefacing her account, however, with a hope that I would not betray her confidence, and saying that it was a relief to have the privilege of unbosoming her troubles to some one whose mind was not warped with the infatuation that had been their ruin.

She had an elegant piano, sofa, and other furniture usual with people in their station of life. The boxes in which they were packed arrived safely at St. Louis, when the Mormon agent, into whose hands they passed, took the liberty of opening and inspecting them. He was delighted with the prospect of plunder, and succeeded in convincing Mrs. C—— that she had better leave the things with him, as the dry air of the plains, and other emergencies, would render them worthless, and that he would give her a draft for their value, to be drawn on the governor. She complied with this proposition, though with great reluctance, but her surprise was greater when arriving at Utah, and presenting her draft, the dignitary protested it, saying that it "wasn't worth the first red cent."

"I wouldn't have minded it so much," she said, "but we really needed the money. We were poor enough I can assure you. I had never before known what poverty was. When we started to cross the plains, a number of wagons drawn by cattle were loaded with our goods, but my husband had not been accustomed to such travelling, or to taking care of cattle. His hired men were brutal. Over-exertion and the want of necessary nutriment reduced the animals to skeletons. They soon gave out, and their bleaching bones mark the path for the future traveller. Worn out with suffering, and destitute, we arrived in the vicinity of the Salt Lake."

It is customary with the Mormon leader, to go out a day's journey to meet an emigrating party, entertaining them with music, and fresh provisions, as a foretaste of the good things in store for them. It enables him to make a show, and gives a certain air of triumph on the acquisition of numbers to his church.

"We were struggling through the mountain passes, weary and despondent," said Mrs. Cunningham, "when our ears were suddenly delighted with the sound of music, breathing and dying away among the hills, or rolling out in waves of harmony, that reverberated from rock to rock. We listened with beating hearts when a courier rode up, and informed us that the Leader was approaching with an escort to conduct us to the city."

"A token of welcome, I suppose."

"And our hearts were gladdened by it; but, oh, sir, it

did not last long. A few days found us living in this little house, so destitute of comfort, that for my children's sake, I know not what to do. For myself, I could bear it, but where are the advantages and accomplishments that I had promised my daughters. What is their prospective future? it makes me shudder to think of it."

This, I am satisfied is the case with many mothers, even of those who sit down quietly themselves under the curse of polygamy. They can bear it, but their hearts bleed for their daughters. And many a father who practises it unhesitatingly himself, shrinks with horror and despair from the immolation of a favorite child.

"My husband," continued Mrs. Cunningham, "is very industrious; yet, not being accustomed to manual labor, he could do little that way. The property he invested in the church has never returned him a cent, and probably never will. A situation was offered him in the theatre, and absolute necessity induced him to accept it. His days are spent copying laws, and his nights are devoted to those dissolute scenes. Oh, sir, my heart aches and my brain is maddened, when I think of it."

The infatuation of this woman was effectually cured, but too late—too late—for all practical purposes. Her hand was fairly in the lion's mouth, and she could not remove it, nor break his teeth.

I subsequently beheld her husband. He looked pale, discouraged, and worn out, though evidently pleased with the attention and respect his presence always commanded. But more substantial comforts were needed to render his life happy, and of these he found few enough.

Few people are more to be pitied than those dupes of Mormon duplicity, who, belonging to the better class of foreigners, and unable from ignorance and the want of habit to obtain a living by manual labor, embark their property as a speculation in the hands of the church, and are then left with their families in a beggarly state of wretchedness. Utah is rife with such examples ; yet the Mormon elders are really kind and generous to such poor emigrants as can work, and thereby increase the productive industry, and consequently the wealth of the country. They are much too politic and observant not to understand the value to any community of a sturdy, hard-working yeomanry.

I was much interested in the story of a rich German family, who had been converted to Mormonism, and the idea of emigration. It is really strange to me how people can be so easily induced to leave their homes, and the sweet associations of their childhood and riper years. But it is the old story of the dog and the bone. Though well off, they concluded that their circumstances might be improved. They saw the shadow in the water, leaped for it, and lost their all. When the various items of their property was collected together, it amounted to the snug sum of 15 or 20,000 dollars in gold, silver, plate, and jewelry. And of all this the silly man was induced to resign possession in favor of the elder to whom he attributed his conversion, that worthy promising, of course, to make all right at a subsequent day, to secure state-rooms for the family on board the ship in which they were to emigrate, and to provide them necessary and respectable accommodations on the entire route.

Imagine, therefore, the surprise and indignation of this husband and father, when he found himself, his family, and all their baggage crowded into the steerage, amid filth, fever, noisome smells, and indescribable indecency. He remonstrated with the captain, but in vain. That dignitary plainly told him that it was too late to make alterations in the arrangements of the ship, and that if he confided his affairs to the discretion of a Mormon priest, there was no alternative but to abide the consequences. The elder, meanwhile, was accommodated with two state-rooms, and every convenience and luxury.

Compelled to submit, but extremely dissatisfied with their treatment, they were landed at New York, and being utter strangers to the language and customs of our country, without means or friends, nothing remained for them, but to float along in the current of emigration to Salt Lake.

Here they were lodged in a wretched hut, without even the commonest necessaries of life, or any prospect of a better condition. They have made some disagreeable discoveries. They have ascertained that the property deposited by the husband in the hands of the elder belongs to the church, that if he wants a house, one can be built for him, for which he will be indebted to the church ; and worse than all, that their daughters are approaching a marriageable age, and will soon be wanted to swell the number of victims to the institution of the church. They knew nothing of polygamy before coming here, and were filled with disgust and terror at the prospect before them. Yet it should not be supposed that these particular cases of individual suffering and discontent are general throughout the community, or that all, without exceptions, are utterly vile and depraved. Many, doubtless, are pure in their feelings, and sincere in their desires to serve God, however mistaken and unfounded the views they have learned to entertain. Many would be glad to be freed from their bonds, and like a liberated bird, exult at their release ; but others are infatuated with their lot, and no inducement could tempt them to abandon it. In the language of the Scriptures, "they are joined to their idols."

What an awful weight of responsibility rests on the heads of the reverend guides and directors of the Mormon people, and what a fearful reckoning will be theirs in the great day of accounts. As usual with their class in all ages and countries, these men are inveterate worshipers of the golden calf. They bow before it, it fills their imaginations, and concentrates their desires. Their cry for gold is incessant, and when this necessary article is not to be had at home in sufficient quantities, they generally start out on a mission, and thus it rarely fails that their pockets are replenished. It is rumored, though whether with truth or not I cannot pretend to say, that some of the elders, who have been best supplied with wives, have disposed of the superfluous to Indian chiefs, or half-breeds in the neighborhood; in all cases for a valuable consideration in horses, furs, or other articles of ready merchandise. Incredible as this might appear, if related of any other enlightened community, I see no reason for disputing its occurrence here. The slavery and merchandise of women is the usual attendant of polygamy. Both are parts of one system, and in all countries where the former is tolerated, the latter comes in as coeval and co-existent. I cannot see why the example of the patriarchs might not be quoted to support the one as well as the other, and with equal propriety.

Parley Pratt, a noted saint in this region, an elder, and the husband of a multitude of wives, is accused of being the originator of this scheme to "raise the wind." At any rate, one or two of the Mrs. Pratts mysteriously disappeared, and the elder immediately came out with a fine stud of horses, known to have belonged to Walker, the Utah Chief. As report goes, a trapper, who visited Walker's lodge sometime afterwards, found it inhabited by two or three white women, and, to his great amazement, learned the particulars of the affair. Parley, however, made a handsome speculation, sold the horses to some California emigrants, and employed the money in furnishing himself with an outfit for a mission to Chili.

The Mormon Missionaries make great pretensions to humility, and of going without purse or scrip, but this is only an excuse for the mendicity they affect and practise. The initiated know very well, that large private resources are at their command, though it is only in cases of emergency that they can be induced to resort to them.

Parley is likewise an inveterate borrower. Mrs. Farrow informed me of several sisters, who having inherited money from Eastern quarters, were immediately assailed by the necessitated priest, whose exceedingly bland and courteous manner is seldom without its influence on the female mind.

But it seems that men sometimes are quite as easily deluded as women, and this redcubtable elder seems to drive a brisk trade at wheedling and swindling them. A poor man at San Bernardina, was induced by the wily hypocrite to trust two or three hundred dollars of hard earnings in his hands. Repayment, though promised at the time, was never performed, and never will be.

This man has a very even flow of language, converses with great ease, has the most perfect suavity of manner, and looks altogether as if he never did and never could do wrong. He has great command of his countenance, never gets angry, though at times you can catch the lurking devil in his eye. Indeed he is a perfect specimen of the class of sanctimonious rascals.

There seems a positive cruelty in the disposition of this man, which manifests itself in the sundering of family-ties and connections. He has persuaded daughters to abandon their homes, wives to forsake their husbands, and mothers their children. He has carried blight and desolation to many a fireside, and caused pangs fiercer than those of death to many a human heart. Many a history of wrong and shame, in which he has been chief actor, might be related. Many a tale of moral delinquency, and mental anguish and bereavement, is connected with his endeavors and success in proselyting unbelievers. Of course, many of the others are equally wicked, and the distress they occasion by the separation of friends and families is actually incalculable. I saw a beautiful young woman, who had abandoned her mother's dying bed, and left her grey-haired father to descend in sorrowful loneliness to the grave, to follow one of these impostors, and become his tenth or twentieth wife. This was vaunted as a great act of heroism on her part, and her praises were sung in all their churches. Another had deserted her lover and prospective husband, who was well nigh distracted; and a third was forcibly plucked from their clutches by her brother, who invoked the aid of the law (*k*). Yet so great was her infatuation, that all his prayers and entreaties were of no avail. In the night she arose, tore the sheets of her bed into strips, let herself down by them from the chamber window, and escaped to them. When sought again, she was not to be found; they had secreted her. Sometimes women, sometimes men, (*l*.) and sometimes children, fall victims to their arts. Their presence in the family circle is the sure prelude of misery and sin. The tale of Mr. Hays, an English cattle-trader, is only one amongst a thousand that might be told of the fanaticism and diabolism that ever attends the hideous and slimy course of Mormonism in its progress over the world.

This gentleman was wealthy and respectable. He had a beautiful cottage, situated on a small stream in the north of England; grounds tastefully laid out, surrounded it, and peace, plenty, and domestic happiness, abode within. The wife was loving and beloved; the daughters beautiful and obedient; the son honorable and intelligent. One stormy night, in the autumn of 1854, two mounted strangers came to the gate, and implored, for the sake of human brotherhood, that shelter and protection might be afforded them for the night. Mr. Hays, who could never find it in his heart to refuse the shelter of his roof even to the wandering mendicant, readily granted their request. His servants were directed to take care of their horses; they were invited to his parlor, and made welcome at his board. The suavity of their manners, their intelligence and apparent respectability won largely on the heart of the good man, and when it came out that they were Americans, and designed to stay some days in the neighborhood, he invited them to consider his house their home. For several days the subject of Mormonism was not broached, indeed their first endeavors seemed to be to gain the good will of the family. In this they fully succeeded, when their designs were gradually unfolded.

However, the strong good sense of Mr. Hays preserved him from falling a victim to the delusion, but the son was easily dazzled with their glowing pictures of Mormon life and libertinism. He deserted his parents, went to Utah, was, it seems, highly delighted, was elevated to posts of dignity and importance, and with each step became more and more in love with the institutions of Mormondom. When his faith was sufficiently established, and it was deemed expedient, he was returned to England as a missionary. His first efforts were against his father's house, but the good man, though receiving his son affectionately, utterly forbade all mention of his heretical doctrines. Opportunities, however, were not wanting; the mother and sisters were duped, and consented to elope and go to Utah, without letting the husband and father into the secret of their designs. Such is the effect of fanaticism; it sears the heart, and renders it insensible to sympathy or natural affection. One Monday, after the arrival of his son, Mr. Hays started on one of his usual expeditions to purchase cattle, leaving a large sum in money, a gold watch, and other valuables in the charge of his wife. He left his home just as years of domestic quiet and happiness had endeared it to him, without a thought or misgiving of the fearful destruction awaiting his treasures. He returned on Saturday, eager to greet his loved ones, and receive their affectionate welcome; but how great was his surprise, how unspeakable his horror! His habitation was stripped and deserted. There was no affectionate greeting, no provision for his comfort. He called, but there was no answer, and to describe his consternation and distress would be impossible. The wife had not only deserted, but robbed her husband, and the son had proved the betrayer of his father. They had likewise induced all the children to accompany them; the money, the jewels, the plate, everything portable, even to the bed-linen, had been removed.

The poor man applied to the police in a state actually bordering on distraction, and without suspecting that Mormonism had wrought his ruin. By careful inquiries, and previous knowledge of the Mormon character, the officers were induced to believe that such might be the case. They hastened to Liverpool, and learning that a large emigrating party of that people had just departed in the ship Good Hope, Captain Sanders, for the New World, it was thought his family might be on board. A steamtug, moored at the dock, with the fires up, was put in requisition, and the pursuit commenced. But the morning was far advanced, and the little party of pursuers were not much encouraged by the captain to hope that they would have any chance of overhauling the Good Hope, for she had been taken out to sea by a strong tug, and had all her sails set to a favoring breeze. After crossing the bar at the mouth of the Mersey, a dark object like a speck was discovered on the horizon, which the captain of the steamtug made out with his glass, and pronounced to be the ship. For two or three hours the chase continued, when it became evident that they were fast gaining on the big ship. When within hailing distance, the captain of the Good Hope slackened sail, supposing that his pursuers were the custom-house officers, and had scented something wrong. Coming alongside, the party jumped aboard, and when they announced their errand, the excitement among the Mormons was intense. The captain received them courteously, invited them into his cabin, and asked to see the warrants under which they were acting. They had none, but that a husband should be so basely deceived and robbed of his household gods and goods at once, was pronounced and felt by the captain, who declared himself no Mormon, and ignorant of the whole affair, an unendurable rascality, and he was evidently anxious to render the bereaved and nearly distracted man all the assistance in his power. The women and children, however, were kept carefully out of sight between decks.

As the search went on, the excitement increased. The poor husband became almost a raving maniac; alternately praying, coaxing, and threatening, sometimes actually kneeling at the feet of the Mormon leaders, and beseeching them with words and gestures that should have melted a heart of stone, to restore his family. His entreaties were seconded by those of the captain and officers; but all were in vain. For two hours this scene continued, the ship all the time being carried further and further out to sea. Finally the officers declared that rather than fail in their mission, they would accompany the vessel to Boston, and denounce the whole gang of Mormon impostors to the British authorities in that city. The firmness of the officers had its effect, and the elders consented to produce the woman, and let her have an interview with her husband. The heartless creature manifested the utmost indifference to his distress, refused even to accept his proffered hand as a token of friendship, and turned a deaf ear to all his remonstrances, until the

officers interposed, telling her that if she persisted in her determination, she would be denounced to the Boston authorities, and probably imprisoned. This information shook her resolution ; with streaming tears and accents of woe, she bade farewell to her deceivers, and was handed into the tug with the youngest child. The husband still knelt on the bulwarks, the very picture of paternal distress, praying and entreating that yet more of his children might be restored to him. Even some of the Mormons were moved at his anguish ; they began to murmur, and say that it was a shame and unnatural to separate a father from his children. At this juncture, the Mormon elders peremptorily ordered their subordinates to go below, but the captain, finding that numbers were on his side, ordered the two little girls of seven and nine years to be handed to their delighted parent.

Two other daughters, seventeen and nineteen years of age, absolutely refused to return. Finding it impossible to break the spell of their infatuation, the tug cast off, and returned to Liverpool, where a large number of people were collected on the docks, anxiously waiting to learn the success of the expedition.

Mr. Hays returned home with a remnant of his family, but scarcely a tithe of his missing property. But his happiness is destroyed for life ;

> "For sharper than a serpent's tooth it is
> To have a thankless child."

The charms of his home have been deranged by the filial ingratitude of his son, the worse than death of his daughters, and the loss of affection and confidence on the part of his wife. She publicly avows her inflexible determination to join the Mormons in Utah with the first opportunity. Her mind, her affections, are all set on them. Oh, the folly, the wickedness, the depravity of human nature, when unpurified and unsupported by grace divine!

CHAPTER XVIII.

THE MORMON PARTY—MORMON BELLES—INCIDENTAL NOTICE OF BRIGHAM YOUNG AND HIS FAMILY, ETC.

I ATTENDED the Mormon party, to which Elder Kimball had been so polite as to extend me an invitation. It was sufficiently unique, and the first thing that surprised me was the great disparity between the numbers of women and the men. In my boyish days I had been accustomed to attend parties of pleasure in country places, where the invitations having been extended almost indiscriminately, resulted in raising three or four young men to every lady. In more select assemblies they were always duly paired, but here each gentleman came attended by two, three, four, or even a greater number of the opposite sex. Ladies were on the sofas, in the chairs, and there was an abundance of wall-flowers. Surely the Mormons have not to complain of a scarcity of women, as is usual with many newly-settled States. Cotillions were the order of the day, and the figures were so arranged, that each gentleman danced with two ladies. A raised platform, well furnished with seats, accommodated the band of music, and more distinguished spectators, whose habits or disinclination forbade their taking part in the dance.

Several of the elders countenanced the proceedings with their presence, attended by their wives, both old and young. A number of Gentiles were present, among whom I noticed some young ladies who were attached to a California caravan, and whose beauty it was evident made a decided impression on the susceptible Mormon elders, and their subjects.

Several Mormon belles were pointed out to me, and constant flirtations and coquetries were carried on in the intervals of the dance. These young ladies, however, either were or appeared decidedly partial to outsiders, and some dashing Californians were evidently made happy by the tokens of their partiality.

One young fellow, ferociously bearded, and dressed in the extreme of Parisian style, attracted much attention. One ungloved hand was literally bespangled with rings, a large gold chain attached to a watch of the same metal, crossed his vest, and a diamond pin glittered on his bosom. He was evidently a gentleman loafer or gambler, and his attentions to the ladies seemed particularly displeasing in certain quarters.

"These girls seem partial to the Gentiles," I observed to one of the bystanders.

"Pshaw," he replied, "that fellow has gold in his pockets, as well as on his person, they are after that."

"Think so?"

"Nothing can be more certain. There will be a row soon. These Mormons are jealous fellows."

Before I had time to reply, supper was announced, and there was a general scramble.

The Californian gave his arm to one of the ladies, the most beautiful in the company. She accepted it with apparent pleasure. He seated himself by her side at table, and helped her to the daintiest viands, receiving the brightest smiles and most beaming glances in return. The feast would have charmed an epicure, and both the elder who gave the party, and his numerous wives, seemed pleased with the hilarity and enjoyment of their guests.

After supper, the dancing was resumed; the Californian meantime monopolizing the beauty, and regarding those around him with a sneer and grin, that showed his white teeth glittering through his moustache, exactly as a wolf might be supposed to regard his compeers, should they approach too near some dainty morsel reserved for himself.

"He'll haul in his horns, when Sam Sloan gets sight of him," said some one at my elbow. "I'll stake my salvation on that, any time."

"Who is Sam Sloan?"

"A young Mormon, who's a match for any Californian," was the answer.

I had before heard of this worthy, and waited with some impatience for his appearance.

I was doomed to disappointment. He did not come, but another young fellow, flush and fiery, walked up to the lady, and asked her hand for the dance. She was engaged for the evening. He turned away, regarding the moustached Californian with a scowl of defiance, quite as black as his own. The fellow clapped his hand to his side, as if to draw thence a concealed weapon, when the Mormon deliberately trod on his toes. There was a low growl of rage, followed by a heavy blow. The Mormon staggered, but recovered in a moment, and returned it with interest. Others rushed in, not to separate, but take part with the combatants.

"As I told you," whispered one beside me.

The dancing ceased; there was a halt in the music; ladies screamed, the elders rose. At length, when the tumult was fast becoming general, a voice rang out above the din in clear, authoritative tones.

"Put those fellows out in an instant," it said, "and proceed with the amusement."

Fifty stout men sprang in a moment to obey the orders, while I turned to look at the speaker, and recognized Brigham Young. He had sat silent and unnoticed, crouched in a dark corner, with his hat on, though the others were uncovered. Whether this was accidental or the result of design, I am unable to say. Certain it is, that his Mormon majesty never removes his hat in public. There he stood, the most conspicuous person in the room, gazing calmly over the scene. In a very few minutes order was restored, and the dancing re-commenced, as if nothing had happened.

Brigham Young is a remarkable man, second to the Mohammed of the Western Continent, and like Abubeker and Ali, abundantly qualified to carry out and perpetuate his scheme of imposture and fanaticism. He can enact the part of chief magistrate and supreme pontiff, or, with equal facility, he turns mountebank and astonishes the world by such antics as few civil and religious functionaries would dare to attempt. He supports by precept and example a domestic institution never before admitted among enlightened people, yet his community receives monthly accessions of strength by the arrival of emigrant converts from the different European nations. Young, beautiful, and accomplished women; men of property and intelligence lay their offerings on the shrine of his faith, solicitous of his benedictions, and obedient to his mandates. Some of his messages from the pulpit are perfect gems in their way, witty, original, in many respects decidedly laughable, and utterly unlike anything of the kind ever heard before. He chooses texts from a Bible, a newspaper, or an almanac. He quaintly touches on every conceivable topic—war, commerce, peace, industry, art, and love. These comprehensive addresses generally include a pretty sharp dig at the President, and rather severe criticism on governmental affairs at Washington. Indeed, it is evident that indistinct visions of future greatness, and supreme independent power, sometimes float through the brain of the distinguished hierarch; yet his strong good sense prevents any undue display of vanity or self-importance. At this time it is impossible to balance his faults and virtues, or to decide whether the title of enthusiast or impostor more properly belongs to him and his predecessor. There is but a step between the two. The warm suggestions of fancy might be mistaken for particular inspirations from heaven ; the labor of thought may expire in rapture and vision, and the inward sensation take, to the deluded understanding, the form and attributes of an angel of God.

History is filled with such instances. Numa, the beloved citizen, good king, and wise legislator, believed in his Egeria, and the demon of Socrates is a memorable example of how a wise man may deceive himself, how a good man may delude others, and how quietly the conscience may slumber in a middle state between self-illusion and voluntary fraud.

It is said that a prophet never has honor in his own country, and with equal propriety might have been added nor in his own time and age. The judgment of contemporaries is generally inflamed by passion and prejudice, and it is a trait of human nature to despise the day of small things. Yet—

> "Large streams from little fountains flow—
> Tall oaks from little acorns grow."

As an evidence of the talent and ability of the Mormon leader, I would let facts speak for themselves. They will reverberate through future ages, and influence the decisions of posterity. Whether famous or infamous, the name of Brigham Young is inseparably connected with the origin and history of a numerous and remarkable sect. When strong enthusiasm impelled from within, and a fiery persecution pressed from without, he led them, then numbering many thousands, to seek a safe home in the distant and almost impenetrable wilderness. Could it have been mere chance or accident, or was it an extraordinary foresight that led them thither to build a city, that, like Tadmor in the Wilderness, should be a half-way house—a grand caravansera, to gather wealth and importance from the hundreds of thousands soon to be on their way to the Pacific shores. Peace with the Mormons was not necessary in Illinois ; it is at the great Salt Lake.

This man likewise has managed to acquire and retain an almost unbounded influence over the minds of his followers. Neither envy, malice, nor rival leaders have succeeded in dethroning him. Even the worthy President seems to have considered the experiment of forcibly ejecting him from authority as an act of dangerous tendency. Why else was the appointment of Colonel Steptoe to the territorial government of Utah and Mormondom suffered to quietly fall to the ground, when it was ascertained that Brigham would not willingly resign. This step affords a dangerous precedent. Either the appointment should never have been made, or else carried out at all hazards. If the general government cannot or does not make them respect its authority now, what are we to expect when the population of Utah has increased sevenfold ?

Yet it must be confessed that Brigham Young has shown

much discretion in the exercise of the one man power, and has maintained a creditable city government at little expense. Setting himself above the laws of his country, and scorning the wisdom of others, his own mother wit readily served as a substitute for both. Yet like many other great men, the Mormon leader is not eminently distinguished for the moral virtues. In fact, he affects no superior sanctity, but is rather all things to all men. To the man of business, he is a man of business ; to the man of pleasure, a man of pleasure ; to that class who, above all others, obtain the first place in the affections of a hero, he is most devoted in his attentions, and liberal of his gifts—here a brooch, and there a ring ; here a collar, and there a muff. To those who have property to sell, he is a liberal buyer, and, to his credit be it spoken, he always pays his debts. He is the munificent patron of artists and mechanics, especially those of his own people, and either employs them himself, or obtains employment for them. Yet Brigham Young would be a dangerous enemy, and many fearful though secret crimes have been imputed to him, with what justice it is impossible to say. Perhaps the greatest evidence that these reports are not without foundation is afforded by the fact, that he is so afraid of assassination, as to be unpleasantly suspicious of strangers. Is this mere frailty of mental constitution, or is there another cause in the promptings of a guilty conscience ?

It is not only in the civil government of a people, or the rise and establishment of a new faith, that the chief of Mormondom is distinguished. In his domestic relations he is equally remarkable. The conjugal ties of Mohammed sink into utter insignificance, when compared with those of the Mormon leader. The Commander of the Faithful, could only boast a daughter, while Brigham can point to his scores of children with the exultation of a Jewish Patriarch.

It is evident, however, that motives of affection have not always governed in his choice of wives; many of these dames being old, ill-formed, and ugly, but it frequently happens in matrimonial affairs, that the solid charms of gold and silver are more highly prized than mental or physical accomplishments. It is said, too, that some of his younger brides have been exceedingly reluctant, and that once or twice a rival disappeared in a remarkable manner. But such reports are speedily hushed up without investigation, and the rumor left to itself soon dies.

The polygamistic tendencies of the Mormon leader have been the occasion of several tragic occurrences. How could it be otherwise when his insatiable appetite seems to increase with what it feeds on, and he is continually looking abroad for beautiful or wealthy women, whose physical or substantial charms can contribute to embellish still farther his domestic establishment. What is worse, the opposition of the female is never suffered to interfere with his arrangements. By fair means or by foul, by harsh or gentle measures, the reluctance of the maiden must be overcome. He never abandons an object of pursuit or desire.

As a general thing, however, the believing sisters consider it a great object to be "sealed" to him, by which, as they suppose, their salvation is ensured; an absurdity worthy of the dark ages, and a slight advance on the doctrine of Mohammedanism, that women have no souls to be saved.

CHAPTER XIX.

EXTERIOR INFLUENCES—YOUNG MEN—DISSATISFACTION WITH POLYGAMY—CHANGES TO BE WROUGHT IN THE SYSTEM OF MORMONISM, AND HOW.

"FAITH, hope, and charity; and the greatest of these is charity," saith the apostle. Faith in the abiding truths of Christianity, and the Rock of Ages; Hope in the strong good sense and principle of the Anglo-Saxon people; and Charity that covereth a multitude of sins, would lead us not to despair even of the Mormons. Influences, both exterior and internal, are at work among them that can scarcely fail to soften and modify the more peculiar doctrines of their faith, and their most obnoxious practices. Could people of other persuasions, with enlarged and benevolent views and motives, be induced to settle among them, establish schools, and erect churches, there can be little doubt that in process of time a radical change might be effected in their peculiar tenets. Already the influence of the emigrants and occasional visitors to the country, has not been lost, and we may confidently anticipate that as travel increases, and facilities for communication with other parts of the world are opened, while other communities and States spring up around them, the Mormons, for the sake of public opinion, and to conciliate the good will of mankind, if for no other purpose, will grow ashamed of their excesses, and lop off such excrescences as must, when known, retard the progress of their faith. Customs now tolerated for mere expedience and the increase of numbers, will be left to become unfashionable, and finally grow obsolete, when the supposed necessity no longer exists.

The younger portions of the community are evidently disaffected to the existing state of things. With the considerate, the thoughtful, and the intelligent, it could scarcely be otherwise. They know it to be an occasion of reproach, and naturally shrink before the contumely and maledictions of the civilized world. Thus far polygamy and its kindred vices have been indebted to the power of priestcraft for their support. When priestcraft falls, as it surely must, in the lapse of generations, we may expect the prohibition of its attendant vice.

There is one class of the community whom hitherto I have not noticed, yet who are destined to act an important part in the future. I allude to the young men, flush, fiery fellows, characterized by a defiant air and independent spirit. Between these and the elders feuds and jealousies have already arisen, in many cases, and we cannot doubt that similar causes will produce the same effects, with still more gratifying results, in the time to come. That the elders should monopolize the youngest, most beautiful, and wealthy women, must of itself be sufficiently displeasing to the young men, without further aggravation from the fact, that as brothers they must witness the humiliation and unhappiness of their sisters, added to the dishonor and domestic annoyances of their mothers. I have heard young fellows anathematize the whole Mormon system on this account; while others would run off to California with their sweethearts, and there abide, in order to preserve the objects of their love from falling beneath the libidinous influence of those they hated. Brothers frequently urge their sisters to depart for California, and escape the contamination of living in a Mormon harem. A young man by the name of Bryce, a Mormon in sentiment, yet independent and, for a backwoodsman, uncommonly intelligent, said that he had a sister whom Elder John Taylor had married for his sixth wife. That he considered such connections abominable, and no marriage at all; that he told his sister so, and offered to bear her expenses wherever she wished to go, if she would only abandon the paramour.

"And did she accept your offer?" I inquired.

"No; she said that here she was as good as the best;" he answered, "but anywhere else she would certainly be despised, and her child called by an opprobrious epithet, which she could not bear."

A young man, whose parents were from Oneida County, in the State of New York, expressed a bitter aversion to polygamy. He had been wounded in the tenderest point.

His affianced bride, within one week of the time appointed for their marriage, jilted him in favor of one of the elders, an old man of forty years, whose house was already shared by four wives. In consideration of her youth and beauty he promised the fifth a separate establishment, which, however, she never obtained.

Another young man with whom I conversed, had suffered severely when a child, from the persecutions of his father's second wife. These women, it seems, are even more cruel and selfish than step-mothers are reported to be, and the helpless children of their rivals are made the subjects of their concentrated jealousy and rage. This, however, must materially depend on the natural dispositions of the females, and would, by the Mormons at least, be referred to the faults of the individual rather than the system.

A highly intelligent young man, a member of the Legislative Assembly, thus expressed himself on the subject of polygamy :

"Polygamy, it must be admitted, is an evil. It is an institution that presses heavily against the best interests of our people. It banishes the best women ; it operates against the increase of our population, instead of assisting it, as has been supposed. It prevents the establishment of families, obstructs the proper education of children, and is the fruitful source of a vast amount of vice and misery. Being thus injurious, have the priests and elders any right to fasten it on our community ? Shall the free Mormon people have their best interests subverted, that these men, fallible and erring like ourselves, may have a better chance to gratify their libidinous desires? What is their sensual gratification compared with the great interests of the common weal? Polygamy was first practised by the priesthood—by the priesthood it has been supported. They have rendered it fashionable, and if its existence be prolonged to futurity, it will be through their influence."

Another one remarked, in language almost equally strong:

"Our females can never take the rank and position among us that properly belong to them, while polygamy is tolerated. Deprived of their legitimate influence as wives and mothers of families, they lose that self-respect which is one of the strongest safe-guards of female virtue, become indolent, careless, and reckless, and it is needless to say that the consequences to the whole community are most disastrous."

And again:

"The experience of ages may be trusted. Polygamy is a curse, a mildew that has blighted every region it has touched since the creation of the world. It presents no new phase, but from the first to the latest periods it has been destructive of the happiness of individuals, the peace of families, and the welfare of communities."

It cannot be believed that many women sit down satisfied under the existing state of things. Womanly nature must rise at times superior to the influence of priestcraft, and though powerless in themselves to effect the change, they will be useful and efficient auxiliaries of reform.

Hence, we may confidently expect that the Mormons of a hundred years hence will be very different from those to-day, and that future generations will redeem, in some degree, the errors of the past and the present.

EXPLANATORY NOTES.

(*a.*) There may be instances of such perverted feelings, though we must hope, for the honor of human nature, that they are of rare occurrence. Married life has its sorrows and evils, but nothing that equals the immorality and crime where a shameless system of polygamy prevails.

(*b.*) This refers to the general external appearance, and every one knows what a vast amount of domestic misery, or social dissatisfaction, may be hidden under a smiling exterior.

(*c.*) These old people had never belonged to the Mormon Church, consequently no Mormon elders attended at their funerals, and they were refused a place in the Mormon cemetery.

(*d.*) This egotism is a peculiar trait of the Mormons; they are excessively fond of talking of themselves, and the questions, What dc you think of us? How do you like our country? What do you think of our institutions? are incessantly asked of a stranger.

(*e.*) In Mormondom the murder of wives is not made a subject of newspaper comment, but the silence of the newspaper is no proof that such crimes do not actually exist. Was there ever a despotic country where the press even hinted at the actually existing state of things? and Mormondom, in its domestic institutions, is a despotism of the very blackest kind, and will probably remain so for some time to come, the efforts of the Federal Government to the contrary notwithstanding.

(*f.*) The better class of English emigrant Mormons should not be confounded with the inhabitants of Brickville. Some of the former are quite as amiable men as it is possible for Mormons to be; while the latter, even in their own country, belonged to the class of loafers and vagabonds.

(*g.*) There are two elders bearing the name of Snow; the one numbered among the Twelve Apostles bears the sobriquet of Lorenzo; the other's name is Erastus.

(*h.*) The Mormons are extremely fond of recommending their practices and opinions by the history of Christianity; and they dwell with great stress on the fact that one or two chapters, and many of the sentences and sentiments, contained in their bible, are faithful copies, word for word, of the Bible of the Christians. I was once somewhat amused while listening to a conversation between a Mormon elder and a Baptist clergyman. The Baptist boldly declared that there was not a word of truth in the Mormon bible.

"Not a word of truth," repeated the Mormon. "Have you ever read it?"

"Never."

The Mormon turned over the leaves of his book to a chapter the exact counterpart of one contained in the Bible of Moses, and presented it to his opponent, inquiring what he thought of that.

(*i.*) It would indeed be a matter for which to thank God were these assertions strictly true; but such is not the fact. They have restored courtesanism to its old Roman dignity, and its female victims, instead of thronging their streets, surround their firesides. This, however, is a subject much too delicate to be enlarged upon; but unfaithfulness in wives is so common, that long ago it ceased to be a disgrace.

(*j.*) Mothers may not sacrifice their offspring, through shame or the sternness of public opinion, but other motives may be quite as potent. Among the poor, want prevails, and the necessity of having so many mouths to fill and backs to clothe is sometimes felt as a serious evil. More than one case of infanticide came beneath my knowledge in Utah, though the affair was never made a subject of public scandal, because this of all things is most carefully avoided.

(*k.*) A similar occurrence happened at Buffalo a short time since, and was widely chronicled by the newspapers of that period.

(*l.*) Mr. Garrison, a resident of Cumberland county, in the State of New Jersey, became infected with the Mormon delusion some years since. He was married, was the father of several children, and the owner of a handsome property. In common with the others, he wished to emigrate, but Mrs. Garrison bitterly opposed the scheme; thus their family peace was destroyed, and their hitherto happy household became the scene of misery and strife.

After a time, the husband commenced turning all his available property into money, besides mortgaging his farm to the full extent of its value. With the proceeds in his pocket, he left the house one night, saying that he was going to call on a neighbor. Time elapsed, still he came not. Mrs. Garrison became alarmed at his prolonged absence, and went in search of him. The neighbor's family had retired, and her husband, they told her, had not been to their house. A search was instituted, but the delinquent could nowhere be found. Why prolong the story? It was subsequently ascertained that he had gone with the Mormons, leaving his family to shift for themselves. This is only one instance among a thousand of equally heartless desertion.

MORMONISM.

SPIRITUAL WIFE SYSTEM.

A REVELATION ON THE PATRIARCHAL ORDER OF MATRIMONY, OR PLURALITY OF WIVES.

Given to Joseph Smith, the Seer, in Nauvoo, July 12th, 1843.

1. Verily, thus saith the Lord unto you my servant Joseph, that inasmuch as you have inquired of my hand, to know and understand wherein I, the Lord, justified my servants, Abraham, Isaac, and Jacob; as also Moses, David, and Solomon, my servants, as touching the principle and doctrine of their having many wives and concubines: Behold! and lo, I am the Lord thy God, and will answer thee as touching this matter: Therefore, prepare thy heart to receive and obey the instructions which I am about to give unto you; for all those who have his law revealed unto them, must obey the same; for behold! I reveal unto you a new and everlasting covenant, and if ye abide not that covenant, then are ye damned; for no one can reject this covenant, and be permitted to enter into my glory; for all who will have a blessing at my hands, shall abide the law which was appointed for that blessing, and the conditions thereof, as was instituted from before the foundations of the world: and as pertaining to the new and everlasting covenant, it was instituted for the fullness of my glory; and he that receiveth a fullness thereof, must and shall

abide the law, or he shall be damned, saith the Lord God.

2. And verily I say unto you, that the conditions of this law are these: All covenants, contracts, bonds, obligations, oaths, vows, performances, connections, associations, or expectations, that are not made and entered into, and sealed, by the Holy Spirit of promise, of him who is anointed, both as well for time and for all eternity, and that too most holy, by revelation and commandment, through the medium of mine anointed, whom I have appointed on the earth to hold this power (and I have appointed unto my servant Joseph to hold this power in the last days, and there is never but one on the earth at a time, on whom this power and the keys of the priesthood are conferred), are of no efficacy, virtue, or force, in and after the resurrection from the dead: for all contracts that are not made unto this end, have an end when men are dead.

3. Behold! mine house is a house of order, saith the Lord God, and not a house of confusion. Will I accept of an offering, saith the Lord, that is not made in my name? Or, will I receive at your hands, that which I have not appointed? And will I appoint unto you, saith the Lord, except it be by law, even as I and my Father ordained unto you, before the world was? I am the Lord thy God, and I give unto you this commandment, that no man shall come unto the Father, but by me, or by my word which is my law, saith the Lord; and everything that is in the world, whether it be ordained of men, by thrones, or principalities, or powers, or things of name, whatsoever they may be, that are not by me, or by my word, saith the Lord, shall be thrown down, and shall not remain after men are dead,

neither in nor after the resurrection, saith the Lord your God: for whatsoever things remaineth, are by me; and whatsoever things are not by me, shall be shaken and destroyed.

4. Therefore, if a man marry him a wife in the world, and he marry her not by me, nor by my word; and he covenant with her so long as he is in the world, and she with him, their covenant and marriage is not of force when they are dead, and when they are out of the world; therefore, they are not bound by any law when they are out of the world; therefore, when they are out of the world, they neither marry, nor are given in marriage, but are appointed angels in heaven, which angels are ministering servants, to minister for those who are worthy of a far more, and an exceeding, and an eternal weight of glory; for these angels did not abide by law, therefore they cannot be enlarged, but remain separately and singly, without examination, in their saved condition, to all eternity, and from henceforth are not Gods, but are angels of God for ever and ever.

5. And again, verily I say unto you, if a man marry a wife, and make a covenant with her for time, and for all eternity, if that covenant is not by me, or by my word, which is my law, and is not sealed the Holy Spirit of promise, through him whom I have anointed and appointed unto this power, then it is not valid, neither of force, when they are out of the world, because they are not joined by me, saith the Lord, neither by my word; when they are out of the world, it cannot be received there, because the angels and the Gods are appointed there, by whom they cannot pass; they cannot, therefore, inherit my glory, for my house is a house of order, saith the Lord God.

6. And again, verily I say unto you, if a man marry a wife by my word, which is my law, and by the new and everlasting covenant, and it is sealed unto them by the Holy Spirit of promise, by him who is anointed, unto whom I have appointed this power, and the keys of this priesthood, and it shall be said unto them, ye shall come forth in the first resurrection; and if it be after the first resurrection, in the next resurrection; and shall inherit thrones, kingdoms, principalities, and powers, dominions, all heights and depths, then shall it be written in the Lamb's Book of Life, that he shall commit no murder whereby to shed innocent blood; and if ye abide in my covenant, and commit no murder whereby to shed innocent blood, it shall be done unto them in all things whatsoever my servant hath put upon them, in time, and through all eternity, and shall be of full force when they are out of the world; and they shall pass by the angels, and the Gods, which are set there, to their exaltation and glory in all things, as hath been sealed upon their heads, which glory shall be a fullness and continuation of the seeds for ever and ever.

7. Then shall they be Gods, because they have no end; therefore shall they be from everlasting to everlasting, because they continue; then shall they be above all, because things are subject unto them. Then shall they be gods, because they have all power, and the angels are subject unto them.

8. Verily, verily I say unto you, except ye abide my law, ye cannot attain to this glory; for straight is the gate, and narrow the way that leadeth unto the exaltation and continuation of the lives, and few there be that find it, because ye receive me not in the world neither do ye know me. But if ye receive me in the world, then

shall ye know me, and shall receive your exaltation, that where I am, ye shall be also. This is eternal life, to know the only wise and true God, and Jesus Christ whom he hath sent. I am He. Receive ye, therefore, my law. Broad is the gate, and wide the way that leadeth to the death; and many there are that go in thereat; because they receive me not, neither do they abide in my law.

9. Verily, verily I say unto you, if a man marry a wife according to my word, and they are sealed by the Holy Spirit of promise, according to mine appointment, and he or she shall commit any sin or transgression of the new and everlasting covenant whatever, and all manner of blasphemies, and if they commit no murder, wherein they shed innocent blood,—yet they shall come forth in the first resurrection, and enter into their exaltation, but they shall be destroyed in the flesh, and shall be delivered unto the buffetings of Satan, unto the day of redemption, saith the Lord God.

10. The blasphemy against the Holy Ghost, which shall not be forgiven in the world, nor out of the world, is in that ye commit murder, wherein ye shed innocent blood, and assent unto my death, after ye have received my new and everlasting covenant, saith the Lord God; and he that abideth not this law, can in nowise enter into glory, but shall be damned, saith the Lord.

11. I am the Lord thy God, and will give unto thee the law of my Holy Priesthood, as was ordained by me, and my Father, before the world was. Abraham received all things, whatsoever he received, by revelation and commandment, by my word, saith the Lord, and hath entered into his exaltation, and sitteth upon his throne.

12. Abraham received promises concerning his seed,

and of the fruit of his loins,—from whose loins ye are, viz.: my servant Joseph—which were to continue, so long as they were in the world; and as touching Abraham and his seed, out of the world, they should continue; both in the world and out of the world should they continue as innumerable as the stars; or, if ye were to count the sand upon the sea-shore, ye could not number them. This promise is yours also, because ye are of Abraham, and the promise was made unto Abraham; and by this law are the continuation of the works of my Father, wherein he glorifieth himself. Go ye, therefore, and do the works of Abraham: enter ye into my law, and ye shall be saved. But if ye enter not into my law, ye cannot receive the promises of my Father, which he made unto Abraham.

13. God commanded Abraham, and Sarah gave Hagar to Abraham, to wife. And why did she do it? Because this was the law, and from Hagar sprang many people. This, therefore, was fulfilling, among other things, the promises. Was Abraham therefore, under condemnation? Verily, I say unto you, *Nay;* for I the Lord, commanded it. Abraham was commanded to offer his son Isaac; nevertheless, it was written, Thou shalt not kill. Abraham, however, did not refuse, and it was accounted unto him for righteousness.

14. Abraham received concubines, and they bare him children, and it was accounted unto him for righteousness, because they were given unto him, and he abode in my law: as Isaac also and Jacob did none other things than that which they were commanded; and because they did none other things than that which they were commanded, they have entered into their exaltation, according to the promises and sit upon

thrones, and are not angels, but are Gods. David also received many wives and concubines, as also Solomon, and Moses my servant; as also many others of my servants, from the beginning of creation until this time; and in nothing did they sin, save in those things which they received not of me.

15. David's wives and concubines were given unto him, of me, by the hand of Nathan, my servant, and others of the prophets who had the keys of this power; and in none of these things did he sin against me, save in the case of Uriah and his wife; and therefore, he hath fallen from his exaltation, and received his portion; and he shall not inherit them out of the world; for I gave them unto another, saith the Lord.

16. I am the Lord thy God, and I gave unto thee, my servant Joseph, an appointment, and restore all things; ask what ye will, and it shall be given unto you, according to my word; and as ye have asked concerning adultery, verily, verily I say unto you, if a man receiveth a wife in the new and everlasting covenant, and if she be with another man, and I have not appointed unto her by the holy anointing, she hath committed adultery, and shall be destroyed. If she be not in the new and everlasting covenant, and she be with another man, she has committed adultery; and if her husband be with another woman, and he was under a vow, he hath broken his vow, and hath committed adultery; and if she hath not committed adultery, but is innocent, and hath not broken her vow, and she knoweth it, and I reveal it unto you, my servant Joseph, then shall you have power, by the power of my Holy Priesthood, to take her, and give her unto him that hath not committed adultery, but hath

been faithful, for he shall be made ruler over many; for I have conferred upon you the keys and power of the priesthood, wherein I restore all things, and make known unto you, all things in due time.

17. And verily, verily I say unto you, that whatsoever you seal on earth, shall be sealed in heaven; and whatsoever you bind on earth, in my name, and by my word, saith the Lord, it shall be eternally bound in the heavens; and whatsoever sins you remit on earth, shall be remitted eternally in the heavens; and whoseever sins you retain on earth, shall be retained in heaven.

18. And again, verily I say, whomsoever you bless, I will bless; and whomsoever you curse, I will curse, saith the Lord; for I, the Lord, am thy God.

19. And again, verily I say unto you, my servant Joseph, that whatsoever you give on earth, and to whomsoever you give any one on earth, by my word, and according to my law, it shall be visited with blessings, and not cursings, and with my power, saith the Lord, and shall be without condemnation on earth, and in heaven; for I am the Lord thy God, and will be with thee even unto the end of the world, and through all eternity: for verily I seal upon you your exaltation, and prepare a throne for you in the kingdom of my Father, with Abraham, your father. Behold, I have seen your sacrifices, and will forgive all your sins; I have seen your sacrifices, in obedience to that which I have told you: go, therefore, and I make a way for your escape, as I accepted the offering of Abraham, of his son Isaac.

20. Verily, I say unto you, a commandment I give unto mine handmaid, Emma Smith, your wife, whom I have given unto you, that she stay herself, and partake not of that which I commanded you to offer unto her;

for I did it, saith the Lord, to prove you all, as I did Abraham; and that I might require an offering at your hand, by covenant and sacrifice; and let mine handmaid, Emma Smith, receive all those that have been given unto my servant Joseph, and who are virtuous and pure before me; and those who are not pure, shall be destroyed, saith the Lord God! for I am the Lord thy God, and ye shall obey my voice; and I give unto my servant Joseph, that he shall be made ruler over many things, for he hath been faithful over a few things, and from henceforth I will strengthen him.

21. And I command mine handmaid, Emma Smith, to abide and cleave unto my servant Joseph, and to none else. But if she will not abide this commandment, she shall be destroyed, saith the Lord; for I am the Lord thy God, and will destroy her if she abide not in my law; but if she will not abide this commandment, then shall my servant Joseph do all these things for her, even as he hath said; and I will bless him, and multiply him, and give unto him an hundred fold in this world, of fathers and mothers, brothers and sisters, houses and lands, wives and children, and crowns of eternal lives in the eternal worlds. And again, verily I say, let mine handmaid forgive my servant Joseph his trespasses, and then shall she be forgiven her trespasses, wherein she has trespassed against me; and I the Lord thy God will bless her, and multiply her, and make her to rejoice.

22. And again, I say, let not my servant Joseph put his property out of his hands, lest an enemy come and destroy him, for Satan seeketh to destroy; for I am the Lord thy God, and he is my servant; and behold! and lo, I am with him, as I was with Abraham thy father, even unto his exaltation and glory.

23. Now as touching the law of the priesthood, there are many things pertaining thereunto. Verily, if a man be called of my Father, as was Aaron, by mine own voice, and by the voice of him that sent me, and I have endowed him with the keys of the power of this priesthood, if he do anything in my name, and according to my law, and by my word, he will not commit sin, and I will justify him. Let no one, therefore, set on my servant Joseph; for I will justify him; for he shall do the sacrifice which I require at his hands, for his transgressions, saith the Lord your God.

24. And again, as pertaining to the law of the priesthood: If any man espouse a virgin, and desire to espouse another, and the first give her consent; and if he espouse the second, and they are virgins, and have vowed to no other man, then is he justified; he cannot commit adultery, for they are given unto him; for he cannot commit adultery with that that belongeth unto him, and to none else; and if he have ten virgins given unto him by this law, he cannot commit adultery, for they belong to him; and they are given unto him—therefore is he justified. But if one, or either of the ten virgins, after she is espoused, shall be with another man, she has committed adultery, and shall be destroyed; for they are given unto him to multiply and replenish the earth, according to my commandment, and to fulfill the promise which was given by my Father before the foundation of the world; and for their exaltation in the eternal worlds, that they may bear the souls of men; for herein is the work of my father continued, that he may be glorified.

25. And again, verily, verily I say unto you, if any man have a wife who holds the keys of this power, and

he teaches unto her the law of my priesthood, as pertaining to these things; then shall she believe, and administer unto him, or she shall be destroyed, saith the Lord your God; for I will destroy her; for I will magnify my name upon all those who receive and abide in my law. Therefore, it shall be lawful in me, if she receive not this law, for him to receive all things whatsoever I the Lord his God, will give unto him, because she did not believe and administer unto him, according to my word; and she then becomes the transgressor, and he is exempt from the law of Sarah, who administered unto Abraham according to the law, when I commanded Abraham to take Hagar to wife. And now, as pertaining to this law: Verily, verily, I say unto you, I will reveal more unto you, hereafter; therefore, let this suffice for the present. Behold, I am Alpha and Omega. Amen.

CELESTIAL MARRIAGE.

A DISCOURSE DELIVERED BY ELDER ORSON PRATT, IN THE TABERNACLE, GREAT SALT LAKE CITY.

It is quite unexpected to me, brethren and sisters, to be called upon to address you this forenoon; and still more so, to address you upon the principle which has been named, namely, a plurality of wives.

It is rather new ground for me; that is, I have not been in the habit of publicly speaking upon this subject; and it is rather new ground to the inhabitants of the United States, and not only to them, but to a portion of the inhabitants of Europe; a portion of them have not been in the habit of preaching a doctrine of this description; consequently, we shall have to break up new ground.

It is well known, however, to the congregation before me, that the latter-day saints have embraced the doctrine of a plurality of wives, as a part of their religious faith. It is not, as many have supposed, a doctrine embraced by them to gratify the carnal lusts and feelings of man; that is not the object of the doctrine.

We shall endeavor to set forth before this enlightened assembly, some of the causes why the Almighty has revealed such a doctrine, and why it is considered a part and portion of our religious faith. And I believe that they will not, under our present form of government (I mean the government of the United States), try us for treason for believing and practising our religious notions and ideas. I think, if I am not mistaken, that the Constitution gives the privilege to all the inhabitants of this country, of the free exercise of their religious notions, and the freedom of their faith, and the practice of it. Then, if it can be proven to a demonstration, that the latter-day saints have actually embraced, as a portion of their religion, the doctrine of a plurality of wives, it is constitutional. And should there ever be laws enacted by this government to restrict them from the free exercise of this part of their religion, such laws must be unconstitutional.

But, says the objector, we cannot see how this doctrine can be embraced as a matter of religion and faith; we can hardly conceive how it can be embraced only as a kind of domestic concern, something that pertains to domestic pleasures, in no way connected with religion. In reply, we will show you that it is incorporated as a part of our religion, and necessary for our exaltation to the fullness of the Lord's glory in the eternal world. Would you like to know the reasons? Before we get through, we will endeavor to tell you why we consider it an essential doctrine to glory and exaltation, to our fullness of happiness in the world to come.

We will first make a few preliminary remarks in regard to the existence of man, to his first existence in his first estate; and then say something in relation to his present state, and the bearing which it has upon his next or future state.

The "Mormons" have a peculiar doctrine in regard to our pre-existence, different from the views of the

Christian world, so called, who do not believe that man had a pre-existence. It is believed, by the religious world, that man, both body and spirit, begins to live about the time that he is born into this world, or a little before; that then is the beginning of life. They believe that the Lord, by a direct act of creation, formed, in the first place, man out of the dust of the ground; and they believe that man is possessed of both body and spirit, by the union of which he became a living creature. Suppose we admit this doctrine concerning the formation of the body from the dust, then how was the spirit formed? Why, says one, we suppose it was made by a direct act of creation, by the Almighty Himself; that He moulded the spirit of man, formed and finished it in a proper likeness to inhabit the tabernacle He had made out of the dust.

Have you any account of this in the Bible? Do the Scriptures declare that the spirit was formed at the time the tabernacle was made? No. All the tabernacles of the children of men that were ever formed, from remote generations, from the days of Adam to this time, have been formed out of the earth. We are of the earth, earthy. The tabernacle has been organized according to certain principles and laws of organization, with bones, and flesh, and sinews, and skin. Now, where do you suppose all these tabernacles got their spirits? Does the Lord make a new spirit every time a tabernacle is made? If so, the work of creation, according to the belief of Christendom, did not cease on the seventh day. If we admit their views, the Lord must be continually making spirits to inhabit all the tabernacles of the children of men; He must make something like one thousand millions of spirits every century; He must be working at it every day, for there are many hundreds of individuals being born into the world every day. Does the Lord create a new spirit every time a new tabernacle comes into the world? That does not look reasonable, nor God-like.

But how is it, you inquire? Why the fact is, that being that animates this body, that gives life and energy, and power to move, to act, and to think: that being that dwells within this tabernacle is much older than what the tabernacle is. That spirit that now dwells within each man, and each woman, of this vast assembly of people, is more than a thousand years old, and I would venture to say, that it is more than five thousand years old.

But how was it made? when was it made? and by whom was it made? If our spirits existed thousands of years ago—if they began to exist—if there were a beginning to their organization, by what process was this organization carried on? Through what medium, and by what system of laws? Was it by a direct creation of the Almighty? Or were we framed according to a certain system of laws, in the same manner as our tabernacles? If we were to reason from analogy—if we admit analogical reasoning in the question, what would we say? We should say, that our spirits were formed by generation, the same as the body or tabernacle of flesh and bones. But what says revelation upon the subject? We will see whether revelation and analogy will agree.

We read of a certain time when the corner stones of the earth were laid, and the foundations thereof were made sure—of a certain time when the Lord began to erect this beautiful and glorious habitation, the earth; then they had a time of joy. I do not know whether they had instruments of music, or whether they were engaged in the dance; but one thing is certain, they had great joy, and the heavens resounded with their shouts; yea, the Lord told Job, that all the sons of God shouted for joy, and the morning stars sang together, when the foundations of this globe were laid.

The SONS of God, recollect, shouted for joy, because there was a beautiful habitation being built, so that they could get tabernacles, and dwell thereon; they expected the time—they looked forward to the period; and it was joyful to them to reflect, that the creation was about being formed, the corner stone of it was laid, on which they might, in their times, and in their seasons, and in their generations, go forth and receive tabernacles for their spirits to dwell in. Do you bring it home to yourselves, brethren and sisters? Do you realize that you and I were there? Can you bring it to your minds that you and I were among that happy number that shouted for joy when this creation was made? Says one, I don't recollect it. No wonder! for your recollection is taken from you, because you are in a tabernacle that is earthly; and all this is right and necessary. The same is written of Jesus Christ himself, who had to descend below all things. Though he had wisdom to assist in the organization of this world; though it was through him, as the great leader of all these sons of God, the earth was framed, and framed too, by the assistance of all his younger brethren—yet we find, with all that great and mighty power he possessed, and the great and superior wisdom that was in his bosom, that after all his judgment had to be taken away; in his humiliation, his reason, his intelligence, his knowledge, and the power that he was formerly in possession of, vanished from him as he entered into the infant tabernacle. He was obliged to begin down at the lowest principles of knowledge, and ascend upward by degrees, receiving grace for grace, truth for truth, knowledge for knowledge, until he was filled with all the fullness of the Father, and was capable of ruling, governing, and controlling all things, having ascended above all things. Just so with us; we that once lifted up our united voices as sons and daughters of God, and shouted for joy at the laying of the foundation of this earth, have come here and taken tabernacles, after the pattern of our elder brother: and in our humiliation—for it is humiliation to be deprived of knowledge we once had, and the power we once enjoyed—in our humiliation, just like our elder brother, our judgment is taken away. Do we not read also in the Bible, that God is the Father of our spirits?

We have ascertained that we have had a previous existence. We find that Solomon, that wise man, says that when the body returns to the dust, the spirit returns to God who gave it. Now all of this congregation very well know, that if we never existed *there*, we could not *return* there. I could not return to California. Why? Because I never have been there. If you never were with the Father, the same as Jesus was before the foundation of the world, you never could return there, any more than I could to the West Indies, where I have never been. But if we have once been there, then we can see the force of the saying of the wise man, that the spirit returns to God who gave it—it goes back where it once was.

Much more evidence might be derived in relation to this subject, even from the English translation of the

Bible; but I do not feel disposed to dwell too long upon any particular testimony; suffice it to say, that the Prophet Joseph Smith's translation of the fore part of the book of Genesis is in print, and is exceedingly plain upon this matter. In this inspired translation we find the pre-existence of man clearly laid down, and that the spirits of all men, male and female, did have an existence, before man was formed out of the dust of the ground. But who was their Father? I have already quoted a saying that God is the Father of our spirits.

In one sense of the word, there are more Gods than one; and in another sense there is but one God. The scriptures speak of more Gods than one. Moses was called a God to Aaron, in plain terms; and our Saviour, when speaking upon this subject, says, "If the Scriptures called them Gods unto whom the word of God came, why is it that you should seek to persecute me, and kill me, because I testify that I am the son of God?" This in substance was the word of our Saviour; those to whom the word of God came, are called Gods, according to his testimony. All these beings of course are one, the same as the Father and the Son are one. The Son is called God, and so is the Father, and in some places the Holy Ghost is called God. They are one in power, in wisdom, in knowledge, and in the inheritance of celestial glory; they are one in their works; they possess all things, and all things are subject to them; they act in unison; and if one has power to become the Father of spirits, so has another; if one God can propagate his species, and raise up spirits after his own image and likeness, and call them his sons and daughters, so can all other Gods that become like him, do the same thing; consequently, there will be many Fathers, and there will be many families, and many sons and daughters; and they will be the children of those glorified celestial beings that are counted worthy to be Gods.

Here let me bring for the satisfaction of the saints, the testimony of the vision given to our Prophet and Revelator Joseph Smith, and Sidney Rigdon, on the 25th day of February, 1832. They were engaged in translating the New Testament, by inspiration; and while engaged in this great work, they came to the 29th verse of the 5th chapter of John, which was given to them in these words—"they who have done good, in the resurrection of the just; and they who have done evil in the resurrection of the unjust." This being given in different words from the English translation, caused them to marvel and wonder; and they lifted up their hearts in prayer to God, that He would show them why it was that this should be given to them in a different manner; and behold, the visions of heaven opened before them. They gazed upon the eternal worlds, and saw things before this world was made. They saw the spiritual creation who were to come forth and take upon themselves bodies; and they saw things as they are to be in the future; they saw the celestial, terrestrial, and telestial worlds, as well as the sufferings of the ungodly; all passed before him in this great and glorious vision. And while they were yet gazing upon things as they were before the world was made, they were commanded to write, saying, "this is the testimony, last of all, which we give of him, that he lives; for we saw him, even on the right hand of God; and we heard the voice bearing record that he is the Only Begotten of the Father; that by him, and through him, and of him, the worlds are and were created; and the inhabitants thereof are begotten sons and daughters unto God." Notice this last expression, "the inhabitants thereof are begotten sons and daughters unto God," (meaning the different worlds that have been created and made). Notice, this does not say, that God, whom we serve and worship, was actually the Father Himself, in His own person, of all these sons and daughters of the different worlds; but they "are begotten sons and daughters unto God;" that is, begotten by those who are made like Him, after His image, and in His likeness; they begat sons and daughters, and begat them *unto* God, to inhabit these different worlds we have been speaking of. But more of this, if we have time, before we get through.

We now come to the second division of our subject, or the entrance of these spirits upon their second estate, or their birth and existence in mortal tabernacles. We are told that among this great family of spirits, some were more noble and great than others, having more intelligence.

Where do you read that? says one. Out of the Book of Abraham, translated from the Egyptian papyrus by the Prophet Joseph Smith. Among the great and numerous family of spirits—"the begotten sons and daughters of God"—there are some more intelligent than others; and the Lord showed unto Abraham "the intelligences that were organized before the world was; and among all these there were many of the noble and great ones." And God said to Abraham, "thou art one of them, thou wast chosen before thou wast born." Abraham was chosen before he was born. Here then, is knowledge, if we had time to notice it, upon the doctrine of election. However, I may just remark, it does not mean unconditional election to eternal life of a certain class, and the rest doomed to eternal damnation. Suffice it to say, that Abraham and many others of the great and noble ones in the family of spirits, were chosen before they were born, for certain purposes, to bring about certain works, to have the privilege of coming upon the stage of action, among the host of men, in favorable circumstances. Some came through good and holy parentages, to fulfill certain things the Lord decreed should come to pass, from before the foundations of the world.

The Lord has ordained that these spirits should come here and take tabernacles by a certain law, through a certain channel; and that law is the law of marriage. There are a great many things that I will pass by; I perceive that if I were to touch upon all these principles, the time allotted for this discourse would be too short, therefore I am under the necessity of passing by many things in relation to these spirits in their first estate, and the laws that governed them there, and come to their second estate.

The Lord ordained marriage between male and female as a law through which spirits should come here and take tabernacles, and enter into the second state of existence. The Lord Himself solemnized the first marriage pertaining to this globe, and pertaining to flesh and bones here upon this earth. I do not say pertaining to mortality; for when the first marriage was celebrated, no mortality was there. The first marriage that we have any account of, was between two immortal beings—old father Adam and old mother Eve; they were immortal beings; death had no dominion, no power over them; they were capable of enduring for ever and ever, in their organization. Had they fulfilled the law, and kept within certain conditions and bounds, their tabernacles would never have been seized by death; death entered entirely by sin, and sin alone. This marriage was celebrated between two immortal beings. For how long? Until death? No. That was entirely out of the question; there could have been no such thing in the ceremony.

What would you consider, my hearers, if a marriage was to be celebrated between two beings not subject to death? Would you consider them joined together for a certain number of years, and that then all their covenants were to cease for ever, and the marriage contract be dissolved? Would it look reasonable and consistent? No. Every heart would say that the work of God is perfect in and of itself, and inasmuch as sin had not brought imperfection upon the globe, what God joined together could not be dissolved, and destroyed, and torn asunder by any power beneath the celestial world, consequently it was eternal; the ordinance of union was eternal; the sealing of the great Jehovah upon Adam and Eve was eternal in its nature, and was never instituted for the purpose of being overthrown and brought to an end. It is known that the "Mormons" are a peculiar people about marriage; we believe in marrying, not only for a time, but for all eternity. This is a curious idea, says one, to be married for all eternity. It is not curious at all; for when we come to examine the Scriptures, we find that the very first example set for the whole human family, as a pattern instituted for us to follow, was not instituted until death, for death had no dominion at that time; but it was an eternal blessing pronounced upon our first parents. I have not time to explain further the marriage of Adam and Eve, but will pass on to their posterity.

It is true, that they became fallen, but there is a redemption. But some may consider that the redemption only redeemed us in part, that is, merely from some of the effects of the fall. But this is not the case; every man and woman must see at once that a redemption must include a complete restoration of all the privileges lost by the fall.

Suppose, then, that the fall was of such a nature as to dissolve the marriage covenant, by death—which is not necessary to admit, for the covenant was sealed previous to the fall, and we have no account that it was dissolved —but suppose this was the case, would not the redemption be equally broad as the fall, to restore the posterity of Adam back to that which they lost? And if Adam and Eve were married for all eternity, the ceremony was an everlasting ordinance, that they twain should be one flesh for ever. If you and I should ever be accounted worthy to be restored back from our fallen and degraded condition to the privileges enjoyed before the fall, should we not have an everlasting marriage seal, as it was with our first progenitors? If we had no other reasons in all the Bible, this would be sufficient to settle the case at once in the mind of every reflecting man and woman, that inasmuch as the fall of man has taken away any privileges in regard to the union of male and female, these privileges must be restored in the redemption of man, or else it is not complete.

What is the object of this union? is the next question. We are told the object of it: it is clearly expressed; for, says the Lord unto the male and female, I command you to multiply and replenish the earth. And, inasmuch as we have proved that the marriage ordinance was eternal in its nature, previous to the fall, if we are restored back to what was lost by the fall, we are restored for the purpose of carrying out the commandment given before the fall, namely, to multiply and replenish the earth. Does it say, continue to multiply for a few years, and then the marriage contract must cease, and there shall be no further opportunity of carrying out this command, but it shall have an end? No, there is nothing specified of this kind; but the fall has brought in disunion through death; it is not a part of the original plan; consequently, when male and female are restored from the fall, by virtue of the everlasting and eternal covenant of marriage, they will continue to increase and multiply to all ages of eternity, to raise up beings after their own order, and in their own likeness and image, germs of intelligence, that are destined, in their times and seasons, to become not only sons of God, but gods themselves.

This accounts for the many worlds we heard Elder Grant speaking about yesterday afternoon. The peopling of worlds, or an endless increase, even of one family, would require an endless increase of worlds; and if one family were to be united in the eternal covenant of marriage, to fulfill that great commandment, to multiply his species, and propagate them, and if there be no end to the increase of his posterity, it would call for an endless increase of new worlds. And if one family calls for this, what would innumerable millions of families call for? They would call for as many worlds as have already been discovered by the telescope; yea, the number must be multiplied to infinity in order that there may be room for the inheritance of the sons and daughters of the Gods.

Do you begin to understand how these worlds get their inhabitants? Have you learned that the sons and daughters of God before me this day, are His offspring —made after His own image; that they are to multiply their species until they become innumerable.

Let us say a few words, before we leave this part of the subject, on the promises made to Abraham, Isaac, and Jacob. The promises were, Lift up your eyes, and behold the stars; so thy seed shall be, as numberless as the stars. What else did He promise? Go to the sea-shore, and look at the ocean of sand, and behold the smallness of the particles thereof, and then realize that your seed shall be as numberless as the sands. Now let us take this into consideration. How large a bulk of sand would it take to make as many inhabitants as there are now upon the earth? In about one cubic foot of sand, reckoning the grains of a certain size, there would be a thousand million particles. Now that is about the estimated population of our globe. If our earth were to continue 8,000 years, or eighty centuries, with an average population of one thousand millions per century, then three cubic yards of sand would contain a greater number of particles than the whole population of the globe, from the beginning, until the measure of the inhabitants of this creation is complete. If men then cease to multiply, where is the promise made to Abraham? Is it fulfilled? No. If that is the end of his increase, behold, the Lord's promise is not fulfilled. For the amount of sand representing his seed, might all be drawn in a one-horse cart; and yet the Lord said to Abraham, thy seed shall be as numerous as the sand upon the sea-shore; that is, to carry out the idea in full, it was to be endless; and therefore, there must be an infinity of worlds for their residence. We cannot comprehend infinity. But suffice it to say, if all the sands on the sea-shore were numbered, says the Prophet Enoch, and then all the particles of the earth besides, and then the particles of millions of earths like this, it would not be a beginning to all thy creations; and yet thou art there, and thy bosom is there; and thy curtains are stretched out still. This gives plenty of room for the fulfillment of the promise made to Abraham, and enough to spare for the fulfillment of similar promises to all his seed.

We read that those who do the works of Abraham, are to be blessed with the blessing of Abraham. Have you not, in the ordinances of this last dispensation, had the blessings of Abraham pronounced upon your heads? O yes, you say, I well recollect, since God has restored the everlasting Priesthood, that by a certain ordinance these blessings were placed upon our heads—the blessings of Abraham, Isaac, and Jacob. Why, says one, I never thought of it in this light before. Why did you not think of it? Why not look upon Abraham's blessings as your own, for the Lord blessed him with a promise of seed as numerous as the sand upon the sea-shore; so will you be blessed, or else you will not inherit the blessings of Abraham.

How did Abraham manage to get a foundation laid for this mighty kingdom? Was he to accomplish it all through one wife? No. Sarah gave a certain woman to him whose name was Hagar, and by her a seed was to be raised up unto him. Is this all? No. We read of his wife Keturah, and also of a plurality of wives and concubines, which he had, from whom he raised up many sons. Here, then, was a foundation laid for the fulfillment of the great and grand promise concerning the multiplicity of his seed. It would have been rather a slow process, if Abraham had been confined to one wife, like some of those narrow, contracted nations of modern Christianity.

I think there is only about one-fifth of the population of the globe, that believe in the one-wife system; the other four-fifths believe in the doctrine of a plurality of wives. They have had it handed down from time immemorial, and are not half so narrow and contracted in their minds as some of the nations of Europe and America, who have done away with the promises, and deprived themselves of the blessings of Abraham, Isaac, and Jacob. The nations do not know anything about the blessings of Abraham; and even those who have only one wife, cannot get rid of their covetousness, and get their little hearts large enough to share their property with a numerous family; they are so penurious, and so narrow and contracted in their feelings, that they take every possible care not to have their families large; they do not know what is in the future, nor what blessings they are depriving themselves of, because of the traditions of their fathers; they do not know that a man's posterity, in the eternal worlds, are to constitute his glory, his kingdom, and dominion.

Here, then, we perceive, just from this one principle, reasoning from the blessings of Abraham alone, the necessity—if we would partake of the blessings of Abraham, Isaac, and Jacob—of doing their works; and he that will not do the works of Abraham, and walk in his footsteps, will be deprived of his blessings.

Again, let us look at Sarah's peculiar position in regard to Abraham. She understood the whole matter; she knew that, unless seed was raised up to Abraham, he would come short of his glory; and she understood the promise of the Lord, and longed for Abraham to have seed. And when she saw that she was old, and fearing that she should not have the privilege of raising up seed, she gave to Abraham, Hagar. Would Gentile Christendom do such things now-a-days? O no; they would consider it enough to send a man to an endless hell of fire and brimstone. Why? Because tradition has instilled this in their minds as a dreadful, awful thing.

It matters not to them how corrupt they are in female prostitution, if they are lawfully married to only one wife; but it would be considered an awful thing by them to raise up a posterity from more than one wife; this would be wrong indeed; but to go into a brothel, and there debauch themselves in the lowest haunts of degradation all the days of their lives, they consider only a trifling thing; nay, they can even license such institutions in Christian nations, and it all passes off very well.

That is tradition; and their posterity have been fostered and brought up in the footsteps of wickedness. This is death, as it stalks abroad among the great and popular cities of Europe and America.

Do you find such haunts of prostitution, degradation, and misery here, in the cities of the mountains? No. Were such things in our midst, we should feel indignant enough to see that such persons be blotted out of the page of existence. These would be the feelings of this community.

Look upon those who committed such iniquity in Israel, in ancient days; every man and woman who committed adultery were put to death. I do not say that this people are going to do this; but I will tell you what we believe—we believe it ought to be done.

Whoredom, adultery, and fornication, have cursed the nations of the earth for many generations, and are increasing fearfully upon the community; but they must be entirely done away from those who call themselves the people of God; if they are not, woe! woe! be unto them, also; for "thus saith the Lord God Almighty," in the Book of Mormons, "Woe unto them that commit whoredoms, for they shall be thrust down to hell!" There is no getting away from it. Such things will not be allowed in this community; and such characters will find that the time will come, that God, whose eyes are upon all the children of men, and who discerneth the things that are done in secret, will bring their acts to light; and they will be made an example before the people; and shame and infamy will cleave to their posterity after them, unto the third and fourth generation of them that repent not.

How is this to be prevented? for we have got a fallen nature to grapple with. It is to be prevented in the way the Lord devised in ancient times; that is, by giving to His faithful servants a plurality of wives, by which a numerous and faithful posterity can be raised up, and taught in the principles of righteousness and truth; and then, after they fully understand those principles that were given to the ancient Patriarchs, if they keep not the law of God, but commit adultery, and transgressions of this kind, let their names be blotted out from under heaven, that they may have no place among the people of God.

But again, there is another reason why this plurality should exist among the latter-day saints. I have already given you one reason, and that is, that you might inherit the blessings and promises made to Abraham, Isaac, and Jacob, and receive a continuation of your posterity, that they may become as numerous as the sand upon the sea-shore. There is another reason, and a good one, too. What do you suppose it is? I will tell you; and it will appear reasonable to every man and woman of a reflecting mind. Do we not believe, as the Scriptures have told us, that the wicked nations of the earth are doomed to destruction? Yes, we believe it. Do we not also believe, as the Prophets have foretold, concerning the last days, as well as what the new revelations have said upon the subject, that darkness prevails upon the earth, and gross darkness upon the minds of the people; and not only this, but that all flesh has corrupted its way upon the face of the earth; that is, that all nations, speaking of them as nations, have corrupted themselves before the Most High God, by their wickedness, whoredoms, idolatries, abominations, adulteries, and all other kind of wickedness? And we furthermore believe, that according to the Jewish prophets, as well as the book of Mormon, and modern revelations given in the book of doctrine and covenants, that the sword of the vengeance of the Almighty is already unsheathed, and stretched out, and will no more be put back into the scabbard until it falls upon the head of the nations until they are destroyed, except they repent. What else do we believe? We believe that God is gathering out from among these nations those who will hearken to his voice, and receive the proclamation of the Gospel, to establish them as a people alone by themselves, where they can be instructed in the right way, and brought to a knowledge of the truth. Very well: if this be the case, that the righteous are gathering out, and are still being gathered from among the nations, and being planted by themselves, one thing is certain—that that people are better calculated to bring up their children in the right way, than any other under the whole heavens. Oh yes, says one, if that is the case—if you are the people the ancient Prophets have spoken of, if you are the people that are guided by the Lord, if you are under the influence, power, and guidance of the Almighty, you must be the best people under heaven, to dictate the young mind: but what has that to do with the plurality of wives? I will tell you. I have already told you that the spirits of men and women, all had a previous existence, thousands of years ago, in the heavens, in the presence of God; and I have already told you that among them are many spirits that are more noble, more intelligent than others, that were called the great and mighty ones, reserved until the dispensation of the fullness of times, to come forth upon the face of the earth, through a noble parentage that shall train their young and tender minds in the truths of eternity, that they may grow up in the Lord, and be strong in the power of His might, be clothed upon with His glory, be filled with exceeding great faith; that the visions of eternity may be opened to their minds; that they may be prophets, priests, and kings to the Most High God. Do you believe, says one, that they are reserved until the last dispensation, for such a noble purpose? Yes; and among the Saints is the most likely place for these spirits to take their tabernacles, through a just and righteous parentage. They are to be sent to that people that are the most righteous of any other people upon the earth; there to be trained up properly, according to their nobility and intelligence, and according to the laws which the Lord ordained before they were born. This is the reason why the Lord is sending them here, brethren and sisters; they are appointed to come and take their bodies here, that in their generations they may be raised up among the righteous. The Lord has not kept them in store for five or six thousand years past, and kept them waiting for their bodies all this time, to send them among the Hottentots, the African negroes, the idolatrous Hindoos, or any other of the fallen nations that dwell upon the face of this earth. They are not kept in reserve in order to come forth to receive such a degraded parentage upon the earth; no, the Lord is not such a being; His justice, goodness, and mercy will be magnified towards those who were chosen before they were born; and they long to come, and they will come, among the Saints of the living God; this would be their highest pleasure and joy, to know that they could have the privilege of being born of such noble parentage.

Then is it not reasonable, and consistent that the Lord should say unto His faithful and chosen servants, that had proved themselves before Him all the day long, that had been ready and willing to do whatsoever His will required them to perform;—take unto yourselves more wives, like unto the patriarchs, Abraham, Isaac, and Jacob, of old—like those who lived in ancient times, who walked in my footsteps, and kept my commands? Why should they not do this? Suppose the Lord should answer this question, would He not say, I have here in reserve, noble spirits, that have been waiting for thousands of years, to come forth in the fullness of times, and which I designed should come forth through these my faithful and chosen servants, for I know they will do my will, and they will teach their children after them to do it? Would not this be the substance of the language, if the Lord should give us an answer upon this subject?

But then another question will arise; how are these things to be conducted? Are they to be left at random? Is every servant of God at liberty to run here and there, seeking out the daughters of men as wives unto themselves without any restriction, law, or condition? No. We find these things were restricted in ancient times. Do you not recollect the circumstance of the Prophet Nathan's coming to David? He came to reprove him for certain disobedience, and told him about the wives he had lost through it; that the Lord would give them to another; and he told him, if he had been faithful, that the Lord would have given him still more, if he had only asked for them. Nathan the Prophet, in relation to David, was the man that held the keys concerning this matter in ancient days; and it was governed by the strictest laws.

So in these days; let me announce to this congregation, that there is but one man in all the world, at the same time, who can hold the keys of this matter; but one man has power to turn the key to inquire of the Lord, and to say whether I, or these my brethren, or any of the rest of this congregation, or the Saints upon the face of the whole earth, may have this blessing of

Abraham conferred upon them; he holds the keys of these matters now, the same as Nathan, in his day.

But, says one, how have you obtained this information? By new revelation. When was it given, and to whom? It was given to our Prophet, Seer, and Revelator, Joseph Smith, on the 12th day of July, 1843; only about eleven months before he was martyred for the testimony of Jesus.

He held the keys of these matters; he had the right to inquire of the Lord; and the Lord has set bounds and restrictions to these things; He has told us in that revelation, that only one man can hold these keys upon the earth at the same time; and they belong to that man who stands at the head to preside over all the affairs of the church and kingdom of God in the last days. They are the sealing keys of power, or in other words, of Elijah, having been committed and restored to the earth by Elijah, the prophet, who held many keys, among which were the keys of sealing, to bind the hearts of the fathers to the children, and the children to the fathers; together with all the other sealing keys and powers, pertaining to the last dispensation. They were committed by that angel who administered in the Kirtland Temple, and spoke unto Joseph the prophet, at the time of the endowments in that house.

Now, let us enquire, what will become of those individuals who have this law taught unto them in plainness, if they reject it? [A voice in the stand, "they will be damned."] I will tell you: they will be damned, saith the Lord God Almighty, in the revelation he has given. Why? Because where much is given, much is required; where there is great knowledge unfolded for the exaltation, glory, and happiness of the sons and daughters of God, if they close up their hearts, if they reject the testimony of His word, and will not give heed to the principles he has ordained for their good, they are worthy of damnation, aud the Lord has said they shall be damned. This was the word of the Lord to His servant Joseph the prophet himself. With all the knowledge and light he had, he must comply with it, or, says the Lord unto him, you shall be damned; and the same is true in regard to all those who reject these things.

What else have we heard from our President? He has related to us that there are some damnations that are eternal in their nature; while others are but for a certain period, they will have an end, they will not receive a restoration to their former privileges, but a deliverance from certain punishments: and instead of being restored to all the privileges pertaining to man previous to the fall, they will only be permitted to enjoy a certain grade of happiness, not a full restoration. Let us inquire after those who are to be damned, admitting they will be redeemed, which they will be, unless they have sinned against the Holy Ghost. They will be redeemed, but what will it be to? Will it be to exaltation, and to a fullness of glory? Will it be to become sons of God, or Gods to reign upon thrones, and multiply their posterity, and reign over them as kings? No, it will not. They have lost that exalted privilege for ever; though they may, after having been punished for long periods, escape by the skin of their teeth; but no kingdom will be conferred upon them? What will be their condition? I will tell you what revelation says, not only concerning them that reject these things, but concerning those that through their carelessness, or want of faith, or something else, have failed to have their marriages sealed for time and for all eternity; those that do not do these things, so as to have the same ordinances sealed upon their heads by divine authority, as was upon the head of old Father Adam—if they fail to do it through wickedness, through their ungodliness, they also will never have the privilege of possessing that which is possessed by the Gods that hold the keys of power, of coming up to the thrones of their exaltation, and receiving their kingdoms. Why? Because, saith the Lord, all oaths, all covenants, and all agreements, etc., that have been made by man, and not by me, and by the authority I have established, shall cease when death shall separate the parties; that is the end; that is the cessation; they go no further; and such a person cannot come up in the morning of the resurrection, and say, Behold, I claim you as my wife; you are mine; I married you in the other world before death; therefore you are mine: he cannot say this. Why? Because he never married that person for eternity.

Suppose they should enter into covenant and agreement, and conclude between themselves to live together to all eternity, and never have it sealed by the Lord's sealing power, by the holy priesthood, would they have any claim on each other in the morning of the resurrection? No; it would not be valid nor legal, and the Lord would say, It was not by me; your covenants were not sealed on the earth, and therefore they are not sealed in the heavens; they are not recorded on my book; they are not to be found in the records that are in the archives of eternity; therefore, the blessings you might have had, are not for you to enjoy. What will be their condition? The Lord has told us. He says these are angels; because they keep not this law, they shall be ministering servants unto those who are worthy of obtaining a more exceeding and eternal weight of glory; wherefore, saith the Lord, they shall remain singly and separately in their saved condition, and shall not have power to enlarge themselves, and thus shall they remain forever and ever.

Here, then, you can read their history; they are not Gods, but they are angels or servants to the Gods. There is a difference between the two classes; the Gods are exalted; they hold keys of power; are made kings and priests; and this power is conferred upon them in time, by the everlasting priesthood, to hold a kingdom in eternity that shall never be taken from them worlds without end; and they will propagate their species. They are not servants; for one God is not to be a servant to another God; they are not angels; and this is the reason why Paul said, know ye not, brethren, that we shall judge angels? Angels are inferior to the saints who are exalted as kings. These angels who are to be judged, and to become servants to the Gods, did not keep the law, therefore, though they are saved, they are to be servants to those who are in a higher condition.

What does the Lord intend to do with this people? He intends to make them a kingdom of kings and priests, a kingdom unto Himself, or in other words, a kingdom of Gods, if they will hearken to His law. There will be many who will not hearken; there will be the foolish among the wise, who will not receive the new and everlasting covenant in its fullness; and they never will attain to their exaltation; they never will be counted worthy to hold the sceptre of power over a numerous progeny, that shall multiply themselves without end, like the sand upon the sea shore.

We can only touch here and there upon this great subject, we can only offer a few words with regard to this great, sublime, beautiful and glorious doctrine, which has been revealed by the Prophet, Seer, and Revelator, Joseph Smith, who sealed his testimony with his blood, and thus revealed to the nations, things that were in ancient times, as well as things that are tc come.

But while I talk, the vision of my mind is opened; the subject spreads forth and branches out like the branches of a thrifty tree; and as for the glory of God, how great it is! I feel to say, Hallelujah to his great and holy name; for He reigns in the heavens, and He will exalt His people to sit with Him upon thrones of power, to reign forever and ever.

INDIAN HOSTILITIES AND TREACHERY—MORMON POLICY TOWARDS THEM.

AN ADDRESS DELIVERED BY PRESIDENT BRIGHAM YOUNG, IN THE TABERNACLE, GREAT SALT LAKE CITY.

I wish to say a few words to the latter-day saints this morning, as there seems to be considerable excitement in the feelings of the people, and many inquiring what will be the result of the present Indian difficulties.

I will give you my testimony, as far as I have one on the subject, concerning these difficulties in this territory, north and south, pertaining to our brethren, the Lamanites. My testimony to all is—IT IS RIGHT, and perfectly calculated, like all other providences of the Lord, of the like nature, to chasten this people until they are willing to take counsel. They will purify and sanctify the Saints, and prepare the wicked for their doom.

There has nothing strange and uncommon to man, yet occurred; nothing has yet happened out of the ordinary providences of the Lord. These common dealings of our great Head with His people have been manifested from days of old, in blessings and chastisements Wars, commotions, tumults, strife, nation contending against nation, and people against people, have all been governed and controlled by Him whose right it is to control such matters.

Among wicked nations, or among Saints, among the ancient Israelites, Philistines and Romans, the hand of the Lord was felt; in short, all the powers that have been upon the earth, have been dictated, governed, controlled, and the final issue of their existence has been brought to pass, according to the wisdom of the Almighty. Then my testimony is, IT IS ALL RIGHT.

There seems to be some excitement among the people, and fears are arising in the breasts of many, as to the general safety. Some person has been shot at by the Indians, or some Indians were seen in a hostile condition. And away go messengers to report to head quarters, saying, "*What shall we do?* for we cannot tell, but we shall all be killed by them; they have stolen our horses and driven off some cattle, which has created a great excitement in our settlement," etc; when, perhaps to-morrow, the very Indians who have committed these depredations will come and say, *How do you do?* We are friendly, cannot you give us some "*Chitcup?*" * They will shake hands, and appear as though it were impossible for them to be guilty of another hostility. And what is the next move? Why, our wise men, the elders of Israel, are either so fluctuating in their feelings, so unstable in their ways, or so ignorant of the Indian character, that the least mark of friendship manifested by these treacherous red men, will lull all their fears, throw them entirely off their guard, saying, "It is all right; wife, take care of the stock, for I am going to the cañon for a load of wood."

Away he goes, without a gun or a pistol to defend himself in case of an attack from some Indian or In-

* Indian language for something to eat.

dians, to rob him of his cattle and perhaps his life. Herds of cattle are driven upon the range, the feelings of the people are divested of all fear by this little show of Indian friendship, and their hearts are at peace with all mankind. They lie down to sleep at night with the doors of their houses open, and in many instances with no way to close them if they were willing, only by means of hanging up a blanket. Thus they go to sleep with their guns unloaded, and entirely without any means of defence, in case they should be attacked in the night. On the other hand, they no sooner discover an Indian in an hostile attitude, than the hue and cry is "*We shall all be murdered immediately.*" That is the kind of stability, the kind of unshaken self-command, the style of generalship and wisdom manifested by elders in Israel. To-day all are in arms, war is on hand; "we are going to be destroyed, or to fight our way through," is in every mouth. To-morrow all is peace, and every man turns to his own way, wherever the common avocations of life call him. No concern is felt as to protection in the future, but "all is right, all is safety, there is no fear of any further trouble," is the language of people's thoughts, and they lie down to sleep in a false security, to be murdered in the night by their enemies, if they are disposed to murder them.

I can tell you one thing with regard to excitement and war. You may take Israel here, as a community, with all their experience, and with all they have passed through in the shape of war, and difficulties of various kinds, and these wild Indians are actually wiser in their generation in the art of war than this people are. They lay better plans, display greater skill, and are steadier in their feelings. They are not so easily excited, and when excited, are not so easily allayed, as the men who have come, to inhabit these mountains, from where they have been trained and educated in the civilization of modern nations. You may not believe this assertion; it is, however, no matter whether you do or do not, the fact remains unaltered, as well as the conviction of my own mind regarding it.

I have been frequently asked, what is going to be the result of these troubles? I answer—*the result will be good.* What did you hear, you who have come to these valleys within the last few years, previous to your leaving your native country? You heard that all was peace and safety among the Saints in these regions; that the earth yielded in her strength, giving an abundance of food; and that this was a splendid country to raise stock. Your determination was then formed to go up to the valleys of the mountains, where you could enjoy peace and quiet, and follow the avocations of life undisturbed. When the people arrive here, many of them come to me and say, "Brother Brigham, can we go here or there to get us farms? Shall we enter into this or that speculation? We have been very poor, and we want to make some money, or we want the privilege of taking with us a few families to make a settlement in this or that distant valley." If I inquire why they cannot stay here, their answer is, "because there is no room, the land is chiefly taken up, and *we* have a considerable stock of cattle, we want to go where we can have plenty of range for our stock, where we can mount our horses, and ride over the prairies, and say, I am lord of all I survey. We do not wish to be disturbed, in any way, nor to be asked to pay tithing, to work upon the roads, nor pay territorial tax, but we wish all the time to ourselves, to appropriate to our own use. I want you, brother Brigham, to give us counsel that we can get the whole world in a string after us, and have it all in our own possession by and by." If there is light enough in Israel, let it shine in your consciences, and illuminate your understandings, and give you to know that I tell you the truth. This is the object many have, in wishing to settle and take in land that is far distant from the main body of the people. I have not given you the language of their lips to me, but the language of their hearts.

Elders of Israel are greedy after the things of this world. If you ask them if they are ready to build up the kingdom of God, their answer is prompt—"Why, to be sure we are, with our whole souls; but we want first to get so much gold, speculate and get rich, and then we can help the Church considerably. We will go to California and get gold, go and buy goods and get rich, trade with the emigrants, build a mill, make a farm, get a large herd of cattle, and *then* we can do a great deal for Israel." When will you be ready to do it? "In a few years, brother Brigham, if you do not disturb us. We do not believe in the necessity of doing military duty, in giving over our surplus property for tithing; we never could see into it; but we want to go and get rich, to accumulate and amass wealth, by securing all the land adjoining us, and all we have knowledge of." If that is not the spirit of this people, then I do not know what the truth is concerning the matter.

Now I wish to say to you who are fearing and trembling, do not be afraid at all, for it is certain if we should be killed off by the Indians, we could not die any younger; this is, about as good a time as can be for us to die, and if we all go together, why, you know, we shall have a good company along with us; it will not be lonesome passing through the valley, which is said to have a vail drawn over it. If we all go together, the dark valley of the shadow of death will be lighted up by us, so do not be scared. But there will not be enough slain by the Indians at this time to make the company very conspicuous in that dark valley. Do you begin to secretly wish you had stayed in the States or in England a little longer, until this Indian war had come to an end? There is a mighty fearing and trembling in the hearts of many. I know what men have done heretofore; when they have seen the enemy advancing, they have skulked, they were sure to be somewhere else than on hand when there was fighting to do, although, upon the whole, I have no fault to find with the latter-day saints, or with the Elders of Israel upon that subject, for they love to fight a little too well. If I were to have fears concerning them, it would not be that they would make war, but in the case of war being made on them, I should have more fear in consequence of the ignorant and foolish audacity of the elders, than of their being afraid. I should fear they would rush into danger like an unthinking horse into battle. So I will not find fault with regard to their courage. On that point I am a coward myself, and if people would do as I tell them, I would not only save my own life, but theirs likewise.

Suppose, now, that we should say to this congregation, and to all the wards of this city, *the time has come for us to fort up;* do you not think a great many persons would come immediately to me, and inquire if I did not think their houses quite safe enough, without being put to that trouble and expense? Yes, my office would be crowded with such persons, wanting to know if they might not live where they were now living, "for," they would say, "we have got good houses, and well finished off, besides, such a course will ruin them, and our gardens will go to destruction; we really cannot fort up." Would there not be a great amount of hard feelings upon the subject? I think so, whether you do or not. I think I should want as many as a legion of angels to assist me to convince every family it was necessary, if it actually was so.

I do not know but that the time may come, and that speedily, when I shall build a fort myself in this city, and those who are disposed can go into it with me, while the rest can stay out. When I see it is absolutely necessary to do this, I shall do it. If the people of Utah Territory would do as they were told, they would always be safe. If the people in San Pete county had done as they were told, from the beginning of that settlement, they would have been safe at this time, and would not have lost their cattle. The day before yesterday, Friday, July 29th, the Indians came from the mountains, to Father Allred's settlement, and drove off all the stock, amounting to two hundred head. If the people had done as they were told, they would not have suffered this severe loss, which is a just chastisement.

I recollect when we were down at Father Allred's settlement last April, they had previously been to me not only to know if they might settle in San Pete, but if they might separate widely from each other, over a piece of land about two miles square, each having a five acre lot for their garden, near their farms. They were told to build a good substantial fort, until the settlement became sufficiently strong, and not live so far apart, and expose themselves and their property to danger. Father

Allred told me they were then so nigh together, they did not know how to live! I told him they had better make up their minds to be baptized into the Church again, and get the Spirit of God, that each one might be able to live in peace with his neighbor in close quarters, and not think himself infringed upon. They wanted to know if they were to build a fort. "Why, yes," I said, "build a strong fort, and a corral to put your cattle, that the Indians cannot get them away from you." "Do you think, brother Brigham, the Indians will trouble us here?" they inquired. I said, "It is none of your business whether they will or not, but you will see the time that you will need such preparations." But I did not think it would come so quickly. There will more come upon this people to destroy them than they at present think of, unless they are prepared to defend themselves, which I shall not take time, this morning, to dwell upon. I said also to the brethren at Utah, "Do you make a fort, and let it be strong enough, that Indians cannot break into it." They commenced, and did not make even the shadow of a fort, for in some places there was nothing more than a line to mark where the approaching shadow would be. They began to settle round upon the various creeks and streamlets, and the part of a fort that existed was finally pulled up, and carried away somewhere else. I have told you, from the beginning, you would need forts, where to build them, and how strong. I told you six years ago, to build a fort that the *Devil could not get into*, unless you were disposed to let him in, and that would keep out the Indians. Excuse me fcr saying devil; I do not often use the old gentleman's name in vain, and if I do it, it is always in the pulpit, where I do all my swearing.

I make this apology because it is considered a sin to say devil, and it grates on refined ears.

I told the settlement in San Pete, at the first, to build a fort. They did not do it, but huddled together beside a stone quarry, without a place of common shelter where they could defend themselves, in case of an Indian difficulty. They had faith they could keep the Indians off. Well, now is the time to call it into exercise. They did, after a while, build a temporary fort at San Pete, which now shields them in a time of trouble.

When the brethren went to Salt Creek, they wanted to make a settlement there, and inquired of me if they might do so. I told them, no, unless they first built an efficient fort. I forbade them taking their women and children there, until that preparatory work was fully accomplished. Has it ever been done? No, but families went there and lived in wagons and brush houses, perfectly exposed to be killed. If they have faith enough to keep the Indians off, it is all right.

From the time these distant valleys began to be settled, until now, there has scarcely been a day but what I have felt twenty-five ton weight, as it were, upon me, in exercising faith to keep this people from destroying themselves; but if any of them can exercise faith enough for themselves, and wish to excuse me, I will take my faith back.

The word has gone out now, to the different settlements, in the time of harvest, requiring them to build forts. Could it not have been done last winter, better than now? Yes. Do you not suppose people will now wish they had built forts when they were told? If they do not, it proves what they have been all the time, shall I say fools? If that is too harsh a term, I will say they have been foolish. It is better for me to labor in building a house or a fort, to get out fencing timber, and wood to consume through the winter, when I have nothing else to do, and not be under the necessity of leaving my grain on the ground to do those things. Harvest is no time to build forts, neither is it the time to do it when we should be plowing and sowing.

Now the harvest is upon us, I wish to say a few words concerning it. I desire you to tell your neighbors, and wish them to tell their neighbors, and thus let it go to the several counties around—now is the time for women and children to assist in the harvest fields, the same as they do in other countries. I never asked this of them before; I do not now ask it as a general thing, but those employed in the expedition south, in the work of defending their brethern from Indian depredations, who have heavy harvests on hand, rather than suffer the grain to waste, let the women get in the harvest, and put it where the Indians cannot steal it. And when you go into the harvest field, carry a good butcher knife in your belt, that if an Indian should come upon you, supposing you to be unarmed, you would be sure to kill him.

Tell your neighbors of this, and go to work, men, women, and children, and gather in your grain, and gather it clean, leave none to waste, and put it where the Indians cannot destroy it.

Does this language intimate anything terrific to you? It need not. If you will do as you are told, you will be safe continually. Secure your bread stuff, your wheat, and your corn, when it is ripe, and let every particle of grain raised in these valleys be put where it will be safe, and as much as possible from vermin, and especially from the Indians, and then build forts.

Let every man and woman who has a house make that house a fort, from which you can kill ten where you now only kill one, if the Indians come upon you. "Brother Brigham, do you really expect Indians to come upon us in this city?" This inquiry, I have no doubt, is at this moment in the hearts of a few, almost breathless with fear. Were I to answer such inquirers as I feel, I should say, it is none of your business; but I will say, you are so instructed, to see if you will do as you are told. Let your dwelling house be a perfect fort. From the day I lived where brother Joseph Smith lived, I have been fortified all the time so as to resist twenty men, if they should come to my house in the night, with an intent to molest my family, assault my person, or destroy my property; and I have always been in the habit of sleeping with one eye open, and if I cannot then sufficiently watch, I will get my wife to help me. Let an hostile band of Indians come round my house, and I am good for quite a number of them. If one hundred should come, I calculate that only fifty would be able to go to the next house, and if the Saints there used up the other fifty, the third house would be safe.

But instead of the people taking this course, almost every good rifle in the Territory has been traded away to the Indians, with quantities of powder and lead, though they waste it in various ways when they have got it. The whites would sell the title to their lives, for the sake of trading with the Indians.

They will learn better, I expect, by and by, for the people have never received such strict orders as they have got now. I will give you the pith of the last orders issued—"That man or family who will not do as they are told in the orders, are to be treated as strangers, yea, even as enemies, and not as friends." And if there should be such a contest, if we should be called upon to defend our lives, our liberty, and our possessions, we would cut such off the first, and walk over their dead bodies to conquer the foe outside.

Martial law is not enforced yet, although the whole Territory is in a state of war, apparently, but it is only the Utah [Indians] who have declared war on Utah [Territory]. Deseret has not yet declared war; how soon it will be declared is not for me to say; but we have a right, and it is our duty, to put ourselves in a state of self-defence.

The few families that settled in Cedar Valley, at the point of the mountains, were instructed to leave there, last spring. They have gone back again, upon their own responsibility, and now want to know what they must do. They have been told to do just as they have a mind to.

Those who have taken their wives and children in the cañons to live, have been told to remove them into the city; and if you want to make shingles, or do any other work that requires you to remain there, have your gun in a situation that an Indian cannot creep up and steal it from you before you are aware, that you can be good for a few Indians if they should chance to come upon you.

If I wished to live away from the body of the people, my first effort should be directed towards building a good and efficient fort. When new settlements were made in the eastern countries, they built them of timber, and they were called "block-houses." I would advise that every house in a new settlement should be made good for all the Indians that could approach it, with an intention to tear it down. If I did not do that, I would go to where I could be safe, I would take up my abode with the body of the people. I would take my family there at least. By taking this course, every person will be safe from the depredations of the Indians, which are generally committed upon the defenceless and unprotected portions of the community.

I know what the feelings of the generality of the people are, at this time—they think all the Indians in the mountains are coming to kill off the latter-day saints. I have no more fear of that, than I have of the sun ceasing to give light upon the earth. I have studied the Indian character sufficiently to know what the Indians are in war, I have been with them more or less from my youth upward, where they have often had wars among themselves. Let every man, woman, and child, that can handle a butcher knife, be good for one Indian, and you are safe.

I am aware that the people want to ask me a thousand and one questions, whether they have done it or not, touching the present Indian difficulties. I have tried to answer them all, in my own mind, by saying, *it will be just as the Lord will.*

How many times have I been asked in the past week, what I intend to do with Walker. I say, LET HIM ALONE, severely. I have not made war on the Indians, nor am I calculating to do it. My policy is to give them presents, and be kind to them. Instead of being Walker's enemy, I have sent him a great pile of tobacco to smoke when he is lonely in the mountains. He is now at war with the only friends he has upon this earth, and I want him to have some tobacco to smoke.

I calculate to pursue just such a course with the Indians, and when I am dictated to by existing circumstances, and the Spirit of the Lord, to change my course, I will do it, and not until then.

If you were to see Walker, do yon think you would kill him? You that want to kill him, I will give you a mission to that effect. A great many appear very bold, and desire to go and bring me Walker's head, but they want all the people in Utah to go with them. I could point out thousands in this Territory who would follow these Indians, and continue to follow them, and leave the cattle to be driven off by the emigrants, and the grain to perish, and thus subject the whole community to the ravages of famine, and its consequent evils. I have been teased and teased by men who will come to me and say, "Just give me twenty-five, fifty, or a hundred men, and I will go and fetch you Walker's head." I do not want his head, but I wish him to do all the devil wants him to do, so far as the Lord will suffer him, and the devil to chastise this people for their good.

I say to the Indians, as I have often said to the mob, go your length. You say you are going to kill us all off, you say you are going to obliterate the latter-day saints, and wipe them from the earth, why don't you do it, you poor miserable curses? The mob only had power to drive the Saints to their duty, and to remember the Lord their God, and that is all the Indians can do. This people are worldly-minded, they want to get rich in earthly substance, and are apt to forget their God, the pit from which they were dug, and the rock from which they were hewn, every man turning to his own way. Seemingly the Lord is chastening us until we turn and do His will. What are you willing to do? Would you be willing to build a fort, and all go in there to live? I tell you, you would have a hell of your own, and devils enough to carry it on. Do you suppose you will ever see the time you would do that, and live at peace with each other, and have the spirit of the Lord enough to look each other in the face, and say, with a heart full of kindness, "Good morning, Mary," or "How do you do, Maria?" You will be whipped until you have the Spirit of the Lord Jesus Christ sufficiently to love your brethren and sisters freely, men, women, and children; until you can live at peace with yourselves, and with every family around you; until you can treat every child as though it were the tender offspring of your own body, every man as your brother, and every woman as your sister; and until the young persons treat the old with that respect due to parents, and all learn to shake hands, with a warm heart, and a friendly grip, and say, "God bless you!" from morning until evening; until each person can say, "I love you all, I have no evil in my heart to any individual, I can send my children to school with yours, and can correct your children when they do wrong, as though they were my own, and I am willing you should correct mine, and let us live together until we are a holy and sanctified society." There will always be Indians or somebody else to chastise you, until you come to that spot; so amen to the present Indian trouble, for it is all right. I am just as willing the rebellious of this people should be kicked, and cuffed, and mobbed, and hunted by the Indians, as not, for I have preached to them until I am tired. I will give no more counsel to any person upon the duties of self-preservation; you can do as you please; if you will not preserve yourselves, I may reason with you until my tongue cleaves to the roof of my mouth, to no avail. Let the Lord extend the hand of benevolence to brother Walker, and he will make you do it by other means than exhortations given in mildness.

This very same Indian Walker has a mission upon him, and I do not blame him for what he is now doing; he is helping me do the will of the Lord to this people, he is doing with a chastening rod what I have failed to accomplish with soft words, while I have been handing out my substance, feeding the hungry, comforting the sick. But this has no effect upon this people, at all, my counsel has not been heeded, so the Lord is making brother Walker an instrument to help me, and perhaps the means that he will use will have their due effect.

Do you suppose I want to kill him? No. I should be killing the very means that will make this people do what we wanted them to do years ago.

There are hundreds of witnesses to bear testimony that I have counselled this people, from the beginning, what to do to save themselves, both temporally and spiritually.

In one of our orders issued lately, the southern settlements were advised to send their surplus cattle to this valley. No quicker had the news reached them, than our ears were greeted with one continued whine, which meant, "We are afraid *you* want them." So we did, to take care of them for you.

When Father Allred was advised to adopt measures *to secure themselves and their property, he replied, "Oh,* I do not think there is the least danger in the world; we are perfectly able to take care of our stock, and protect ourselves against the Indians." All right, I thought, let circumstances prove that.

Now, as difficulties surround them, they say to me, "Why, brother Brigham, if you had only told us what to do, we would have done it. Were we not always willing to take your counsel?" Yes, you are a great deal more willing to take it, than to obey it. If people are willing to carry out good counsel, they will secure themselves accordingly.

I have thought of setting a pattern, by securing myself; but were I to build a fort for myself and family, I should want about a legion of angels from the throne of God, to stay nine months with me, to get my folks willing to go into it. But I am so independent about it, I care not the snap of my finger for one of them. If my wives will not go into a place of security with me, it is all right, they can stay out, and I will go in and take my children with me. I say, I do not know but I may take a notion to set a pattern by building a fort; if I do, some one in in this city may follow my example, and then somebody else, etc., until we have a perfect city of forts.

"Brother Brigham, do you really think we shall ever need them?" YES, I DO. All the difficulties there is in the community this year, is not a drop in comparison to the heavy shower that will come. "Well, and where is it coming from?" From hell, where every other trouble comes from. "And who do you think will be the actors?" Why, the Devil and his imps. [W. W. Phelps in the stand. We could not do very well without a Devil.] No, sir, you are quite aware of that; you *know* we could not do without him. If there had been no devil to tempt Eve, she never would have got her eyes opened. We need a devil to stir up the wicked on the earth to purify the saints. Therefore, let the devils howl, let them rage, and thus exhibit themselves in the form of those poor, foolish Lamanites. Let them go on in their work, and do you not desire to kill them, until they ought to be killed, and then we will extinguish the Indian title, if it is required.

Did you never feel to pity them, on viewing their wretched condition? Walker, with a small band, has succeeded in making all the Indian bands in these mountains fear him. He has been in the habit of stealing from the Californians, and of making every train of emigrants that passed along the Spanish trail to California pay tithing to him. He finally began to steal children form those bands to sell to the Spaniards; and through fear of him, he has managed to bring in subjection almost all the Utah tribes.

I will relate one action of Walker's life, which will serve to illustrate his character. He, with his band, about last February, fell in with a small band of Payedes, and killed off the whole of the men, took the squaws prisoners, and sold the children to the Mexicans, and some few were disposed of in this Territory. This transaction was told by Arapeen, Walker's brother, though he was not at the affray himself.

The Indians in these mountains are continually on the decrease; bands that numbered 150 warriors when we first came here, number not more than 35 now; and some of the little tribes in the southern parts of this Territory, towards New Mexico, have not a single squaw amongst them, for they have traded them off for horses, etc. This practice will soon make the race extinct. Besides, Walker is continually, whenever an opportunity presents itself, killing and stealing children from the wandering bands that he has any power over, which also has its tendency to extinguish the race.

Walker is hemmed in, he dare not go into California again. Dare he go east to the Snakes? No. Dare he go north? No, for they would rejoice to kill him. Here he is, penned up in a small compass, surrounded by his enemies; and now the elders of Israel long to eat up, as it were, him and his little band. What are they? They are a set of cursed fools. Do you not rather pity them? They dare not move over a certain boundary, on any of the four points of the compass, for fear of being killed; then they are killing one another, and making war upon this people that could use them up, and they not be a breakfast spell for them if they felt so disposed. See their condition, and I ask you, do you not pity them? From all appearance, there will not be an Indian left, in a short time, to steal a horse. Are they not fools, under these circumstances, to make war with their best friends?

Do you want to run after them to kill them? I say, let them alone, for peradventure God may pour out His Spirit upon them, and show them the error of their ways. We may yet have to fight them, though they are of the house of Israel to whom the message of salvation is sent; for their wickedness is so great, that the Lord Almighty cannot get at the hearts of the older ones to teach them saving principles. Joseph Smith said we should have to fight them. He said, "When this people mingle among the Lamanites, if they do not bow down in obedience to the Gospel, they will hunt them until there is but a small remnant of them left upon this continent." They have either got to bow down to the Gospel or be slain. Shall we slay them simply because they will not obey the Gospel? No. But they will come to us and try to kill us, and we shall be under the necessity of killing them to save our own lives.

I wished to lay these things before the people this morning, to answer a great many questions, and allay their fears. Yesterday, brother Kimball heard at his mill, ten miles north, that I had sent word to him, that the mountains were full of Indians, and he and the families with him were to move into the city; so they immediately obeyed this report. Brother Kimball came to me and inquired if I had sent such orders. I said, no. But it is all right, for I wanted the women and children from there. This shows the excited state of the people.

One thing more. I ask you men who have been with Joseph in the wars *he* passed through, and who were with him at the time of his death, what was it that preserved us, to all outward appearances? It is true, in reality, God did it. But by what means did He keep the mob from destroying us? *It was by means of being well armed with the weapons of death to send them to hell cross lots.* Just so you have got to do.

And for this people fostering to themselves that the day has come for them to sell their guns and ammunition to their enemies, and sit down to sleep in peace, they will find themselves deceived, and before they know, they will sleep until they are slain. They have got to carry weapons with them, to be ready to send their enemies to hell cross lots, whether they be Lamanites, or mobs who may come to take their lives, or destroy their property. We must be so prepared that they dare not come to us in a hostile manner without being assured they will meet a vigorous resistance, and ten to one they will meet their grave.

The Lord will suffer no more trouble to come upon us than is necessary to bring this people to their senses. You need not go to sleep under the impression that it is the north and south only that is in danger, and we are all safe here. Now *mind*, let this people here lie down to sleep, and be entirely off their watch, and the first thing they know, they are in the greatest danger. You must not desert the watch tower, but do as I do—keep some person awake in your house all night long, and be ready, at the least tap of the foot, to offer a stout resistance, if it is required. Be ready at any moment to kill twenty of your enemies at least. Let every house be a fort.

After the cattle were stolen at San Pete, a messenger arrived here in about thirty hours to report the affair, and obtain advice. I told brother Wells, "you can write to them, and say, 'Inasmuch as you have no cows and oxen to trouble you, you can go to harvesting, and take care of yourselves.'" If you do not take care of yourselves, brethren, you will not be taken care of. I take care of them that help themselves. I will help you that try to help yourselves, and carry out the maxim of Doctor Dick—"God helps them that help themselves."

I am my own policeman, and have slept, scores of nights, with my gun and sword by my side, that is, if I slept at all. I am still a policeman. Now is the day to watch. It is as important for me to watch now, as well as pray, as it ever has been since I came into this kingdom. It requires watching, as well as praying men; take turns at it, let some watch while others pray, and then change round, but never let any time pass without a watcher, lest you be overtaken in an hour when you think not; it will come as a thief in the night. Look out for your enemies, for we know not how they will come, and what enemy it will be. Take care of yourselves.

Again, let me reiterate to the sisters, do not be afraid of going into the harvest field. If you are found there helping your, sons, your husbands and your brethren, to gather in the harvest, I say, God bless you, and I will also.

Take care of your grain, and take care of yourselves, that no enemy come to slay you. Be always on hand to meet them with death, and send them to hell, if they come to you. May God bless you all. Amen.

USE AND ABUSE OF BLESSINGS.

AN ADDRESS DELIVERED BY PRESIDENT B. YOUNG, IN THE TABERNACLE, GREAT SALT LAKE CITY.

I FEEL disposed to say a few words on the present occasion. It is said, that "at the sight of the eyes the heart is made to rejoice." This is truly the case with me this afternoon, when I look upon the congregation to see this spacious hall filled with the Saints of the Most High, for the purpose of partaking of the Sacrament of the Lord's Supper. It is a sight which I have not had the privilege of seeing before, only on Conference days. This morning I looked round to see how the house was crowded, which was packed to that extent, that scores could not be seated. I looked if peradventure I could designate any person that did not belong to the Church, that did not profess to be a Saint; but I could not see a single person of that description, that I knew of. I thought, why not be as diligent to attend the afternoon meetings, to partake of the Sacrament of the Lord's Supper, as to attend the morning meetings? Hitherto it has not been the case, but my heart rejoices to see the house so well filled this afternoon. I feel in my heart to bless you: it is full of blessings and not cursings. It is something that does not occupy my feelings to curse any individual, but I will modify this by saying *those who ought not to be cursed.* Who ought to be? Those who know their master's will, and do it not; they are worthy of many stripes; it is not those who do not know, and do not do, but those who know it, and do not do it—they are the ones to be chastised.

While the brethren have been speaking upon the blessings the Lord bestows upon this people, my mind has reflected upon many of the circumstances of life, and upon certain principles. I will ask you a question—*Do you think persons can be blessed too much?* I will answer it myself. Yes, they can, they can be blessed to their injury. For instance, suppose a person should be blessed with the knowledge of the holy Gospel, whose heart is set in him to do evil. We esteem this as a blessing, and would not the Lord consider it a blessing to bestow His favors and mercies upon any individual, by giving him a knowledge of life and salvation? But suppose He bestowed it upon persons whose hearts were set in them to do evil, who would by their wickedness turn these blessings into curses, they would be blessed too much. It is possible to bless people to death, you can bless them to everlasting misery by heaping too many blessings upon them. Perhaps this is what is meant by the saying—It is like heaping coals of fire upon their heads; it will injure them, consume them, burn them, destroy them. Suffice it to say, that people can be blessed too much. Can you bless a wise man too much? a man who knows what to do with his blessings when they are bestowed upon him? No, you cannot. Can you bless a wise people too much? No, it is impossible, when they know how to improve upon all blessings that are bestowed upon them. But the Lord does and will bless the inhabitants of the earth with such great and inestimable blessings, in the proclamation of the Gospel, that they will be damned who reject them, for light brings condemnation to men who love darkness rather than light.

Have this people been blessed too much? I will not positively say, but I think they have, inasmuch as their blessings in some instances have been to their injury. Why? Because they have not known what to do with their blessings.

While the brethren were speaking of the liberal hand of Providence in bestowing abundantly the products of the earth, it occurred to me, that this people, to my certain knowledge, had felt that they had too much, and they esteemed it as good for nothing. It is true what brother Jedediah Grant said with regard to wheat, and other grains, for I have seen it myself. I have seen hundreds, and thousands, and scores of thousands of bushels of grain lying to waste and rot, when it has not brought a great price. Many of this people have thought, and expressed themselves in language like this —"I can go to California, and get so much gold, or I can trade and make so much gold, I cannot therefore spend time to take care of wheat, nor to raise it; let it lie there and rot while I go and accumulate riches," They were then wealthy, for their granaries and barns were full of the blessings of the Lord, *but now they are empty*, because they did not know what to do with their blessings.

I can tell this people how to dispose of all their blessings, if they will only allow me time enough; and if I cannot tell them how, I can show them. For instance, you who have fields of wheat, beyond the limits of grasshoppers. will have considerable crops when it is harvested and perhaps so much that you will not know what to with it. I know what you ought to do with it; you ought to say to your poor brethren—"Come and help take care of my grain, and share with me, and feed yourselves and your families." If you have so much that you cannot take care of it, and your neighbor is not without bread, tell Bishop Hunter that you have got so many hundred bushels to lay over in the store, and you will have the benefit of it on your tithing. That is what I recommend you to do with your blessings, when you have more than you can take care of yourselves. I say, hand it over and let your neighbors take care of it for you.

This makes me think of what I saw the first year I came into this valley, the same year I moved my family, which was the next season after the pioneers arrived here. It was late in the season when I arrived, but from the ground where this house now stands, there had been two crops of wheat. They had harvested the first crop very early, and the water being flooded over, it again started from the roots, and produced a fair crop, say from ten to twelve bushels to the acre. That was harvested, and it was coming up again. I said to the brethren, "Let these my brethren who have come with me gather up this wheat," but they would not suffer *them* to do it. Some of the brethren had gathered their crops of grain, and left a great deal wasting on the fields, I said, "Let the poor brethren, who have come in from abroad, glean in your fields." You can bear me witness that a great many widows and poor men came here, and brought but very little with them, and there never was a man, to my knowledge, ever expressed a desire to let them glean in his field. "All right," I said, "we can live on greens," while at the same time there was more wasted that season than to make up the deficiency, that all might have been comfortable. Late in the fall I saw one man working among his corn; he had a large crop, more than a single man could take care of. I saw he was going to let it go to waste; I said to him, "Brother, let the brethren and sisters help you to husk your corn, to gather it and put it safely away, for so much it will benefit them and help you. "O," he replied, "I have nothing to spare, I can take care of it myself." I saw it wasting, and said to him, "Brother, get your corn husked immediately, and let the brethren do it, and pay them with a portion of it." He replied, "I cannot spare a bit of it." I have no question of it at all in my mind, but three-fourths of his corn went into the mud, and was trampled down by the cattle; and women and children went without bread in consequence of it. That man had no judgment, he knew not what to do with his blessings the Lord had bestowed upon him.

Were I to ask the question, how much wheat or anything else a man must have to justify him in letting it go to waste, it would be hard to answer; figures are inadequate to give the amount. *Never let anything go to waste.* Be prudent, *save everything*, and what you get more than you can take care of yourselves, ask your neighbors to help you. There are scores and hundreds of men in this house, if the question were asked them if they considered their grain a burthen and a drudge to them, when they had plenty last year and the year before, that would answer in the affirmative, and were ready to part with it for next to nothing. How do they feel now, when their granaries are empty? If they had a few thousand bushels to spare now, would they not consider it a blessing? They would. Why? Because it would bring the gold and silver. But pause for a moment, and suppose you had millions of bushels to sell, and could sell it for twenty dollars per bushel, or for a million of dollars per bushel, no matter what amount, so that you sell all your wheat, and transport it out of the country, and you are left with nothing more than a pile of gold, what good would it do you? You could not eat it, drink it, wear it, or carry it off where you could have something to eat. The time will come that gold will hold no comparison in value to a bushel of wheat. Gold is not to be compared with it in value. Why would it be precious to you now? Simply because you could get gold for it? Gold is good for nothiug, only as men value it. It is no better than a piece of iron, a piece of limestone, or a piece of sandstone, and it is not half so good as the soil from which we raise our wheat, and other necessaries of life. The children of men love it, they lust after it, are greedy for it, and are ready to destroy themselves and those around them, over whom they have any influence, to gain it.

When this people are blessed so much that they consider their blessings a burden and a drudge to them, you may always calculate on a cricket war, a grasshopper war, a drought, too much rain, or something else to make the scales preponderate the other way. This people have been blessed too much, so that they have not known what to do with their blessings.

What do we hear from the inhabitants of the different settlements? The cry is—"I do not wish to live out yonder, for there is no chance to speculate and trade with the emigrants." Have you plenty to eat? Have you plenty of wheat, fowls, butter, cheese, and calves? Are you not raising stock in abundance for flesh meat of different kinds? What use is gold if you get enough to eat, drink, and wear without it? What is the matter? "Why, we are away off, and cannot get rich all at once." You are lusting after that which you do not know what to do with, for few men know what to do with riches when they possess them. The inhabitants of this valley have proved it. They have proved it. by their reckless waste of the products of the earth, by their undervaluing the blessings conferred upon them by the emigration, which has administered clothing and other necessaries to them. We can see men who can clothe themselves and their families easily, go into the cañons in their broad cloth pantaloons to get wood, or you may see them take a horse, and ride bare-backed until they tare them to pieces, that they are not fit to come to meeting in. They do not know how to take care of good clothing. Again, if we were digging in a water-ditch to-morrow, that required all hands, in consequence of the rising of the water, I have no doubt but you would see what I saw the other day—one of our young dandies, who was perhaps not worth the shirt on his back, came to work in a water-ditch, dressed in his fine broad-cloth pantaloons, and a fine bosomed shirt, and I have no doubt he would have worn gloves too if he had been worth a pair. You would see men of this description, who are without understanding, whole hearted, good fellows, and ready to do anything for the advancement of the public good, commence to dig in the mud and wet, in their fine clothes, and go into the water, up to their knees, with their fine calf-skin boots. This is a wanton waste of the blessings of God, that cannot be justifiable in His eyes, and in the eyes of prudent, thinking men, under ordinary circumstances. If prudence and economy are necessary at one time more than another, it is when a family or a nation are thrown upon its own resourses, as we are. But you may trace the whole lives of some men, and it will be impossible for you to point out a single portion of time, when they knew how to appreciate and how to use even the common comforts of life, when they had them, to say nothing of an abundance of wealth.

Again, there have been more contention and trouble between neighbors, in these valleys, with regard to surplus property, which was not needed by this people, than any other thing. For instance, a widow woman comes in here from the United States, and turns out on the range beyond Jordan, three yoke of oxen and a few cows, for she considers she is too poor to have them herded. Again, a man comes in with ten yoke of oxen; he also turns them out to wander where they please. If he is asked why he does not put them in a herd, he will tell you, "I do not want to pay the herding fee." Another comes on with three or four span of horses, and twenty or thirty yoke of cattle. Has he any for sale? No, but he turns them all out upon the range and they are gone. By and by he sends a boy on horseback to hunt them, who is unsuccessful in finding them after a week's toil. The owner turns out himself, and all hands, to hunt up his stock, but they also fail in finding them, they are all lost except a very few. He was not able to have them herded, he thought, though he possessed so much property, and knew nothing more than to turn them out to run at large. Thus he consumes his time, running after his lost property. He frets his feelings, for his mind is continually upon it; he is in such a hurry in the morning to go out to hunt his stock, that he has no time to pray; when he returns home late at night, worn out with toil and anxiety of mind, he is unfit to pray; his cattle are lost, his mind is unhinged and darkened through the neglect of his duty, and apostacy stares him in the face, for he is not satisfied with himself, and murmurs against his brethren, and against his God. By and by some of his cattle turn up with a strange brand upon them; they have been taken up, and sold to this person or that one. This brings contention and dissatisfaction between neighbor and neighbor. Such a person has too much property, more than he knows what to do with. It would be much better for a man who is a mechanic, and intends to follow his business, to give one out of two cattle which he may possess, to some person, for taking care of the other. It would be better for those who possess a great quantity of stock, to sell half of them to fence in a piece of land, to secure the other half, than to drive them all out to run at large, and lose three-fourths of them. If there are half-a-dozen men round me, and I can put a cow in their way or anything else that will do them any good, for fencing up a lot for me, the property I thus pay is not out of the world, but is turned over to those men who had not a mouthful of meat, butter, or milk; it is doing them good, and I am reaping the profit and benefit of their labors in exchange. If I did not do this, I must either see them suffer, or make a free distribution of a part of what I have among them.

It is impossible for me to tell you how much a man must possess to entitle him to the liberty of wasting anything, or of letting it be stolen and run away with by the Indians. The surplus property of this community, as poor as we are, has done more real mischief than everything else besides.

I will propose a plan to stop the stealing of cattle in coming time, and it is this—let those who have cattle on hand join in a company, and fence in about fifty thousand acres of land, make a dividend of their cattle, and appropriate what they can spare, to fence in a large field, and this will give employment to immigrants who are coming in. When you have done this, then get up another company, and so keep on fencing until all the vacant land is substantially enclosed.

Some persons will perhaps say—"I do not know how good and how high a fence it will be necessary to build to keep thieves out. I do not know either, except you build one that will keep out the devil. Build a fence which the boys and the cattle cannot pull down, and I will ensure you will keep your stock. Let every man lay his plans so as to secure for his present necessities, and hand over the rest to the laboring man; keep making improvements, building, and making farms, and that will not only advance his own wealth, but the wealth of the community.

A man has no right with property, which, according to the laws of the land, legally belongs to him, if he does not want to use it; he ought to possess no more than he can put to usury, and cause to do good to himself and his fellow-man. When will a man accumulate money enough to justify him in salting it down, or, in other words, laying it away in the chest, to lock it up, there to lie, doing no manner of good either to himself or his neighbor? It is impossible for a man ever to do it. No man should keep money or property by him that he cannot put to usury for the advancement of that property in value or amount, and for the good of the community in which he lives; if he does, it becomes a dead weight upon him, it will rust, canker, and gnaw his soul, and finally work his destruction, for his heart is set upon it. Every man who has got cattle, money, or wealth of any description, bone and sinew, should put it out to usury. If a man has the arm, body, head, the component parts of a system to constitute him a laboring man, and has nothing in the world to depend upon but his hands, let him put them to usury. Never hide up anything in a napkin, but put it forth to bring an increase. If you have got property of any kind, that you do not know what to do with, lay it out in making a farm, or building a saw mill or a woollen factory, and go to with your mights to put all your property to usury.

If you have more oxen and other cattle than you need, put them in the hands of other men, and receive their labor in return, and put that labor where it will increase your property in value.

I hope you will now lay your plans to set men to work who will be in here by and by, for there will be a host of them, and they will all want employment, who trust to their labor for a subsistence; they will all want something to eat, and calculate to work for it. In the first place keep the ground in good order to produce you plentiful crops of grain, and vegetables, and then take care of them.

Let me say to the sisters, those who have children, never consider that you have bread enough around you to suffer your children to waste a crust or a crumb of it. If a man is worth millions of bushels of wheat and corn, he is not wealthy enough to suffer his servant girl to sweep a single kernel of it into the fire; let it be eaten by something, and pass again into the earth, and thus fulfill the purpose for which it grew. Some mothers would fill a basket full of bread to make a plaything for their children, but I have not had flour enough in the time of my greatest abundance, to let my children waste one morsel of bread with my consent. No, I would rather feed the greatest enemy I have on the earth with it, than have it go into the fire. *Remember it*, do not waste anything, but take care of everything; save your grain, and make your calculations, so that when the brethren come in from the United States, from England, and other places, you can give them some potatoes, onions, beets, carrots, parsnips, watermelons, or anything else which you have, to comfort them, and cheer up their hearts, and if you have wheat, dispose of it to them, and receive their labor in return. Raise enough and to spare of all the staple necessaries of life, and lay your plans to hire your brethren who will come in this fall to fence your farms, improve your gardens, and make your city lots beautiful. Lay your plans to secure enough to feed yourselves, and one or two of the brethren that are coming to dwell with us.

When we first came into the valley, the question was asked me, if men would ever be allowed to come into this Church, and remain in it and hoard up their property. *I say*, NO. That is a short answer, and it is a pointed one. The man who lays up his gold and silver who caches it away in a bank, or in his iron safe, or buries it up in the earth, and comes here, and professes to be a Saint, would tie up the hands of every individual in this kingdom, and make them his servants if he could. It is an unrighteous, unhallowed, unholy, covetous principle; it is of the devil, and is from beneath. Let every person who has capital, put it to usury. Is he required to bring his purse to me, to any of the twelve, or to any person whatever, and lay it at their feet? No, not by me. But I will tell you what to do with your means. If a man comes in the midst of this people with *money*, let him use it in making improvements, in building, in beautifying his inheritance in Zion, and in increasing his capital by thus putting out his money to usury. Let him go and make a great farm, and stock it well, and fortify it all around with a good and efficient fence. What for? Why for the purpose of spending his money. Then let him cut it up into fields, and adorn it with trees, and build a fine house upon it. What for? Why for the purpose of spending his money. What will he do when his money is gone? The money thus spent with a wise and prudent hand, is in a situation to accumulate and increase a hundred fold. When he has done making his farm, and his means still increase by his diligent use of it, he can then commence and build a woollen factory, for instance, he can send and buy the sheep and have them brought here, have them herded here, and shear them here, and take care of them, then set the boys and girls to cleaning, carding, spinning and weaving the wool into cloth, and thus employ hundreds and thousands of the brethren and sisters who have come from the manufacturing districts of the old country, and have not been accustomed to dig in the earth for their livelihood, who have not learned anything else but to work in the factory. This would feed them, and clothe them, and put within their reach the comforts of life; it would also create at home a steady market for the produce of the agriculturist, and the labor of the mechanic. When he has spent his hundred and fifty thousand dollars, which he began business with, and fed five hundred persons, from five to ten years, besides realizing a handsome profit from the labor of the hands employed, by the increased population, and consequent increased demand for manufactured goods, at the end of ten years his factory would be worth five hundred thousand dollars. Suppose he had wrapped up his hundred and fifty thousand in a napkin, for fear of losing it, it would have sent him down to perdition, for the principle is from beneath. But when he puts forth his money to usury, not to me or any other person, but where it will redouble itself, by making farms, building factories for the manufacture of every kind of material necessary for home consumption, establishing blacksmiths' shops and other mechanical establishments, making extensive improvements to beautify the whole face of the earth, until it shall become like the garden of Eden, it becomes a saving blessing to him and those around him. And when the kings, princes, and rulers of the earth shall come to Zion, bringing their gold, and silver, and precious stones with them, they will admire and desire your possessions, your fine farms, beautiful vineyards, and splendid mansions. They will say—"*We have got plenty of money, but we are destitute of such possessions as these.*" Their money loses its value in their eyes when compared with the comfortable possessions of the Saints, and they will want to purchase your property. The industrious capitalist inquires of one of them—"Do you want to purchase this property? I have obtained it by my economy and judgment, and by the labor of my brethren, and in exchange for their labor I have been feeding and clothing them, until they also have comfortable situations, and means to live. I have this farm, which I am willing to sell to enable me to advance my other improvements." "Well," says the rich man, "how much must I give you for it?" "Five hundred thousand dollars," and perhaps it has not cost him more than one hundred thousand. He takes the money and builds up three or four such farms, and employs hundreds of his brethren who are poor.

Money is not real capital, it bears the title only. True capital is labor, and is confined to the laboring classes. They only possess it. It is the bone, sinew, nerve, and muscle of man that subdue the earth, make it yield its strength and administer to his varied wants. This power tears down mountains and fills up valleys, builds cities and temples, and paves the streets. In short, what is there that yields shelter and comfort to civilized man, that is not produced by the strength of his arm the making elements bend to his will?

I will not ask the question again—*How much must a man possess to authorize him to waste anything?* Three or four years ago money was of little value in this country; you might go round exhibiting a back load of gold, and hold out a large piece to a man, I was going to say, almost as big as this Bible, and ask him to work for you, but he would laugh at your offer, and tell you he was looking for some one to work for him. He would then hail another man who had been in Nauvoo, and passed through the pinches there, and had scarcely a shirt to his back, but he would reply—"I was looking for some man to work for me." Gold could not purchase labor, it was no temptation whatever, but those times are passed. It is not now as it was then. I consequently alter my counsel to the brethren. I used to command you to hand over your surplus property, or that which you could not take care of, to me, and I would apply it to a good purpose, but now I counsel you to put it into the hands of men who have nothing at all, and let them pay you for it in labor.

I have never been troubled with thieves stealing my property. If I am not smart enough to take care of what the Lord lends me, I am smart enough to hold my tongue about it, until I come across the thief myself, and then I am ready to tie a string round his neck.

I have not the least hesitation in saying that the loose conduct, and calculations, and manner of doing business, which have characterized men who have had property in their hands, have laid the foundation to bring our boys into the spirit of stealing. You have caused them to do it, you have laid before them every inducement possible, to learn their hands, and train their minds to take that which is not their own. Those young men who have been taken up the past season and condemned to ignominious punishment, may trace the cause of their shame to that foundation. *Distribute your property.* The man that thinks he requires ten yoke of cattle, and can only use one yoke, is laboring under a mistake, he ought to let nine yoke go to the laboring community. If every man would do this with the property which he is not using, all would be employed and have sufficient. This would be the most effectual means of bringing the vile practice of stealing cattle and other property to a termination, which, as I have already said, has been encouraged by covetous, selfish men, who have refused to use their property for their own good, or the community's.

Let us hold before our mind the miser. If the people of this community feel as though they wanted the whole world to themselves, hate any other person to possess anything, and would hoard up their property, and place it in a situation where it would not benefit either themselves or the community, they are just as guilty as the man who steals my property. You may inquire—"What should be done with such a character?" Why, CUT HIM OFF FROM THE CHURCH. *I would disfellowship a man who had received liberally from the Lord, and refused to put it out to usury.* We know this is right.

I recollect well the days brother Grant was telling of, when it was so hard to raise fifty dollars for brother Joseph. I also remember we had a man for trial before the high council, a man who had plenty of money, and refused to loan it, or use it for the advancement of the cause of truth. He would not put his money out to usury. I was going into the council when he was making his plea, and he wept and sobbed. His name was Isaac McWithy, a man about fifty-three years of age. I knew him when he lived on his farm in York State. He told them, in his plea, what he had done for the cause, that he had always been a Christian, and had done so much for the churches, and for the priests, and been so liberal since he had been in this church, which was between three and four years. Some of the brethren said—"Brother McWithy, how much do you suppose you have ever given for the support of the Gospel?" The tears rolled down his cheeks, and he said, "Brethren, I believe I have given away in my lifetime two hundred and fifty dollars." I spake out and said, "If I could not preach as many months each year in this kingdom as you have been years in this Church, and give no more than two hundred and fifty dollars, I should be ashamed of myself."

On one occasion, brother Joseph Young and myself had travelled more than two hours among snow, and in a piercing cold, to preach in his neighborhood one evening. Having had no dinner or supper, we went home with him, and he never asked us to eat a mouthful of supper, though he did muster courage enough to go into the cellar with a little basket, he came up with the tears almost running down his cheeks, and said with some difficulty—"Brethren, have some apples." He held out the basket to us, and when we were about to help ourselves, his niggardly soul made him draw it back again, for fear we should take any. I saw he did not intend us to have any apples, so I put my hand on the basket, and drew it out of his hand, saying—"Come here." I took it on my knees, and invited brother Joseph to eat some apples. He did make out to give us some breakfast in the morning, and even then he got up from the table before we had time to half finish our breakfast, to see if we would not give over eating. Said I—"Never mind, I shall eat what I want before I stop."

I am happy to say, through your trustee in trust, that the latter-day saints, in the capacity of a church and kingdom, do not owe near as much money as they have on hand. A year ago last April conference, we owed over sixty thousand dollars, but we do not now owe a single red cent.

May God bless us, that we may always have enough, and know what to do with what we have, and how to use it for the good of all, for I would not give much for property unless I did know what to do with it.

"MORMONISM."

A DISCOURSE DELIVERED BY PARLEY P. PRATT, IN THE TABERNACLE, GREAT SALT LAKE CITY.

I HOPE the congregation will lend us their undivided attention, and exercise their faith and prayers for those that speak, that the truth may be drawn out to the edification of all.

I always feel diffident to address the assemblies of the people of God, at the seat of the government of the Church, knowing that there are many that can edify and enlighten our minds better than I can. I always feel that I would sooner hear than speak. But nevertheless, I feel it my duty to impart my testimony, and exercise my gift among my brethren, according to my calling; I therefore shall address you for awhile this morning.

There may be many strangers assembled with us at this season of the year; many are passing through this city from different parts of the world. The members of the Church need not complain, if I should address myself to the people as if they were all strangers, on the principles that are sometimes designated "MORMONISM;" and confine myself to some of the plain, simple, introductory principles of that system. It will refresh the minds of those acquainted with them, and perhaps edify them, and at the same time edify others.

Suppose I were to ask a question this morning, as a stranger, "What is Mormonism?" I suppose it is known to most men at all conversant with principles classed under that name, that it is a nickname, or a name applied to the public, and not used officially by the Church so called. Mormon was a man, a prophet, an author, a compiler, and a writer of a book. Mormon was a teacher of righteousness, holding certain doctrines. The Church of Jesus Christ of latter-day saints are agreed with Mormon, as well as with many other ancient writers, and hold to the same principles; therefore their neighbors have seen fit to call those principles they hold, "MORMONISM." They might as well have called them, *Abrahamism*, *Enochism*, or *Isaiahism;* because the ancient prophets, patriarchs, and apostles, held to the same truths in general terms, only differing in circumstances, in distant countries and ages of the world, and acted upon the same general principles, according to the particular circumstances that surrounded them. But the world, out of all the ancients, have selected one called *Mormon*, and all the principles held by all good inspired men of all ages and countries they have seen fit to sum up, and call "Mormonism." Well, it is as well as anything else, for aught I know; name does not affect the principles.

The word of God, as written in the good old Book, designates the people of God by the name of Saints; which name is almost or quite as ancient, as any writings extant. Saint was spoken of by Enoch long before the flood. The same term was applied to the people of God by the prophets, the psalmist, and by the writers of the New Testament.

Not only was this term applied to saints in ancient

days, but the patriarchs, prophets, and apostles applied it prophetically, speaking of the people of God in the latter days, when the kingdom should be given to the people of God, and the principles of God should bear rule over all the earth. Daniel and the other prophets, in speaking of this subject, always call them the saints of the Most High. They do not call them "Mormonites," Methodists, Presbyterians, Congregationalists, Jews, Pagans, or Mohammedans, nor yet Catholics; but the language of the apostles and prophets is, that the SAINTS of the Most High shall prevail—prevail over the world, establish a true order of government, and, in short, rule the lower world; and that all the nations shall bow to him who is at their head, and to the principles held by them.

Why not this be continued and sustained, Oh ye people of Christendom, and, letting these party names go by the board, and be classed among the things that were in the darker ages, come to the proper and correct Scripture language, and when we speak of the people of God, call them SAINTS OF THE MOST HIGH?

Well, then, such is the name that the Church which I represent, do their business in. As such, they are known on their own records, and on the records of heaven, inasmuch as they are recognized there. But we know what the world mean when they say "Mormonism," and "Mormon." What are the principles called "Mormonism?" You may ask those who profess to be instructors of the people abroad in the States, and elsewhere—and very few of them will give you one correct idea in regard to the doctrines of the latter-day saints. Indeed, they have not informed themselves, but remain in ignorance on the subject; and when they would show others, of course, they cannot inform them correctly on that subject. But you will generally be informed, that "Mormonism" is a new religion, that it is something new under the sun, and of course is an innovation —a kind of trespass on Christianity, on the Bible, or on the good old way. "Oh," say some of the editors that ought to be the most enlightened, and that profess to be, "if Mormonism prevails, Christianity will come down."

Now suppose that we examine, principle by principle, some of the fundamental principles of "Mormonism," and see whether there is one item that is new, or that is in any way an innovation on Christianity.

What is the first start towards an introduction of these principles in this age, and the organization of a people? What is it that first disturbed the world, or any part of it, or called the attention of the people towards it, giving rise to the system now called "Mormonism?" It was the ministration of angels to certain individuals; or in other words, certain individuals in this age enjoyed open visions.

Now we will stop, right at this point; it is called "Mormonism." Let us dwell on it. Is that a new principle? Is it adding something to Christianity, or taking something from it? Do not let our modern notions weigh anything, but come right to the fact of the matter. If Peter the apostle were here to-day, and a person were to relate to him a vision wherein an angel appeared to him and said something to him, would Peter call together the rest of the apostles, and sit in council on that man's head for error? Would they say to that man, "Sir, you have introduced something here in your experience that is derogatory to Christianity, and contrary to the system of religion we have taught, and introduced into the world?" I need not answer this question, neither need I bring Scripture to show what were the teachings and experience of Peter and the rest of the apostles on this subject. The Bible is too common a book, too widely circulated in the world, and the people of the United States, especially, are too well read in its contents to suppose, for a moment, that Peter or the rest of the apostles would condemn a man because he believed in the ministration of angels, because he related an experience wherein he had had a vision of an angel.

Now that was the principle that disturbed this generation, in the commencement of the introduction of that which is now called "Mormonism"—a principle as common in the ancient church as the doctrine of repentance. I will say more—it is a principle that has been common in all dispensations; it is a principle which was had before the flood, and fully enjoyed by the ancient saints, or at least held to by them; a principle that was common among them; not that every man attained to it.

But where can we read, under the government of the patriarchs, before the flood or after it; before Moses or after him; before Christ or after Christ—where can we read in sacred history of a people of God by whom the doctrine of visions and ministering of angels would be discarded, or be considered erroneous? It was common to all dispensations, it was enjoyed by the patriarchs and prophets under the law of Moses, before it and after it, and by the people of God among the ten tribes, and among the Jews. We will carry it still further. It was enjoyed among the Gentiles, before there was a people of God fully organized among them in the days of

Christ. Cornelius had the ministering of angels before he became a member of the Christian Church, or understood there was a crucified and risen Redeemer. He prayed to the living God, and gave alms of such things as he had. He was a good man, and an angel came to him and told him his prayers were heard, and his alms had come up as a memorial before God.

It is astonishing then, to me, that the modern Christian world consider this a new doctrine, an innovation—a trespass on Christianity. No! it is as old as the world, and as common among the true people of God, as His every day dealings with man. We will leave that point, and say, it is the Christian world, and not the latter-day saints, that have a new doctrine, provided they discard that principle.

What next? Why, that man, by vision, the ministering of angels, and by revelation, should be called with a high and holy calling—commissioned with a holy mission to preach, and teach, and warn, and prophesy, and call men to repentance. That was one of the first principles introductory to what is now called "Mormonism" in this age.

Is there anything new about that, anything strange, anything that differs from the patriarchal ages, from the Jewish economy, the Mosaic dispensation, or from the dispensation called Christian? Similar things happened before Moses, in his day, and after his day; and among the prophets, and in different ages. Were not such things common in the days of Jesus Christ, and after that in the days of the apostles? Was not John the Baptist thus commissioned? Was not Jesus thus commissioned. And were not His apostles, elders, and seventies? After his resurrection and ascension into heaven, were not others called, and ordained under the hands of those who were thus commissioned, and called sometimes by visions and revelations directing them to those who were thus commissioned in order to be ordained? That was no new doctrine, no innovation on Christianity, no perversion of the Scriptural system, nor was it anything new, unless you call the old principle new.

Well, then, that the man thus commissioned should call upon others to turn from their sins; and that an individual, a government, a house, a city, a nation, or a world of people should perish unless they did turn from their sins—is that anything new? No. Every one conversant with the Bible will say, that such things took place frequently under all the different dispensations. The heathen were warned in this way. Individuals, households, cities, nations, and the world have to be warned in this way, and especially under the Christian dispensation. So there was a special commission given to the servants of God, to go to all the world, and call upon everybody to repent, or whole nations should become disfranchised, scattered, and millions be destroyed, as for instance the Jews at Jerusalem, because they would not hearken to it. It is nothing new, to cry to all men to repent, and warn different cities and nations of wars coming upon them, or that they will be damned if they do not repent. This is one of the early principles called "Mormonism." Is there anything new in this? Is there anything strange or unscriptural? No; no sensible professing Christian will maintain such a point for a moment.

Suppose that some people should hearken, when the ministering of angels takes place. Among many men one certain man is commissioned by revelation to preach the Gospel, and cry repentance. Suppose that some persons should hearken and repent, and he should take them and walk down to the water, and bury them in the water in the name of the Father, and of the Son, and of the Holy Ghost, and raise them again out of the water, to represent the death and burial of Jesus Christ, and his resurrection from the dead; and to represent the faith of the individual thus ministered to, that he does believe in Jesus Christ, that he died, and that he did rise from the dead, and that he, the individual, does put his trust and confidence in him for the remission of sins and eternal life—is that anything new? Would that be new to Peter? Suppose some person was to relate before Peter and Paul to-day, and the Christians with them, that lived when they lived—suppose they were all present, and this person told them that a man came along preaching repentance, and he called upon us to believe in Jesus Christ, and we did so, believing their testimony, and they took us and buried us in water, and raised us again out the water unto newness of life—would Peter or John blame him? Would Paul say, "It is something new?" Or would he say, "Brother, thousands of us received the very same thing in ancient days?"

The Catholic Church profess to be the true church—the ground and pillar of the truth, handed down by regular succession from the ancient church, of which they are still members; and their priesthood and apostles are now of the very same church which the New Testament calls the true Church at Rome. These Roman Catholics of modern times profess to be members of that very same church that Paul wrote that epistle to. If they are, I will show you to demonstration, if the

Scriptures be true, that this doctrine called "Mormonism" is not a new doctrine, Paul, writing to that church, of which they profess to be members, says, Know ye not, brethren, ye Romans, that as many of you as have been baptized into Christ have been baptized into his death, being buried with him by baptism into death, that like as Christ rose from the dead, even so ye may walk in newness of life? Now this epistle containing this doctrine was written by Paul to the Church at Rome, and which these modern people called Roman Catholics profess to be members of. If they are what they profess to be, every one of them have been buried with Christ in baptism, and have risen again to newness of life. We will, however, leave them to describe whether that is really the case, or whether they are contented to sprinkle a few drops of water on an infant's face and call that a burial! Paul said that was a principle of the true Church of Rome that had been buried with Christ by baptism into death, and had risen to newness of life. Have these modern Roman Catholics gone forward repenting of their sins, and been buried in water, in the likeness of Jesus Christ according to this pattern? If they have not, they are a spurious Church of Rome, and not real. Therefore, if they be the real Church of Rome, it will be no new thing to them when the latter-day saints inform them upon being buried with Christ in the likeness of his death, etc. If this is a new doctrine to them, they had better be looking about them to see if they have not got up a counterfeit Church of Rome, for Paul knew of only one, and the members of it were all buried with Christ in baptism.

If 500 persons here were to say they came repenting of their sins, and went down and were buried in the waters of baptism, and had risen again to walk in newness of life, Paul would say, if he were here, "It is just what we used to do in ancient times; and I wrote to the Church of Rome, telling them that as many as were baptized into Christ were baptized into his death, buried with him by baptism into death," etc.

Now if this doctrine is new to the Church of Rome, then that is that church, that priesthood, and those members that have introduced something new, who are departing from the old Christian religion, and not the "Mormons."

This reasoning applies just the same to the Church of England. They have just as good a right to have a Church in England as anywhere else—to have a national Church of England by law established, but if they are a true Church of God, all of them have been buried with Christ in baptism, etc., or the apostle must have been mistaken, or there are two different kinds of Gospel.

Now if I were speaking to the state Church of England, or the state churches of the Catholic world, I would tell them in the name of the Lord Jesus Christ to repent of their new doctrine, and come back to the old standard spoken of by the Apostle, when he says, "though we or an angel from heaven preach any other Gospel unto you than that which we have preached unto you, let him be accursed," etc.

I need not go through with this same application upon the Lutherans, upon the Presbyterians, upon the Methodists, and others, for all these people sprinkle infants; for the principle once carried out will apply to the whole. If they are Christians according to the doctrine of the ancient church, they hold the doctrine of the apostles, they have repented of their sins, after believing on the Lord Jesus Christ, and have been BURIED with Christ by baptism into death, etc If not, they may judge themselves, for I will not judge them. If they have got a new doctrine, different from that believed by the apostles, and the latter-day saints have got the old one, why not say, then, "If sectarianism prevails, Christianity, as held by the Mormons will be in danger," instead of saying the opposite? Why not turn the thing right about? If we have no one new principle in our religion, why are we considered innovators, and opposed to Christianity? And why is Christianity in the world in danger if "Mormonism" prevails? It is because that floating Christianity, called so by the world, is a spurious one; they have departed from the doctrine of the apostles. Then, I ask again, why say, "If Mormonism prevails, Christianity is in danger?" for if it is a false Christianity, the quicker it falls the better.

We have examined three general principles, to see if there is anything new in "Mormonism." First, the ministering of angels. Second, the commission of ministers, apostles, prophets, and elders to administer in holy things, by revelation and the authority of heaven. Third, that all those that hear them, believe their words, and repent of their sins, shall go down into the waters of baptism, and be immersed or buried in the name of the Father, and of the Son, and of the Holy Ghost, and thus show that they do believe in a crucified and risen Redeemer, and in the remission of sins through His name. So far, I think, we have fairly stated some of the first principles of what the world calls "Mormonism;" and every one who has heard us, must decide that there is nothing new in these principles, but rather, that those who have departed from them, are justly chargeable with introducing new things, and innovations on Christianity.

Now suppose that one, two, or a dozen, or a hundred thousand, or even millions of individuals thus baptized, should all come together, in their several congregations, and should unite in earnest prayer, and a man commissioned in the ministry of Jesus Christ should rise and lay his hands on them, praying the Almighty God to give the Holy Spirit, and it be given as in days of old, and he confirms that promise upon them according to the pattern in the New Testament—would that be something new? Would it be an innovation upon Christianity? Would it be right to say "this is Mormonism, come to do away with Christianity?" Why, no! Every sensible man at all acquainted with the Holy Scriptures, would laugh at the idea. If the ancient saints were here, they would tell you it was their ancient manner; they would ask you if you had not read over their history, which describes how the Holy Spirit was administered in days of old. Every man who has read the Bible, knows it.

Well, then, the different sections of what is called Christianity, never do this, and call it something new. When the "Mormons" do it, they are at once charged with innovation; and yet we have not got anything new in that respect, but simply a restoration of that which was. They are the persons chargeable with new doctrine, and not the latter-day saints.

Well, then, suppose that after this ordinance, the Holy Spirit falls upon these congregations, or upon these individuals thus baptized and confirmed, and fills them, and enlightens their minds, and bears testimony to them of the truth which they have received, and confirms them in the faith of it, and fills them with the spirit of utterance and prayer, and with gifts whereby they prophesy, or speak in tongues, lay hands on the sick and they recover, in the name of Jesus, or whereby they are filled with the spirit of any gift, renewed in their utterance, strengthened in their powers of intellect, so as to be able to speak with eloquence to the edification of others by the word of wisdom, knowledge and prophecy; or peradventure some one, two, or three of them have a heavenly vision, and happen to relate it—is this something new? Are these things an innovation on Christianity?

Let the apostles of the ancient church come up now, and be judges, not these innovators. Oh yes, saints of ancient days, are these things new to you? "No," they reply, "but just exactly what we used to have among us; and you who have read the New Testament know it is so." If this, then, is Mormonism, it is nothing new, but simply that which should have been in the world in order to constitute true Christianity.

Now suppose, after all these have been established, the people organize on them; and that in the enjoyment and cultivation of them, this people unite their efforts, both temporally and spiritually, to build up themselves as a people, and each other as individuals, in righteousness upon the earth; and the Spirit of the Lord God into which they were all baptized, should make them very great in union—in union of effect, in counsel, in operation, in fellowship, in temporal things in a great measure, and in spiritual things, by which they are all of one heart and mind to a great degree, and growing in it every day—is this something new, because it is "Mormonism?" Or is this the very doctrine which was inculcated in days of old by the apostles of Jesus Christ?

It was the main object for which the Holy Spirit was given, that they might all grow up in union, in fellowship, in co-operation, in holiness in the Lord. No man who has read the New Testament, will say this is NEW, when we say that the great object of the Gospel is, that we may all become one in Christ Jesus—one in knowledge, and in the love and practice of the peaceable things of God. Is it anything new? No. Well, it is a part of what the world calls "MORMONISM;" and I would to God it was more perfected among this people than it is.

If any one of these principles in practice, should prevail over the whole world, it would be nothing new; but the world only hold this last as a theory; as to the practice of it, they are strangers.

We have examined five or six general principles, called "Mormonism," and found nothing new in them. "But," says one, "I heard you had got a new Bible; that is certainly an innovation." But stop; suppose, on inquiry, you become as much surprised and disappointed as many have who have asked for a "Mormon Bible," and when we have presented them with one, behold it is King James' translation of the Scriptures, the standard we read, containing the covenants, predictions, and hopes of the ancients, and the doctrines of Jesus Christ, just as we believe them, and hope for their fulfillment. Is that anything new?

"Well, if you have not a new Bible, you have certainly got a new book." Is that any thing strange? Have not other societies got new books? The Church of England have not only the Scriptures, but the book of Common Prayer, and the time was when they did not have such a book, therefore when they made that, it was something new. They are not alone in that, however, for the Methodists have a new book called the "Methodist's Discipline." One hundred and twenty years ago there was no such thing in existence. If having a new book be an innovation, then all are guilty of it as well as the "Mormons."

"But those other people do not profess that their books are inspired, and we have learned that you have a book that you believe is inspired. What is it, any how?" This is all a fact, and if it is wrong we will cheerfully plead guilty. We have got another book besides the Bible, that was an ancient book, and profess that it was inspired, and was written by prophets, and men that enjoyed the ministering of angels, more or less of them, and had communion with the heavens, and the spirit of prophecy. And moreover, we profess that this ancient book was restored to the knowledge of the modern world by inspiration, and the ministering of angels. Is that something new? It may be new to the world in its history, and in its bearings; in that respect it may be new to them; but suppose, after all, it should contain no new doctrine, no new principle, no new prophecy, that is differing from or doing away that which is already extant in the Bible? Well, then, I do not say that it would be a new doctrine. Men had books revealed in the days of old.

"If it is no new doctrine, and if its predictions do not differ from those contained in the old and new Testaments, what is the use of it?" The same question was investigated in ancient times. A great conqueror had taken possession of an ancient library, when there were no printing presses, containing one hundred thousand volumes, all in manuscript, comprising more history than was in any library extant in the ancient world. The conqueror was a Mahommedan. He wrote to the head of the department to know what he would do with this library. It was invaluable in its cost and intrinsic worth. "What shall I do with it?" The reply was, "If it agrees with the Koran, we have no use for it; and if it does not agree with the Koran, it is false anyhow; so in either case burn it."

"Now if these latter-day saints have a book extant among them, and it agrees with the Bible, there is no kind of use for it," says the opposer, "for the Bible contains all that is necessary; if it does not agree with the Bible, it is false anyhow; so in either case burn it." This was a principle of Mahommedanism, and may be a principle of what is called modern Christianity. I hope not, however.

"What is the use of the book in question, anyhow?" Why, in the first place, it differs in its history from the Bible. The Bible is a history of things that took place in Asia principally, and a little of what took place in Europe and Africa. The book of Mormon is a history of things in another hemisphere. The one book is the ancient history of the eastern hemisphere, in part; and the other is a history of the western hemisphere, in part. Shall we say, because we have the history of one part of the world, that the history of the other part of the world is good for nothing? Could the rulers of nations realize that fact, and could they only have a copy in their libraries at the cost of $100,000, they would appropriate it for this history of the western hemisphere.

Discredit it as you will, we have it in genuineness

and in truth, written by the ancient prophets that lived upon this land, and revealed in modern times by the ministering of angels, and inspiration from the Almighty. It is in the world, and the world cannot get it out of the world. It is in the world in six or seven languages of Europe. It is as important in its history as the Bible, and it is just as interesting and as necessary for men to get an understanding of the ancient history of America, as it is for them to get an understanding of the history of Asia.

"But are the merits of history all that it is good for?" It is good in doctrine also. If two or more writers, one living in Asia, and the other in America, and cotemporary, have the same doctrine revealed to them, and both bear record of the same plan of salvation, who is he that shall say that the record of one is of no worth?

Is it not a satisfaction to sit down and read that a country far removed from Bible scenes, from that part of the stage on which figured the patriarchs of old, with Moses and the Jewish prophets, John the Baptist, Jesus Christ, and the apostles, was also the theatre of revelation, prophecy, visions, angels, of the ministration of the doctrine of Christ, of the organization and government of his true church? that there too were angels, that there too were apostles, that there too was the word of God, that there too faith came by hearing, and salvation by faith? Shall we say that such things and such good news are worth nothing, when that very news corroborates the song of the heavenly hosts, when they declared to the shepherds of Judea, in joyful songs, that they brought glad tidings of great joy, that should be to all people! And here comes a book informing us that these glad tidings were also to another hemisphere at the same time.

Now, stop a moment, and let us reason. Suppose yourself an angel of God at that time, full of benevolence, full of joy, full of a soul-inspiring hope, full of charity for poor, ignorant, perishing mortals, and you felt so full of poetry, and song, and gladness, that you could scarcely hold your peace. Suppose you had a bird's eye view of our little, dark, benighted world, by soaring above it, and in a moment you could light down upon any part of it. You come to Palestine, in Asia; that part of the globe is rolling under your feet; you visit it, and sing to the shepherds the glorious tidings of great joy, which shall be to all people: "for unto you is born this day in the city of David, a Saviour which is Christ the Lord." The earth rolls on about half way round, you look down again with a bird's eye view, and you discover the western hemisphere, and it is full of people; I wonder whether your soul would still swell with the same glad tidings—or would your charity have become exhausted? Would you not fly and declare these glad tidings to them also, and sing them a song of joy, and tell them what day the Saviour was born, that would reach their case as well as the case of those who dwelt upon the continent of Asia? "Yes," you reply, "if I were an angel, and had liberty to tell these glad tidings, I would never tell them to one part of the earth and go to sleep there, while the other part rolled under my feet unnoticed."

Were those angels commissioned and endowed to bear glad tidings to ALL PEOPLE, that the Saviour was born? I say that the choir of angels which sang that song, had full liberty, not only to tell the plan of salvation to chosen vessels of the Lord in one country, but also to another country—not only that the Saviour was born, in general terms, but the place where, and the time when, he was born. These were the tidings, "Go to all people." An angel must be a limited being, or be very ignorant in geographical knowledge, or partake largely of sectarian feelings of heart, to bear such tidings to one half of the globe, and not to the other.

I knew an infidel once, that did not believe in the Christian religion, nor in the New Testament, nor in the Saviour of the world. I asked him why he did not believe this. "Because," says he, "according to the New Testament the manifestation of such an important affair was so limited. Here was half of the world, according to the New Testament, that never heard of it. A message so important should have been made more public.'

"Well," said I, "if I will produce you a record, and a history, as well authenticated as the New Testament, showing that angels, the risen Saviour, holy inspired prophets and apostles, ministered in the western hemisphere, and preached the gospel to every creature, and handed it down, to ages, will you then believe?" "Yes," he answered, "I will." I presented him the Book of Mormon, which he perused. I inquired if he now believed. "Yes." he said, "I do;" and he has lived a Christian until now, for ought I know. I have seen him in this congregation, and he may be here today. His name is Alger.

What objection have you to the hope of eternal life being as widely developed as the ravages of death, sorrow, and mourning? What objection have you to the angels of God, apostles of God, the Son of God, or to the Holy Spirit of prophecy being poured out in more countries than one? You may say the keys of the Gospel were given to the Jewish apostles, but they were so far off as not to be able to reach the western hemisphere, even if they had had a knowledge of it. Were there ships and steam vessels to bear them to this country? No. Was there any communication kept up, or was this country known to them? No. But the waves, and winds, and elements, and the great depths that intervened, even the unexplored ocean, said to the ancient apostles, "Thus far shall ye go, and no further." This ocean, however, was no barrier to the fleet-footed angel of God, to the risen Jesus, and to immortal man. They could come to this hemisphere, and reveal the things of heaven to the people, and could rejoice in the same glad tidings, whether it was here or in Jerusalem, or if it were in the uttermost parts of the earth.

Though Peter was crucified at Rome, and Paul suffered in the same manner; though saints of the Most High were slaughtered by thousands and tens of thousands, and bled at the feet of Roman altars; yet a crucified and risen Redeemer, angels of God, and the Holy Spirit of truth that fills all things, were not thus curtailed and limited, but could minister truth to the uttermost bounds of the universe of God, where intelligences were mourning in darkness; wherever the ravages of death had spread sorrow, wherever there was a broken heart to be bound up, or wherever there was a despairing mortal to be inspired with hope, they could go and tell the glad tidings of life and salvation. The Book ot Mormon says they did come to this continent. It is a history of their coming, and contains the doctrine taught to the people here by the risen Jesus, and by his predecessors. In short, the doctrine taught and practised in ancient America is there portrayed, together with the history of the people.

Again, is this book of no interest with regard to the prophetic value? It reveals many things not noticed by the Jewish prophets. Did the old prophets touch upon every item that pertains to man in other countries? No, they did not, only in general terms together with the rest of the world. These other prophets portrayed many things not in their book, though agreeing with it as far as it goes, but touching events on which their book is silent.

Has any person any cause to say that there has not been a multiplicity of revelations, testimony, prophecy, history and doctrine, developed in various countries by the same Spirit of God, and by angels? And is not all this of great worth, to compare, in order to blend it together, that we may see more clearly the principles of the doctrines of salvation, and understand prophecy more extensively, especially in an age when the mind has been obscured by priestcraft.

If these are the principles of "Mormonism," where can you point out an innovation on Christianity? But is this all? No, this is not all, and I shall not tell it all today. I do not know it all yet. I have been twenty-three years learning "Mormonism," and I know but little of it. If any one expects to learn all the doctrines of "Mormonism," he must learn more than twenty-three years. For be it known unto you all, that "Mormonism," instead of being confined to a few dogmas or general truths, opens the flood-gates of all truth and knowledge, and teaches mankind to retain all the truth they can already comprehend, and comprehend as much more as they can all the time.

"Have you not other books?" Yes, we have histories and compilations of the dealings of God with us as a people. We keep a record, if you must know, not only individually some of us, but as a church, as a body, or community. We have revelation penned, revelations and visions penned, we have revelation and prophecy penned, we have knowledge penned, we have knowledge and principle penned, we have principle and history penned; the history comprising but a small portion, such as can be written, revealed to us latter-day saints, and practised upon; so that our modern books are like the ancient books—a mixture of revelation, prophecy, history, and doctrine. Has any person any objections to this? I ask, should an angel administer to this or that man, or suppose an open vision was manifested to him, revealing many precious truths, would he not be a simpleton not to write it? If the power of God, and the ministering of God, and the visions of the Almighty are extant in the world, these will be written. The practical part of history will be written, for if all were written, the world would not contain the books. The ancient apostles and prophets wrote a few of the items revealed to them, and a history of the practical workings of the system over which they presided. Do we differ from them? No.

"Well," says one, "to be plain with you, Mr. Speaker, we have been taught to believe that the one book, called the Bible, contains all the revelations that God ever revealed to man, therefore it is an innovation to offer anything else to the world as a revelation." This is a tradition of your own, so I have nothing to do with it. The Bible never taught that to you, nor angels, neither did any minister of God ever teach it to you; and if it is a modern sectarian tradition, it is calculated to bind men into a cast iron creed, and the sooner you break the fetters the better; burst them asunder, and come out into liberty and freedom, and know and understand that there is no such doctrine in the broad principles of eternal truth, that heaven is full of knowledge, and the earth ought to be full of prophets, heaven and earth full of angels, and both full of inspiration; and if the inhabitants of all the worlds of the universe were scribes, every blade of grass a pen, and every ocean ink, they could not write all the doings of the Almighty, of His servants, and of His angels. If I were to live for millions of years to come, and then millions of millions more, I expect there would always be some being ready to reveal something new, and somebody would write it. The art of writing will never cease. We may not have pens and ink, but we may have something better. Suffice it to say, that the arts and sciences will not come to an end, yet man may have been traditionated to believe that one small book contains all that God ever said or did. Such persons are to be pitied, and not to be reasoned with.

What is "Mormonism?" It is a restoration by new revelation, by the authorities of heaven, by the ministration of angels, by the ordination of prophets and apostles, and ministers or elders, by their testimony and ministry on the earth, by the organization of saints, by the administration of ordinances, by the operations of the Holy Spirit; it is a restoration of these ancient principles revealed from heaven, for the government of man.

Says one, "You have said you are not going to tell the whole system to-day." I do not know it all, and I shall not state the half I do know. What I have said are a few every day items, a few of the first principles of the Gospel of Christ, as believed and practised by the "Mormons."

I will tell one more before I close. "Your marriages," says the objector, "are founded upon principles entirely new, and different from the Christian world." I say, without any hesitancy, I defy the world to establish that assertion. I say our marriage relations are nothing new at all. There is no man, or set of men, or nation of men, where the Bible is extant, and they are readers, but what know that the institutions of marriage contained in the Bible, and the organization of families, differ widely from modern Christianity. We differ from modern Christianity, but not from the Bible. Patriarchs of the remotest ages, that obeyed the Lord God in regard to their marriages and family organizations, have not disagreed with us, nor we with them, so far as we and they have obeyed the law of God. If there is any difference at all, it was more developed among them than it is among us, we being in our infancy. If it should happen to be, that the whole modern world differ from the Bible—have done away with the law of God, and we have come in contact with them, instead of with the word of God, then the boot is on the other foot, and in reality what is said to us applies to them. It is like the farmer and the lawyer. A certain farmer came to a neighboring lawyer, and frankly confessed that his bull had had the misfortune to kill one of his (the lawyer's) oxen. The lawyer replied, "Thou art a very honest fellow, and will not think it wrong that I have one of thy oxen in return." "But," said the farmer, "I am mistaken, it was thy bull that killed my ox." "O," replied the lawyer, "that alters the case, and if—if—i-f—."

Now, then, if it is the whole Christian world, from Catholicism down to the latest of her daughters, that have made void the law of God, and trampled under foot the institutions of heaven, the holy principles of matrimony and family government, and have made them void also, by their traditions, and introduced that which God never did; and "Mormonism" has restored the law of God, in theory and practice, then it is the so-called Christian world, and not us, that are wrong. Whether it regards family organization, the law of God, patriarchal government, ordinances, principles and prophecy, I know of nothing new, or of nothing wherein we are innovators.

As I said before, and I am able to maintain it when called upon, "Mormonism" is a system which was understood and enjoyed by the ancients, and restored unto us by revelation. And if carried out, what will it do? It will simply fulfill the sayings of the prophets, both ancient and modern, put down all wickedness, abuse, proscription, misrule, oppression, ignorance, darkness, and tyranny, and restore mankind to righteousness, truth, liberty, law and government, in which the Lord's will will be done on the earth as it is in heaven. That is what "Mormonism" will do, when carried out.

May God bless you all. Amen.

LEGITIMACY AND ILLEGITIMACY.

A SERMON DELIVERED BY ELDER JOHN TAYLOR, AT THE GENERAL CONFERENCE, IN THE TABERNACLE, GREAT SALT LAKE CITY.

It rejoices my heart to hear the principles that have been advanced this day by our President, because they have their foundation in truth, and based upon the principles of equity, and are calculated to promote the happiness, well-being, exaltation and glory of man, in time, and throughout eternity. They lead us back into eternity: they existed with us there, and in all the various stages of man's existence they are calculated to elevate and ennoble him, and place him in a proper position before God, angels and men. They will put him in possession of his legitimate right, save him from the grasp of the adversary, from every subtle strategem of the powers of darkness, and place him in his proper station in time and in eternity.

I have been much pleased with and edified by the remarks that have been made upon this stand during the conference. Wisdom has been displayed in them; from them the intelligence of heaven have beamed forth, the mysteries of eternity have been spread before our minds, and we have had a view of heavenly things, that has fil' -ur hearts with joy and our mouths with praise.

It has made us feel as though we were upon the threshold of eternity; as though we were eternal beings, and had to do with eternal things; as though the things of this world were short, fleeting and evanescent, not worthy of a thought when compared with those things that are calculated to exalt and ennoble us in time and in eternity.

The principles of justice, righteousness, and truth, which have an endless duration, can alone satisfy the capacious desires of the immortal soul. We may amuse ourselves like children do at play, or engage in the frivolities of the dance. We may take our little enjoyments in our social assemblies, but when the *man* comes to reflect, when the *Saint of God* considers, and the visions of eternity are open to his view, and the unalterable purposes of God are developed to his mind—when he contemplates his true position before God, angels and men, then he soars above the things of time and sense, and bursts the cords that bind him to earthly objects; he contemplates God and his own destiny in the economy of heaven, and rejoices in a blooming hope of an immortal glory.

Such have been some of our feelings, while our minds have been carried away from the things of earth to contemplate the things with which eternal beings are associated, and the glories that await us in the everlasting mansions of the Gods.

The principles that we have to do with, then, are eternal, and not simply to play a game upon the checker of mortality, on which people can win and lose for the time being. We have to do with that which shall continue

> "While life, and thought and being last,
> Or immortality endures."

We seek not to build our hopes upon things that are evanescent, fleeting and transitory.

It is not he that can play the best game at checkers, that can take the most advantage of his neighbor, that can grasp the most earthly good, or that can put himself in possession of anything his heart desires pertaining to time, that is the most happy; but it is *he* who does to that which will *last*, *live* and *continue* to abide with him while "*immortality endures*," and still be on the increase, worlds without end.

If we can possess principles of this kind, then we are safe, everything else amounts to an illusion or a delusion, which cannot satisfy the desires of the mind, but, as the prophet says, it is like a thirsty man who dreams he is drinking, but when he awakes, he is faint, and his soul is thirsty; he dreams that he is eating, and when he awakes his soul is empty. This is the true situation of all men who are without God in the world; and nothing but a knowledge of eternal principles, of eternal laws, of eternal governments, of eternal justice and equity, and of eternal truth, can put us right, and satiate the appetite of the immortal soul.

If we make not a just estimate of these things, it is in vain that we attempt to say, "Lord, Lord," because we do not the things which he says. Every thing associated with the Gospel of salvation is eternal, for it existed before the "morning stars sang together for joy," or this world rolled into existence. It existed then, just as it exists now with us, and it will exist the same when time with us is no more. It is an eternal principle, and every thing associated with it is everlasting. It is like the priesthood of the Son of God, "without beginning of days or end of years." It lives and abides for ever.

If there is any principle that is not eternal, it is not a principle of the gospel of life and salvation.

There are many changes and shifting scenes that may influence the position of mankind, under different circumstances, in this state of mortality; but they cannot influence or change the gospel of the Son of God, or the eternal truths of heaven; they remain unchangeable; as it is said very properly by the Church of England, in one of their homilies, "as it was in the beginning, is now, and ever shall be, worlds without end." If nothing else they say is true, that is, and I can say amen to it with all my heart. All true principles are right, and if properly understood and appreciated by the human family, to them they are a fountain of eternal good.

The principle of "heirship," which President Young preached about to-day, is a principle that is founded on eternal justice, equity and truth. It is a principle that emanated from God. As was said by some of our brethen this morning, there may be circumstances arise in this world to pervert for a season the order of God, to change the designs of the Most High, apparently, for the time being, yet they will ultimately roll back into their proper place—justice will have its place, and so will mercy, and every man and woman will yet stand in their true position before God. If we understand ourselves correctly, we must look upon ourselves as eternal beings, and upon God as our Father, for we have been taught when we prayed to say, "Our Father, which art in heaven, hallowed be thy name." We have fathers in the flesh, and we do them reverence, how much more shall we be in subjection to the Father of Spirits and life. I need not enter into any proof in relation to this, for it is well understood by the Saints that God is the

Father of our spirits, and that when we go back into His presence, we shall know Him, as we have known our earthly parents. We are taught to approach Him as we would an earthly parent, to ask of Him such blessings as we need; and He has said, "If a son ask bread of his father shall he give him a stone, or if he ask for fish, a scorpion? If ye then, being evil, know how to give good gifts unto your children, how much more will your Heavenly Father give His holy Spirit to them that ask Him."

We have a Father, then, who is in heaven. He has placed us on this earth for some purpose. We found ourselves in posession of bodies, mental faculties, and reasoning powers. In a word, we found ourselves intelligent beings, with minds capable of recalling the past and launching into the unborn future with lightning speed; and were it not for this earthly tabernacle, this tenement of clay, they would soar aloft and contemplate the unveiled purposes of Jehovah in the mansions of the redeemed. We found ourselves here with minds capable of all this and more. God, who has ordained all things from before the foundation of the world, is our Father. He placed us here to fulfill His wise and unerring counsels, that we might magnify our calling, honor our God, obtain an exaltation, and be placed in a more glorious, exalted and dignified position than it would have been possible for us to enjoy if we had never taken upon us these bodies. This is my faith; it is the faith of this people.

I have no complaints to make about our father Adam eating the forbidden fruit, as some have, for I do not know but any of us would have done the same. I find myself here in the midst of the creatures of God, and it is for me to make use of the intelligence God has given me, and not condescend to anything that is low, mean, grovelling and degrading—to anything that is calculated to debase the immortal mind of man, but to follow after things that are in their nature calculated to exalt, ennoble and dignify, that I may stand in my true position before God, angels and men, and arise to take my seat among the Gods of eternity.

We will now come to the principles of *legitimacy*, which was the text given out this morning—to our rights, privileges, priesthoods, authorities, powers, dominions, etc., etc. And as some of us are Scriptorians, and all profess to believe the Bible, I feel inclined to quote a text from it. Paul, when speaking of Jesus Christ, gives us to understand that he is the first-born of every creature, for by him were all things made that were made, and to him pertains all things; he is the head of all things, he created all things, whether visible or invisible, whether they be principalities, powers, thrones, dominions; all things were created by him and for him, and without him was not anything made that was made. If all things were created by him and for him, this world on which we stand must have been created by him and for him; if so, he is its legitimate, its rightful owner and proprietor; its lawful sovereign and ruler. We will begin with him, then, in the first place, in treating on the subject of legitimacy.

But has he had the dominion over all nations, kindreds, peoples and tongues? Have they bowed to his sceptre, and acknowledged his sway? Have all people rendered obedience to his laws, and submitted to his guidance? *Echo* answers "No!" Has there ever been a kingdom, a government, a nation, a power, or a dominion in this world that has yielded obedience to him in all things? Can you point out one?

We read of the Jews who where a nation that submitted only in part to his authority, for they rebelled against his laws, and were placed under a schoolmaster until the Messiah should come. We read also, in the Book of Mormon, of some Nephites that dwelt upon this land, who kept the commandments of God, and perhaps were more pure than any other nation that history gives an account of. But, with these exceptions, the nations, kingdoms, powers, and dominions of the world have not been subject to the law, dominion, rule or authority of God; but, as it is expressed by one of the ancients, the prince and power of the air, the god of this world has ruled in the hearts of the children of disobedience, and led them captive at his own will. Where is the historian, the man acquainted with ancient lore, who can point me out one government, nation, power or dominion, that has been subject to the rule of God, to the dominion of Jesus Christ, with the exception of those Jews and Nephites which I have referred to? If there has been any such nation, the history of it has escaped my notice. I have never been able to obtain such information.

What has been the position of the world for generations past? They have been governed by rulers not appointed by God; if they were appointed by Him, it was merely as a scourge to the people for their wickedness, or for temporary rulers in the absence of those whose right it was to govern. They had not the legitimate rule, priesthood, and authority of God on the earth, to act as his representatives in regulating and presiding over the affairs of His kingdom.

Perhaps it may be well, at this stage of my remarks, to give you a short explanation of my ideas of government, legitimacy, or priesthood, if you please. The question, "What is priesthood?" has often been asked of me. I answer, it is the rule and government of God, whether on earth, or in the heavens; and it is the only legitimate power, the only authority that is acknowledged by Him to rule and regulate the affairs of His kingdom. When every wrong thing shall be put right, and all usurpers shall be put down, when he whose right it is to reign shall take the dominion, then nothing but the priesthood will bear rule; it alone will sway the sceptre of authority in heaven and on earth, for this is the legitimacy of God.

In the absence of this, what has been the position of nations? You have made yourselves acquainted with the political structure and the political intrigues of earthly kingdoms; I ask, from whence did they obtain their power? Did they get it from God? Go to the history of Europe, if you please, and examine how the rulers of those nations obtained their authority. Depending upon history for our information, we say those nations have been founded by the sword. If we trace the pages of history still further back to the first nation that existed, still we find that it was founded upon the same principle. Then follow the various revolutions and changes that took place among the subsequent nations and powers, from the Babylonians through the Medo-Persians, Grecians, Romans, and from that power to all the other powers of Europe, Asia and Africa, of which we have any knowledge: and if we look to America from the first discoveries by Columbus to the present time, where are now the original proprietors of the soil? Go to any power that has existed upon this earth, and you will find that earthly government, earthly rule and dominion, have been obtained by the sword. It was the sword of men that first put them in possession of this power. They have walked up to their thrones through rivers of blood, through the clotted gore and the groans of the dying, and through the tears and lamentations of bereaved widows and helpless orphans; and hence the common saying is "thrones won by blood, by blood must be maintained." By the same principle that they have been put in possession of territory, have they thought to sustain themselves—the same violence, the same fraud and the same oppression have been made use of to sustain their illegitimacy.

Some of these powers, dominions, governments and rulers, have had in their possession the laws of God, and the admonitions of Jesus Christ; and what have they done to his servants in different ages of the world, when he has sent them unto them? This question I need not stop to answer, for you are already made too familiar with it. This, then, is the position of the world. Authority, dominion, rule, government has been obtained by fraud, and consequently is not legitimate. They say much about the ordination of kings, and their being anointed by the grace of God, etc. What think you of a murderer slaying hundreds and thousands of his fellow-creatures because he has the power, and while his sword is yet reeking with human blood, having a priest in sacerdotal robes to anoint him to the kingship? They have done it. What think you of the cries of the widows, the tears of the orphans, and the groans of the dying, mingling with the prayers and blessings of the priest upon the head of the murderer of their husbands and their fathers?

It is impossible that there can be any legitimate rule, government, power or authority, under the face of the heavens, except that which is connected with the kingdom of God, which is established by new revelation from heaven.

In a conversation with some of our modern reformers in France, one of their leaders said, "I think you will not succeed very well in disseminating the principles of your religion in France." I replied, "you have been seeking to accomplish something, for generations, with your philosophy, your philanthropic societies, and your ideas of moral reform, but have failed; while we have not been seeking to accomplish the thing that you have, particularly, and yet have accomplished it." We began with the power of God, with the government of heaven, and with acknowledging His hand in all things; and God has sustained us, blessed and upheld us to the present time; and it is the only government, rule and dominion under the heavens that will acknowledge His authority.

Brethren, if any of you doubt it, go into some of those nations, and get yourself introduced into the presence of their kings and rulers, and say, "Thus saith the Lord God." They would at once denounce you as a madman, and straightway order you into prison. What is the matter? They do not acknowledge the legitimacy, the rule and government of God, nor will they inquire into them. They receive not their authority from Him. Nations honor their kings, but they do not honor the authority of their God in any instance, neither have they from the first man-made government to the present time. If there has been such a nation, or if there is at this time such a government, it is a thing of which I am ignorant.

The kings and potentates of the world profess to be anointed by the grace of God. But the priests who anoint them have *no authority* to do it. No person has authority to anoint a king or administer in one of the least of God's ordinances, except he is legally called and ordained of God to that power; and how can a man be called of God to administer in His name, that does not acknowledge the gift of prophecy to be the right of the children of God in all ages? It is impossible. These men have been grasping after power, and for this they have laid waste nations and destroyed countries. Some of them possessed it for awhile, and others were on the eve of getting it when they were cut off, and down they went. What became of them afterwards? Isaiah in vision saw the kings of the earth gathered together as prisoners in a pit, and after many days they were to be visited.

Having said so much in relation to other governors and governments, we will now notice the difference between them and Abraham of old. Abraham was a man who contended for the true and legitimate authority. God promised to him, and to his seed after him, the land of Canaan for their possession. "The Lord said unto Abraham, after that Lot was separated from him, lift up now thine eyes, and look from the place where thou art northward, and southward, and eastward, and westward; for all the land which thou seest, to thee will I give it, and to thy seed for ever." What did Stephen say generations afterwards? That God "gave him none inheritance in it, no, not so much as to set his foot on;

yet he promised that he would give it to him for a possession, and to his seed after him, when as yet he had no child." Ezekiel's vision of the dry bones explains this seeming contradiction. The Lord said to him, "Son of man, can these bones live?" etc. Who are they? We are told, in the same chapter, that they are the whole house of Israel, and that they shall come out of their graves, bone come to its bone, and sinew to sinew, and flesh come upon them, and they shall become a living army before God, and they shall inherit the land which was given to them and their fathers before them. The measuring line shall again go forth upon those lands, and mark out the possessions belonging to the tribes of Israel.

Abraham was a man who dared fear God, and do honor to His authority, which was legitimate. God tried and proved him, the same as He has tried many of us, and felt after his heart-strings, and twisted them round. When He had tried him to the utmost, He swore by Himself, because He could swear by no greater, saying, "That in blessing I will bless thee, and in multiplying I will multiply thy seed." "And in thy seed shall all the nations of the earth be blessed." Abraham obtained his dominion by legitimate authority; his priesthood was obtained from God; his authority was that which is associated with the everlasting Gospel, which was, and is, and is to come, that liveth and abideth for ever. And the promises made to him will rest upon him and his posterity, through every subsequent period of time, until the final winding up scene of all things. Will he ever obtain them? Yes. For we are eternal beings, and I am now talking as though we were in eternity. We shall wake up in the morning of the resurrection, attain to all the blessings which have been promised to us, and strike hands with Abraham, and see him inherit the promises. Abraham and all his children will then inherit the promises, through the principle of legitimacy. And there are many of the sons and daughters of Abraham among us at the present time; these will be baptized for their dead brethren and sisters, and by this means bring them unto Christ, beginning on the outside branches of the tree, and so progressing to the main stock, and from that to the root. And it shall come to pass that all Israel shall be saved. Why? Because it is their legitimate right. And they are Israel who do the works of Abraham.

Thus it is, then, with Abraham. The old man feels perfectly easy about the matter; and if he does see many of his descendants existing as a cursed race on account of their transgressions, many of them enjoying no higher avocation than crying "old clothes," still the time of their redemption will come, and by means of the eternal Gospel and priesthood, they with us will be made perfect, and we with them. While the faithful are operating in heaven to bring this about, the saints are operating on earth; and by faith and works we will accomplish all things, we will redeem the dead and the living, and all shall come forth, and Abraham will stand at the head of his seed as their ruler. This is his legitimate position.

We will now notice those men who are contending for it without any authority, and make a contrast between the two. We see them gathering their forces, and using their influence to destroy the poor among men. How long will the kings and rulers of the earth do this? Until they are dead and damned. And what then? They will be cast down into a pit. Isaiah saw them there, along with many other scoundrels, murderers and scamps. After many days they will be visited, but they have got to lie in prison a long time for their transgressions. The one is legitimacy, and the other is illegitimacy; the one is the order of God, and the other is the order of the devil.

Such is the position of things in relation to the world, to legitimacy and illegitimacy, in regard to things that are right, and things that are wrong. Jesus Christ created all things, and for him were they made, whether it be principalities, powers, thrones or dominions. Now the question is, is he going to be dispossessed of his right, because scoundrels exist in the world, and stand in power and dominion; because his subjects have rebelled against him from time to time, and usurpers have taken his place, and the dominion is given to another? Verily, no. But the time will come when the kingdom and the greatness of the kingdom under the whole heaven will be given to the saints of the Most High, and they will possess it for ever and ever.

We will now notice some of the acts of God, and some of the acts of those who have been under the dominion of Satan, those who have had dominion over the world—the proud and haughty usurpers, and the shedders of innocent blood. These are they that have lived in the world, and possessed all the good things of it. And what has been the situation of the saints in every age? All those who dared acknowledge that God lived, that this kingdom belonged to Him, that it was His right, and that He would without doubt possess it, have been trodden under foot, persecuted, cast out, hated, killed; "they wandered about in sheep-skins and goat skins; being destitute, afflicted and tormented." As one of old says, in speaking of the Jews, which of the prophets have not your fathers killed, who testified before the coming of the Just One?

This was the case in ancient days, and has been carried on in modern times. I have, with my own eyes, seen holy prophets expire, who were killed by the hands of a murderous gang of blood-thirsty assassins, because they bore the same testimony that the holy prophets did in days of old. How many more of their brethren who dared to acknowledge the truth, have fallen beneath the same influences—have been shot, whipped, imprisoned, and put to death in a variety of ways, while hundreds of others, driven from their homes in the winters, have found their last bed; they were worn out with suffering and fatigue, the weary wheels of life stood still; they were obliged to forsake the world, in which they could no longer remain, because of the persecution heaped upon them by the enemies of the truth.

The reason of all this vile outrage upon innocent men, women and children, is because there is no legitimate rule upon the earth. God's laws and government are not known, and His servants are despised and cast out.

Legitimacy and right, whether in heaven or on earth, cannot mix with anything that is not true, just and equitable; and truth is free from oppression and injustice, as is the bosom of Jehovah. Nothing but that will ultimately stand. What has been the position of the world generally, among themselves? You see men marshalling armies, and making war with one another to destroy each other, and take possession of their territory and wealth. One man who is in possession of wealth, power and authority, sees oppression exercised by kings; so he follows the example, as do rulers who exercise authority under their sovereign; then others in a still lower degree do the same; thus oppression treads upon the heels of oppression, and distress follows distress. You will find this to exist in a great measure through every grade of society, from the king on his throne, down to the match-maker or the chimney-sweep.

To ameliorate the condition of man, there are a great many institutions introduced into the world in the shape of Tract Societies, Bible Societies, and many more too numerous for me to name. Many of them are founded by sincere men, but commencing on the wrong foundation, they keep wrong all the time, and fail to accomplish the object desired. If any one of these different institutions were to carry out their own principles, they would not only fail in accomplishing the object they have in view, but ultimately destroy themselves.

There are Peace Societies among the rest; their object is to bring peace into the world, without the Spirit of God. They see plainly that peace is desirable, but they wish to graft it on to a rotten stock. In Europe they had a "Peace Congress," and sent their representatives to all parts of the world; and of course this "Congress of Peace" wished to regulate the world, make an end of war, and bring in universal peace.

Talk about peace, when rancorous discord makes its nest in the councils and cabinets of all nations, and the hearts of their statesmen are steeped in hatred one to another! Jealousy, animosity and strife, like the influence of a deadly contagion, may be found in almost every family; brother rising up against sister, sister against brother, the father against the mother, and the mother against the father, etc. We can find discord reigning even in the "Peace Society" itself.

Jesus Christ says, "My peace I give unto you; not as the world giveth, give I unto you," etc. Wherever this peace exists, it leaves an influence that is comforting and refreshing to the souls of those who partake of it. It is like the morning dew to the thirsty plant. This peace is alone the gift of God, and it can only be received from Him through obedience to His laws. If any man wishes to introduce peace into his family or among his friends, let him cultivate it in his own bosom; for sterling peace can only be had according to the legitimate rule and authority of heaven, and obedience to its laws.

Everything is disordered, and in confusion in the world. The reason is, because no legitimate authority has been known or acknowledged on the earth. Others have been trying to build up and establish what they supposed to be the kingdom of God. The socialists of France call themselves religious people, and they also expect to bring about a reign of glory through a species of Robespierreism. I was told by a man well acquainted with matters of fact in relation to these things, that if they gained the ascendancy in France, their first object would be to erect a statue to Robespierre. They were going to cut off thousands of people, to accomplish their designs; and had not Napoleon taken active measures to head them, bands of men were ready on a moment's warning to cut off the heads of thousands, and among these, I was informed, fifty thousand priests were doomed.

These are some of the principles and ideas that exist in the world, among the various nations and institutions of men, which are framed according to illegitimate principles. A change of government changes not the condition of the people, for all are wrong, and acting without God.

Our ideas are, that the time has come to favor God's people; a time about which prophets spoke in pathetic strains, and poets sung. These men of God looked through the dark vista of future ages, and being wrapped in prophetic vision, beheld the latter day glory—the time of the dispensation of the fullness of times, spoken of by all the holy prophets since the world began; for they all looked forward with joyful anticipations to the things which have commenced with us; they all had their eye upon the time when legitimacy would obtain its proper place upon the earth, in the shape of the kingdom of God established in the world, when all false rule and dominion would be put down, and the kingdoms of this world would become subject to God and His Christ. These are the ideas that they had, and these are the things we are seeking to carry out.

If we look at what illegitimacy has done in former times, we shall see the absolute necessity of the restitution spoken of by the prophets, for it has filled the earth with evil, it has caused the world to groan in bondage, laid millions in the cold embrace of death, and caused disease to spread its pestiferous breath among the nations, leaving ruin, misery and desolation in its path, and made this fair earth a howling wilderness. And nothing but the wisdom and intelligence of God can change it. The kingdom of God will establish truth and correct principles—the principles of truth, equity and justice; in short, the principles that emanate from God, principles that are calculated to elevate man in time and through all eternity. How shall this be? It will be by a legitimate rule, authority and dominion.

Who have we for our ruling power? Where and how did he obtain his authority? Or how did any of this Church and kingdom obtain it? It was first obtained by a revelation from the Lord of the universe, by the opening of the heavens, by the voice of God, and by the ministering of holy angels. It is by the voice of God and the voice of the people, that our present President obtained his authority. Many people in the world are talking about mis-rule and mis-government. If there is any form of government under the heavens where we can have legitimate rule and authority, it is among the Saints. In the first place, we have a man appointed by God, and, in the second place, by the people. This man is chosen by yourselves, and every person raises his hand to sanction the choice. Here is our President, Brigham Young, whom we made choice of yesterday, who is he? He is the legitimate ruler among this people. Can anybody dispossess him? They cannot, because it is his legitimate right, and he reigns in the hearts of the people. He obtains his authority first from God, and secondly from the people; and if a man possesses five grains of common sense, when he has a privilege of voting for or against a man, he will not vote for a man that oppresses the people; he will vote according to the dictates of his conscience, for this is the right and duty of this people in the choice of their President, and other leading officers of the kingdom of God. While this is being done here, it is being done in every part of the world, wherever the Church of Jesus Christ of latter-day saints has a footing. Is there a monarch, potentate or power under the heavens that undergoes a scrutiny as fine as this? No, there is not; and yet this is done twice a year, before all the saints in the world. Here are legitimacy and rule. You place the power in their hands to govern, dictate, regulate and put in order, the affairs of the kingdom of God. This is *Vox Dei vox populi.* God appoints; the people sustain. You do this by your own act; very well, then, it is legitimate, and must stand, and every man is bound to abide it if it takes the hair off his head. I know that there are things sometimes that are hard, tough and pinching; but if a man is a man of God, he has his eyes upon eternal things, and is aiming to accomplish the purposes of God, and all will be well with him in the end.

What advantage is there, then, between this government and others? Why we have peace, and as eternal beings we have knowledge of eternal things. While listening to the remarks made on this stand, what have we not heard—what have we not known? The curtains of heaven have been withdrawn, and we have gazed as by vision upon eternal realities. While, in the professing world, doubt and uncertainty throw their dark mantle over every mind.

Let us now notice our political position in the world. What are we going to do? We are going to possess the earth. Why? Because it belongs to Jesus Christ, and he belongs to us, and we to him; we are all one, and will take the kingdom and possess it under the whole heavens, and reign over it for ever and ever. Now, ye kings and emperors, help yourselves, if you can. This is the truth, and it may as well be told at this time as at any other.

"There's a good time coming, Saints,
A good time coming,
There's a good time coming, Saints,
Wait a little longer."

Having said so much on this point, we will return to the principle of legitimacy. God is our legitimate Father, and we are His children, and have a claim upon Him, and He has a claim upon us. We have come into this world to accomplish a certain purpose, and we have come in the dispensation of the fullness of times, when God decreed to gather all things together into one, whether they be things in heaven or on earth; and everything that has been in existence in any age of the world, or that is, or will be, which is calculated to benefit and exalt men, we shall have; consequently, it is for us to look after anything and everything that ever has been true, or that ever has been developed in any period of the history of man, for it all belongs to us, and has got to be restored, for restitution means bringing back that which was lost. If the antedeluvians enjoyed anything that was good, true and eternal, which is not yet made known to us, it has to be restored; or if anything existed among the ancient patriarchs and prophets, that has been lost, it has to be restored. If there are any people of God upon any detached part of this world, they with it have got to be restored. God's word will also be gathered into one, and His people and the Jews will hear the words of the Nephites, and the ten tribes must hear the words of the Jews and Nephites, and God's people be gathered and be one. All things will be gathered in one, and Zion be redeemed, the glory of God be revealed, and all flesh see it together. God's dominion will be established on the earth, the law go forth from Zion, and the word of the Lord from Jerusalem, and the kingdoms of this world will become subject to God and His Christ.

As eternal beings, then, we existed with our Father in the eternal worlds. We came on to this earth, and obtained tabernacles, that through taking possession of them, and passing through a scene of trial, and tribulation, and suffering, we might be exalted to more glory, dignity and power, than would have been possible for us to obtain had we not been placed in our present position. If any of you do not believe this, let me refer you to a passage of Scripture or two. How was man created at first? We are told that God made man a little lower than the angels; then says Paul, "Know ye not that we shall judge angels." What through? It is through the atonement of Jesus Christ, through the taking of our bodies, the powers of the holy priesthood, and the resurrection of Jesus Christ, that we shall obtain a higher exaltation than it would have been possible for us to enjoy, if we had not fallen. To do right in our present state, then, we must carry out the principle of legitimacy according to a correct rule, and, if we profess to be subjects of the kingdom of God, we must be subject to the dominion, rule, legitimacy, and authority of God. No person can escape from this unless he apostatizes, and goes to the devil, like a fool. He must be a fool who would barter away eternal life, thrones, principalities and powers in the eternal world, for the paltry trash which exists in the shape of wealth and worldly honor; to let go his chance of heaven and of God, of being a king and priest unto Him, of living and reigning for ever, and standing among the chiefs of Israel. I cannot help calling such men fools, for they are damned now in making such choice, and will be hereafter.

I will say a little more on legitimacy and right to rule. What would be the position of a man who would take a course to rob his neighbor, or take advantage of him in the case of his legitimacy, which you have heard of this morning? Such a man must be a greater fool than the other. For instance, a good man dies, who has served God in righteousness all his days; the weary wheels of life stand still, and he goes to the world of spirits. He believed in the principles of justice, equity, righteousness, and truth, and that his rights would be held sacred to him by his brethren after he was gone. But some professed man of God comes to his widow, and wants to steal her away from him; he would rob the dead with impunity, under the ostensible garb of justice to her and her dead husband; he will tell her he is doing it out of pure love to them both, and he is going to exalt them in the kingdom of God. We read of the kingdom of God suffering violence; if violence is ever attempted, it is in a case of this kind. It is bad enough to steal from a man his earthly property; his oxen, his cow, his horse, his harness, his wagon wheels, and other paraphernalia; but what think you of a man that would rob the dead of a treasure which he holds the most dear, and prized as the most precious thing he possessed on earth—his affectionate wife! Such a person will assuredly miss his figure.

You will find in the ancient laws of Israel, there were proper rules in relation to these matters; one was, that if a man died without a child, his brother or the nearest relation of the husband should take the widow, and raise up seed to the husband, that his name might be continued in Israel, and not be blotted out. Where did these laws come from? We are told they came from God. But instead of doing this, suppose he should try to steal this woman away, and rob his brother—how would he get along, I wonder, with such a case against him, at the bar of justice? The laws and ordinances that exist in the eternal world have their pattern in the things which are revealed to the children of men on earth. The priesthood as it exists on the earth is a pattern of things in heaven. As I said in a former part of this discourse, priesthood is legitimate rule, whether on earth or in heaven. When we have the true priesthood on earth, we take it with us into the heavens; it changes not, but continues the same in the eternal world.

There is another feature of that ancient law which I will mention. It was considered an act of injustice for the nearest relation not to take the wife of the deceased if he refused to do it, he was obliged to go before the elders of "Israel, and his brother's wife shall loose his shoe from off his foot, and spit in his face, and shall answer and say, So shall it be done unto the man that will not build up his brother's house; and his name shall be called in Israel, The house of him who hath his shoe loosed." If the restitution of all things is to be brought to pass, there must be a restitution of these things; everything will be put right, and in its proper place.

There is another thing which is most grievous, afflicting and distressing so contemplate. When a man takes to himself a woman that properly belongs to another, and defiles her, it interferes with the fountain of life, and corrupts the very source of existence. There is an offspring comes forth as the fruit of that union, and that offspring is an eternal being—how can it be looked upon? To reflect upon it, wounds the finest feelings of human nature in time, and will in eternity. For who can gaze upon the degradation of their wife, and the corruption of their seed, without peculiar sensations? How much more is this feeling enhanced when the wronged man considers that he has been robbed by one who professed to be his friend? This thing is not to be trifled with, but is of the greatest importance; hence the necessity of the sealing powers, that all things may be pure, chastity maintained, and lasciviousness be rooted out from among the saints. Why so? That we may have a holy offspring, that shall be great, and clothed with the mighty power of God, to rule in His kingdom, and accomplish the work we propose they shall fulfill; and that when we go to sleep, we may sleep in peace, knowing that justice will be administered in righteousness. We shall know that we have a claim upon our own in the first resurrection; we shall know that our wives and our children will be there to join us, justice will be administered, and we shall have a claim upon them in the eternal world, and that no unprincipled scoundrel will be permitted to set his foot on another, or rob him of his just claims. Why is a woman sealed to a man for time and all eternity? Because there is legitimate power on earth to do it. This power will bind on earth and in heaven; it can loose on earth, and it is loosed in heaven; it can seal on earth, and it is sealed in heaven. There is a legitimate, authorized agent of God upon earth; this sealing power is regulated by him; hence what is done by that, is done right, and is recorded. When the books are opened, every one will find his proper mate, and have those that belong to him, and every one will be deprived of that which is surreptitiously obtained.

Let us do righteously, and you who would seek to injure another, and take advantage of one who was just and faithful to his God in his day, how would you like, when you get a few years older and drop into eternity, for somebody to come and serve you the same? You could not expect anything else, you could not die without being menaced by this supposition, and your dying pillow would be made unhappy, you would know you had done wrong, and would expect somebody to measure to you the same measure pressed down, shook together, and running over.

We have been told to preach confidence; correct principles and just dealings alone will inspire it. If a man speaks that which is not true about another, can you have confidence in him? No. If a man defrauds another, can you have confidence in him? No. But if you would, through a principle of covetousness, seek to sap the foundation of another's happiness, by trying to wrench from him those sacred rights which pertain to his interest in the eternal world, how much greater will be your condemnation? Nothing but truth, integrity, virtue, honor, and every pure principle, will stand in the great day of God Almighty. If such a person happens to get through this world, he will find barriers in the next, and probably miss a chance of obtaining a place in the first resurrection. Nothing contrary to the authority, rule, and government of heaven, will stand in time or in eternity; and if any man wants to be blessed and honored, and to obtain a high place in the eternal world, let him pursue a course of honor, righteousness, and virtue before his God; and if he wants to find himself amongst usurpers, defrauders, oppressors, and those in possession of illegitimate claims, let him take an opposite course. If time would permit, much more might be said about social, family and individual legitimate rights; but as time hastens, I forbear for the present.

Well, brethren and sisters, may God bless you. Amen.

THE END.

www.ingramcontent.com/pod-product-compliance
Lightning Source LLC
LaVergne TN
LVHW021139110826
845150LV00005B/1070

* 9 7 8 1 4 2 5 5 4 8 4 7 6 *